POLYMER CLAY ART

QUARRY

First published in the United States of America by
Quarry Books, a member of
Quayside Publishing Group
33 Commercial Street
Gloucester, Massachusetts 01930-5089
Telephone: (978) 282-9590
Fax: (978) 283-2742
www.rockpub.com

Library of Congress Cataloging-in-Publication Data available

ISBN-13: 978-1-59253-357-2
ISBN-10: 1-59253-357-4

10 9 8 7 6 5 4 3 2

Design: Bob's Your Uncle
        Susan Raymond Art & Design
        tabula rasa graphic design
Cover Design: Dania Davey
Illustrations by: Lorraine Dey

Grateful acknowledgment is given to Ellen Marshall for her work from *Polymer Clay Surface Design Recipes* on pages 9–25, 28–101, 270–287, and 300; to Georgia Sargeant, Celie Fago, and Livia McRee for their work from *Polymer Clay* on pages 7–8, 102–195 and 288-299; and Dinko Tilov for his work from *Creating Fantasy Polymer Clay Characters* on pages 26–27 and 196–269.

Printed in China

POLYMER CLAY ART

Projects and Techniques for Jewelry, Gifts, Figures, and Decorative Surfaces

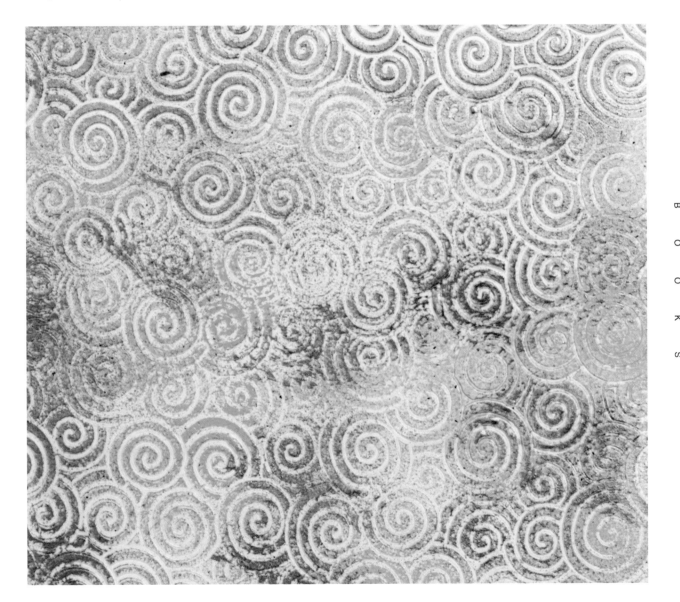

GLOUCESTER MASSACHUSETTS

QUARRY BOOKS

by Celie Fago, Ellen Marshall, Livia McRee, Georgia Sargeant, and Dinko Tilov

Contents

Exploring Polymer Clay

by Georgia Sargeant

Polymer clay is solid color—color you can knead, twist, pull, mold, layer, and cut. You can make it look like ancient amber, glowing glass, engraved ivory, or modern steel. You can use it to make delicate miniatures or large folding screens, wrap it around an armature, or stretch it out to airy thinness. You can layer it with metal leaf, blend in scented spices or delicate sparkles, transfer photocopied images on to it, or tint the surface with paint and colored pencil. It is wonderfully convenient because it will harden in twenty minutes in a home oven, so expensive studio space and fiery kilns are not needed. A corner of a table in a small apartment will do just fine.

In recent years, polymer clay has been transformed from a child's toy to a mature art medium, yet its delightful playfulness has not been lost. It can be bright or dull, large or small, realistic or abstract, down to earth or fantastical. It has been used to make jewelry, dolls, sculptures, accessories, wearable art, lamps, books, boxes, and bowls; it has been turned into mosaics, plaques, wall hangings, furniture, and decorations.

Polymer clay is a modern material that combines well with other media, allowing you to borrow techniques and tools from other arts and industries and use them in your own creations. In turn, modeling and construction techniques devised for polymer clay can be applied to other media, especially precious metal clay, producing metal objects with a fluidity and freshness seldom attained before. In one section of this book, eleven artists will introduce you to decorative and structural techniques for polymer clay. In another section, master craftsman Celie Fago will show you how to work in PMC and how to combine it with polymer clay. In yet another, Dinkov Tilov will show you how to create strange and fantastical creatures. In the Gallery section, many artists will show you examples of how some of these techniques have been used in creating marvelous and evocative objects to delight the senses and entice the imagination.

The projects in this book are intended to explore the wide-ranging possibilities of this versatile medium. There is something for everyone—from those just starting to discover polymer clay to those who have been creating with it for a while and are ready to experiment with new techniques. Keep in mind that the most beautiful and ingenious polymer clay techniques were developed by fellow enthusiasts—we hope that this book inspires you to develop a few of your own.

Polymer Clay Basic Techniques

Polymer clay is a brilliantly colored modern modeling material that bakes hard in a home oven. Its star feature is its compatibility with other art and craft materials, from acrylic paints to glues to glitter to metal leafing to rubber-stamping supplies. With polymer clay, sturdy and colorful three-dimensional art is within everyone's reach. It's widely available in art and craft stores.

The basic ingredient of polymer clay is polyvinyl chloride (PVC), the same sturdy stuff that water pipes are made of. The other ingredients are inert fillers to give it bulk (and sometimes texture), dyes and pigments to give it color, and a plasticizer—an oily chemical that allows the microscopic chains of PVC molecules to slide over each other at room temperature but lock onto each other when the clay is heated.

This clay, also known to its fans as "polyclay" and "PC," comes in many of the colors you find on the artist's paint rack—not only in standard colors like red, white, and brown, but also in flesh tones (developed for doll making) and in translucent clays that are milky when raw but almost clear when baked properly (and in a thin enough layer, they're absolutely transparent). With many brands, you can mix the package colors and get attractive intermediate shades.

Manufacturers also make some wonderful specialty clays. There are pearlescent and metallic colors incorporating tiny mica flakes that give a shimmery luster. There are fluorescent colors using brilliant pigments; a dab added to a dull color will perk it up. There are glow-in-the-dark colors that shine at night. There are glitter clays—tinted translucent clays with heat-resistant microfine glitter mixed in. There are clays that contain short colored fibers that make them look like stone. You can even make your own stone clays by mixing embossing powder from the rubber-stamp counter into translucent clay. Or you can mix in other grains or powders, from coffee grounds to aromatic herbs to iridescent pigments to children's tinted play sand.

A Helpful Note to Readers

This book presents a wide array of techniques and inspirations for creating unique surface designs in polymer clay. We have made an attempt to tell you very specifically what materials we have used to get a particular effect, so that if desired, you can try to duplicate a result exactly. If a product has a certain property or characteristic that makes it especially suitable for a particular effect, we have made a point to tell you. In many cases, another brand may work just as well, but we still tell you exactly what we used, in case you want to match a particular color or design.

Please note: None of this specificity should discourage you from substituting similar products that are easier to find or that you may already have. You may discover that your results are exactly the same, or you may find completely unexpected results that make you just as happy. We have tried to design this book so that the information provided, based on the authors' extensive experience and testing, is as detailed and as helpful as we can make it, but we also encourage you to conduct your own experimentation and to not feel limited by the suggested products in any way.

A majority of the materials used in this book are available internationally or can be easily ordered on the Internet. A resources section is included for your reference on page 301.

Chapter 1
Getting Started

A Guide to Using This Book

I hope you find this book inspiring and informative whether you are familiar with polymer clay or not.
If you are already acquainted with surface design from the paper or textile arts, I hope you will see
surface techniques in a new light. One goal of this book is to illustrate how anyone interested in surface design, regardless of their experience, can develop or expand their repertoire of surface treatments by using artist media in different ways and by combining surface and polymer clay techniques.
Stamps can be used to apply images or texture. Paints and inks can be used in silk-screening, monoprinting, or masking. Acrylic media can be used to create faux suede, raku, or paste paper surfaces.
The other goal of this book is to spark ideas for using surface design. There are a number of creative
designs in the project and gallery sections of this book. From a simple card (page 84) to an elaborate
necklace with beaded fringe (page 88), you'll find a variety of ways to use decorated clay in creating
mixed-media pieces of art.

Polymer clay is our foundation material, so we begin this chapter with an overview of the material
and methods for working with it. To create successful surface designs, it is important to become
familiar with the properties of different media and how they interact with clay. Information about
how particular materials, such as paints, inks, and acrylic media, work on clay is given in the technique
and project instructions.

It is difficult to provide blanket rules about how artist materials work on clay. For example, acrylic paints and inks generally dry on raw or unbaked clay and bond permanently to clay when baked. But not all acrylic paints and inks dry completely on raw clay; some remain a little tacky. There is a variation in how products perform because manufacturers use different formulations. This is actually a welcome fact. It is precisely because of the differences in how materials work with clay that result in not only the surface techniques you'll find in this book, but also the techniques you may discover as you try various ideas. Note, too, that new products are being introduced to the market constantly, which offer the opportunity to create new techniques or apply current ones in different ways.

In my favorite section, Surface Technique Intensives (page 60), I invite you to use your surface-design knowledge and work with abandon. Mix materials! Mix techniques! Do the unthinkable—cut up that breathtaking decorated sheet you've just made! You'll appreciate how working in this way can fuel your creativity.

About Polymer Clay

Polymer clay is a brilliantly colored modern modeling material that bakes hard in a home oven. Its star feature is its compatibility with other art and craft materials, from acrylic paints to glues to glitter to metal leafing to rubber-stamping supplies. With polymer clay widely available in art and craft stores, sturdy and colorful three-dimensional art is within everyone's reach.

The basic ingredient of polymer clay is polyvinyl chloride (PVC), the same sturdy stuff that water pipes are made of. It also contains inert fillers to give it bulk (and sometimes texture), dyes and pigments to give it color, and a plasticizer—an oily chemical that allows the microscopic chains of PVC molecules to slide over each other at room temperature but lock onto each other when the clay is heated.

This clay, also known to its fans as "polyclay" and "PC," comes in many of the colors you find on the artist's paint rack—not only standard colors like red, white, and brown, but also flesh tones (developed for doll making) and translucents which are milky when raw but almost clear when baked properly (and in a thin enough layer, they're absolutely transparent). With many brands, you can mix the package colors and get attractive intermediate shades.

Manufacturers also make some wonderful specialty clays. There are pearlescent and metallic colors that incorporate tiny mica flakes to provide a shimmery luster. There are clays that remain flexible and rubbery and act like a pencil eraser when baked. There are glow-in-the-dark colors that shine at night. You can even make your own stone clays by mixing embossing powder from the rubber-stamp counter into translucent clay. Or you can mix in other grains or powders, from coffee grounds to aromatic herbs to iridescent pigments to children's tinted play sand.

With this book you'll learn many techniques for decorating the surface of opaque, translucent, and metallic clays. But feel free to experiment with other custom-color and specialty clays. The only rule in working with polymer clay is to create joyously!

Polymer Clay Basics

Which Clay Should You Use?

Polymer clay is colorful, adaptable, and compatible with many other art and craft materials. It's heat sensitive, which means it's stiff when cold and more malleable when warm. As you knead and condition it, especially by hand, it gets warmer, softer, and stickier, but it does firm up again when it cools.

The different brands on the market are similar enough to be blended successfully, but they do have different characteristics. When you become familiar with the various properties of each, it will be easy to choose the right clay for the job. Manufacturers do change clay formulas from time to time, and they're always releasing new products, so test clays yourself to discover your favorites.

❖ **Sculpey** is an inexpensive, soft, brittle, white clay that is popular with railroad and dollhouse modelers for making buildings and landscape figures that will not receive wear and tear. It takes paint well.

❖ **Premo Sculpey** is a fine, all-purpose clay that is strong and slightly flexible when properly baked. Many of the colors are the same as artist's paint colors, making paint-mixing savvy useful. It's a good caning clay. Some sculptors and doll makers find it too soft and sticky.

❖ **Sculpey III** bakes to an attractive matte finish, and its translucent clay becomes the clearest of all. It's often given to children because it's soft

out of the package. However, it can accidentally "toast," or turn brown, if the oven temperature is too high. Even when properly baked, it's relatively chalky and brittle and breaks easily if dropped.

❖ **Sculpey Super Flex** is a very soft, sticky clay when uncured that remains highly flexible even after it's baked. When making a mold from an existing object, ensure the clay won't stick to the object by first coating the clay with a release agent, such as cornstarch, baby powder, talcum powder, water, or glycerin.

❖ **Super Sculpey** is a very strong, hard clay designed for doll making. It's sold only in large packages.

❖ **Fimo Classic** is a firm clay, valued by cane makers for its ability to hold fine patterns and by sculptors for its ability to take sharp details and hold its shape.

❖ **Fimo Soft** is firm in the package, but it is pressure-sensitive, so it softens readily under a roller. The transparent colors are brilliant, like stained glass. The glitter colors are made from tinted transparent clay blended with fine, heat-tolerant glitter.

❖ **Cernit** is formulated for doll making. It's soft to handle, but it's the hardest of the polymer clays when cured. Most colors are slightly translucent, like porcelain.

❖ **Creall-Therm** is excellent for making miniatures because it can safely be rolled out into tiny threads without breaking, and it isn't overly sticky.

❖ **Kato Clay** is the newest clay on the market. This clay conditions easily and is strong and durable when cured. The clay is also good for caning, and it requires less sanding and buffing to achieve a polished finish.

Fimo, Kato, and Sculpey all make a translucent liquid clay. Kato liquid clay (also known as **Kato Sauce**) and **Translucent Liquid Sculpey** (TLS) are products used in this book primarily as a finish to seal powders or crayon on the surface of clay. Liquid translucent clay has a variety of decorative and utilitarian uses. Powders, alcohol, acrylic inks, and oil-based artist paint can be mixed into TLS and applied on clay as a paint or glaze. Mix oil-based paint in liquid clay for consistent results. You can get bubbling or crackle effects when baking liquid clay mixed with acrylic paint depending of the grade and chemistry of the paint. Liquid clay can also be used to fill in small crevices or to assure adhesion between baked and unbaked clay. See the section about sanding and buffing liquid clay to a glasslike shine (see page 26).

Polymer Clay Equipment and Supplies

Experiment and you'll soon discover which tools work best for you. Below are the essential items you'll need to begin, including some household items adaptable for use with polymer clay.

Safety Tip: Polymer clay is certified nontoxic, so it's safe for adults and supervised children to use. However, once you use a kitchen tool with polymer clay, don't use it for preparing food again, and don't place foods on polymer clay surfaces.

Basic Kit (shown on right)
❖ **Work surface (A)** You'll need a large, smooth, and solvent-proof work area as your base. It can be made of Lucite, tempered glass, marble, tile, Formica, (or similar kitchen counter material); a flexible polypropylene plastic cutting board, or even heavy paper or cardboard will work. Don't use a varnished tabletop; as raw clay will damage varnish and acrylic plastics such as those used for inexpensive picture frames. Bare wood isn't ideal either because clay will stick in the pores. If you use paper for your work area, you'll need a separate cutting surface made from Lucite, glass, or a self-healing craft cutting board.

❖ **Rolling tools (B)** An acrylic pipe or rod, a brayer, a heavyweight straight-sided drinking glass or jar, a thick wooden dowel, or a marble rolling pin will all work. To make large, even, thin sheets, a pasta machine is extremely helpful.

❖ **Cutting tools (C)** Sharp scissors with smooth blades, craft knives with pointed and rounded blades, and long, thin tissue blades specially made for polymer clay are all useful.

❖ **Needle tools (D)** These are available from ceramics suppliers and can also be found in the sculpting section of art supply stores. You can also make your own by placing a large darning needle in a polymer clay ball, baking it, then pulling out the needle, washing off any oil, and gluing it back in place with cyanoacrylate glue.

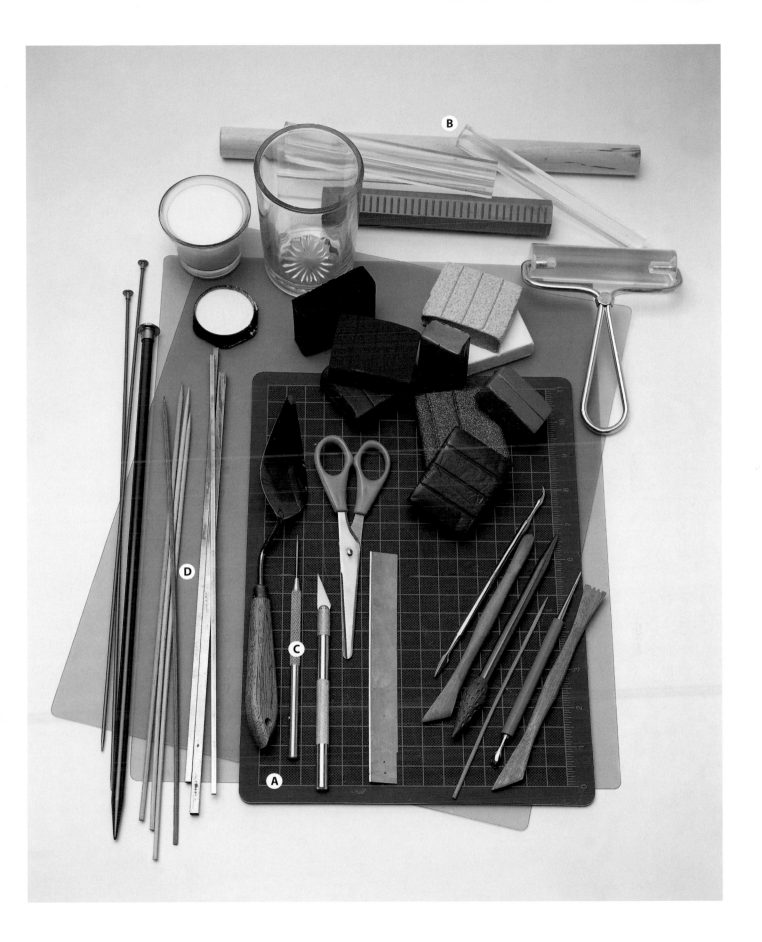

❖ **Oven** When you're first getting to know polymer clay, a home oven may be used, then wiped out and washed down carefully afterward. Once hooked, most cautious clay lovers obtain a small portable toaster oven or convection oven and use it only for art.

❖ **Oven thermometer** To properly cure polymer clay, you'll need a thermometer to check and calibrate your oven's temperature.

❖ **Rubbing alcohol** Tools and surfaces can be cleaned easily with rubbing alcohol.

❖ **Finishing materials** Sanding with wet/dry sandpaper followed by buffing with a cotton wheel gives polymer clay a polished, glasslike finish. You'll need sandpaper grits ranging from 320 to 600, which you can buy from home-improvement stores. For an even shinier finish, extrafine grades from 800 to 2,000 are available at auto-supply stores.

❖ **Latex or plastic gloves** Polymer clay is certified nontoxic, but like all art materials, it should be used with care. Some people find that it irritates their skin, so protect your hands with latex or plastic gloves or an artist's or mechanic's cream.

Safety Tip: Tissue blades are extremely sharp, and the dull and cutting edges look similar. Paint the dull side with nail polish, or bake a strip of polymer clay onto it, remove the clay, then glue this new "handle" into place on the tissue blade.

Intermediate Kit

Shown on page 19 are some of the things that can also be used with polymer clay. Many of the items pictured are called for in the techniques and projects that follow. Once you've assembled a basic kit, start experimenting with other materials to assemble a more sophisticated, personalized kit.

Working With Polymer Clay

Conditioning

Polymer clay can be used right out of the package, but conditioning the clay makes it more pliable. (Some artists say that conditioning also makes it stronger.) During conditioning, the plasticizer is distributed more evenly, bubbles are driven out, and the clay warms up and softens. When it cools, it will firm up again, but the other improvements will remain.

To condition clay by hand, it's best to start with the clay at body temperature. To get it there, you can put the packages in your clothing for a while, place them in a gentle warming device such as a baby-bottle warmer or a barely warm heating pad, or seal them in a resealable plastic bag and submerge the bag in lukewarm water.

Remove the wrapper and lay about 1 oz (28 gm) of clay (half a block) on your work surface. Roll over it heavily with a strong roller: an acrylic rod or pipe, a brayer, a thick wooden dowel, or a rolling pin. (An acrylic rod is preferable because clay will not stick to it with repeated use.) Fold it, squash it flat, and roll again. When it's a bit softer, form it into a log, and roll it out into a snake. Fold it over, twist it, and ball it up. Repeat until the clay has the texture and elasticity you want—approximately fifteen to twenty times.

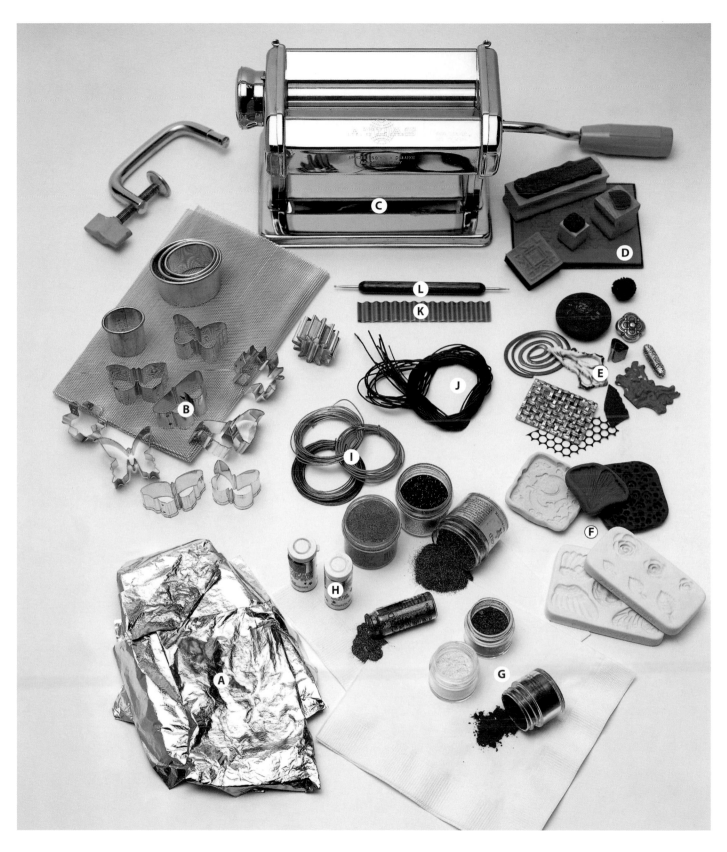

A metallic leaf

B cookie and hors d'ouevres cutters

C pasta machine (durable Italian model)

D deep-cut rubber stamps

E texturing tools, such as beads, charms, and found objects

F molds, handmade and commercial

G powders and pigments, such as metallic, mica, and embossing powders

H inclusions, such as ultrafine glitters and tiny beads

I plastic-coated craft wire

J rubber and leather cording

K wavy blade

L ball-end stylus

To condition clay with a pasta machine, lay half a block of clay on your work surface and flatten it to make it thin enough to feed into the pasta machine's rollers. Crank it through. Fold the resulting sheet in half and feed it through again, fold side first. Repeat about twenty times.

It takes the same amount and kind of work to mix colors uniformly as is does to condition clay. If you want to mix colors, begin when you start conditioning.

Leaching

Clay that is fresh from the factory may be too soft and sticky to work with. To harden it a bit, roll it into sheets (using the middle setting on a pasta machine). Place the sheets on clean office paper, then sandwich them between absorbent newspapers, and weigh them down with books for at least 24 hours. Some of the oily plasticizer will leach into the papers. In some cases, you may have to do this more than once before the clay is firm enough.

Softening

All clay becomes firmer over time, as polymerization slowly advances. Some clays are inherently stiffer than others. Two proprietary softeners—Sculpey Diluent or Clay Softener and Fimo Mix Quick—can be used to soften clay that is too hard. Artists have also used vegetable oil or mineral oil. The translucent liquid clays can also be used for this purpose. You can mix any brand of liquid clay with any brand of solid clay, but you may develop a preference for a particular combination.

First, chop up the hard clay, place it in a resealable plastic bag, add a few drops of softener, and leave it to soak overnight. The next day, compress the bag to adhere the clay scraps together. Take them out and place them on a sheet of fresh clay, fold the sheet around the scraps, and condition the whole "sandwich."

Storing Opened Packages

Don't leave raw clay on a painted or varnished surface, because the plasticizer will mar the surface. Instead, store the clay in the original package, a resealable plastic bag, or a polyethylene shoebox, which protects the clay from dust.

Baking

Each manufacturer provides specifications for baking, or curing, their brand of polymer clay properly so that it hardens and fuses throughout without burning. These specifications are printed on the packages, and they vary from brand to brand. If the directions are missing, a good rule of thumb is to bake your clay project for thirty minutes per ¼" (6 mm) of thickness at 265°F to 275°F (129°C to 135°C). Some of the translucent clays may brown at this temperature, so first bake a test tile the same thickness as your project.

Most ovens cycle, first heating above the designated temperature, then turning off the heat and cooling down, then heating again, so most oven thermometers are inaccurate. To control the temperature, preheat the oven and use a separate oven thermometer to calibrate it: Adjust the dial on the oven until the oven thermometer reads 265°F (129°C), and don't worry about what the dial says.

If your oven has an overhead heating element, you may want to protect your project from scorching with an aluminum foil tent. The clay shouldn't go above 300°F (149°C), because it will begin to scorch and emit unpleasant fumes.

During baking, the clay goes through a soft stage when it can sag or slump under gravity and conform to the surface supporting it. To prevent this, thin strands or sheets should be supported with a curl of paper, and to avoid getting glassy spots where the clay piece touched a polished glass or metal baking surface, it's a good idea to lay the clay on a piece of plain paper or cardboard for baking.

Beads can be set on pleated paper or cardstock, which will yield while supporting them; or they can be held up on a bamboo skewer, a stiff wire, or 00 aluminum knitting needles. Large rounded objects can be supported during baking by a nest of quilt stuffing, which won't melt or stick to the clay.

Ceramic tiles make an excellent, inexpensive, portable baking surface, and they're available in both glossy and matte finishes. Many clayers bake on metal or tempered glass pans or sheets of cardboard. Don't bake on Teflon, which can fuse with polymer clay.

After baking, most projects should be allowed to cool slowly to room temperature. But translucent clay benefits from being dropped into ice water while still hot; if you do this, the final project will appear more translucent.

Safety Tip: Bake polymer clay with the best ventilation you can manage. Turn on a fan and open the windows.

Cleaning Up

Your work surface and pasta machine should be kept clean to avoid having one color of clay contaminate the next one. Many clayers wipe down their machines with baby wipes or rubbing alcohol on a paper towel.

The warmer your hands, the more likely they are to acquire a sticky film of clay as you work. Massaging in a bit of hand lotion and wiping it off with a paper towel, then washing with cool water and dish detergent that cuts grease should do the trick.

Choosing Glue

PVA-Based White Craft Glues

Use this basic glue to help raw clay bond to baked clay or stick to paper. PVA stands for polyvinyl acetate, a close chemical cousin to the PVC (polyvinyl chloride) that is the basis of polymer clay. Coat the cured surface with the glue and allow it to dry, then affix the raw clay.

Cyanoacrylate Glue

This glue, commonly called SuperGlue or Krazy Glue, can be used to bond baked clay to metal, glass, or other pieces of baked clay. The cyanoacrylate glue bond fails at high temperatures, however, there is now an exception to this: Poly Bonder by Lisa Pavelka, Heart in Hand Studio, is effective up to 300°F (149°C).

E6000 Silicon Glue

This heavy-duty glue is extremely effective, but it contains harsh solvents. Use it outdoors.

Two-Part Epoxy Glues

These are the best glues for bonding baked clay to metal, such as jewelry findings.

Basic Techniques

Making Sheets

All the surface techniques in this book require that you make polymer clay sheets. The easiest way to control this is to pinch and pull your conditioned clay into a rough rectangle about the thickness of a dinner plate, then roll it through a pasta machine, which is designed to roll out even, consistent layers of dough. Pasta machines take so much of the labor out of clay work that they're well worth the investment—and they can often be found at secondhand stores and yard sales.

But even if you don't have a pasta machine, you can still make thin, even sheets by using bakers' techniques and treating your clay like piecrust dough. With your hands, roll a lump of conditioned clay into a fat cylinder, dust it with cornstarch or talc, and flatten it with a thick roller. You can pull on the edges with your hands to help the process.

To roll the clay out to an even thickness, tape down two long rods, skewers, or chopsticks beside the clay in a parallel orientation. (Many hobby shops sell foot-long sections of squared-off brass and aluminum tubing in different diameters that would be ideal for this.) Place the roller on top of the rod and roll out the clay that is positioned between them. You can get clay sheets that vary in thickness by varying the thickness of the rods. Then roll your clay out even with the rods.

Settings for Rolling Sheets

This chart, devised by Dottie McMillan, lists the corresponding thickness for each pasta machine setting. (Some machines have more than seven settings.) It is a useful guide when you need to prepare relatively thick or thin sheets.

Setting	Inches	Millimeters
1	$\frac{1}{8}$ "	3.2 mm
2	$\frac{7}{64}$ "	2.8 mm
3	$\frac{3}{32}$ "	2.4 mm
4	$\frac{5}{64}$ "	2.0 mm
5	$\frac{1}{16}$ "	1.6 mm
6	$\frac{1}{32}$ "	0.8 mm
7	$\frac{1}{40}$ "	0.6 mm

Millefiori (Canework)

One of the most popular polymer clay techniques comes from the clay's ability to stretch evenly and smoothly. It shares this quality, technically known as "thixotropicity," with hot glass and hard candy. This stretchiness makes it possible to layer several colors together in a pattern, consolidate the layers into a multicolored loaf, then stretch out the loaf without changing the proportions of the colors.

Long pieces of different-colored polymer clay can be assembled into many-colored "canes" that keep the same pattern throughout the length, even after you compress the sides and stretch the cane out long and narrow. This is called "reducing" the cane—really you're reducing the diameter but increasing the length. The great thing is that with clay, you can do it all at room temperature! And once you have made a cane, you can make many thin slices with the same pattern, just as slicing a jellyroll dessert yields the same spiral pattern in every slice. In fact, one of the most common canes is called a "jellyroll" cane.

Cane patterns can be as simple as stripes, checks, bull's-eyes, and swirls. And because you can stack and pack simple canes together, they can also add up to complex canes of flowers, faces, and even landscapes. A combination of simple and complex canes are displayed in Clay as Surface Media, page 54.

Color Mixing, Marbling, and Blends

You can mix two or more colors during the conditioning process simply by flattening each color and stacking the layers at the start; by the time you have finished conditioning, the colors will be mixed.

One of the simplest decorative techniques is to marble clay. Start by making small snakes of different colors of conditioned clay. Bundle them, pack them, and twist them together. Roll the bundle on your work surface to lengthen it, then fold it and twist again. Stop when you like the marbled effect; if you go too far, the clay will start to look blended rather than marbled.

For a simple blend—often called "Skinner blend" in reference to the technique's developer, Judith

Skinner—start by rolling out two colors of clay sheets about the same size. (The clay doesn't have to be conditioned in advance, because it will be conditioned by the blending process.) Trim them into rectangles. Slice one sheet diagonally, and stack the two triangles; repeat with the other sheet. Butt the two double triangles together so they make a rectangle, one color on each side; overlap the edge a bit, and press them so they stick together. Feed the double-thick rectangle through the rollers of a pasta machine. This will stretch out the rectangle twice as long but a single thickness. Fold it in half again at the "waist," and roll it through again, fold side first. Repeat about fifteen times, always folding at the waist and sending it through fold side first. By the time you have finished, you'll have a smooth color blend with one color down one vertical edge and the other color down the other vertical edge; the upper and lower edges will show the blend. If you stop early—after about ten times—you'll have an incomplete blend with a cross-section that looks streaky, like ikat cloth.

For a complex blend, start by rolling out a clay sheet at least 6" (15 cm) long in each color you want to use. From each sheet, cut out two long triangles about 2" (5 cm) wide at the base. Assemble them together, head to foot, into a rectangle the width of your pasta machine; overlap the edges of the pieces, and pinch them together. Send the whole piece through the pasta machine. Fold the long rectangle at the "waist," and send it through the pasta machine, fold side first. Repeat as above. You'll have a blended sheet with one color down one side, another down the other side; the top and bottom edges will show the blend. The ikat technique and complex color blending are shown in the final surface treatment on page 74.

Metallic Effects

Some of the Premo Sculpey clays contain so much mica that they look like mother-of-pearl or metal. Mica is formed of flat plates, and remarkably, when you run the metallic or pearl clays through the pasta machine, the pressure seems to make the plates line up and face the surface of the sheet. Because the little plates reflect light, the surface looks brighter and brighter the more you send it through the pasta machine. Conversely, the edges of the sheet look darker because you're looking between the little plates.

Acrylic floor finish and metallic powders are used to create a crackled effect on the handle of this ice cream scoop.

Artist: Mona Kissel

Artists discovered this effect and figured out many ways to use it. Most rely on making sheets of brightened clay, cutting them into uniform pieces, stacking them, and then manipulating the stack in various ways to take advantage of the contrast between the brightened surface and the darkened edges.

Mokumé Gané

An ancient Japanese metalworking technique inspired the artists who developed these methods. The original involved soldering and compressing layers of several colored metals into one fused piece, punching into them from both sides to make bumps and hollows, then sanding off the bumps to reveal the layers beneath.

In clay, of course, it's easy to get different layers to stick together, and clay artists have a rainbow of colors, translucents, pearly clays, paints, inclusions, and metal leaf to work with. Many artists have developed special variations on this theme. Layer work shows how different artists can take a basic idea, play with it, and come up with utterly different results.

The core mokumé gané technique is to stack different colored sheets of unbaked clay, rumple them like a bed after a restless night or punch into them, then take thin slices from the top. Because the layers are no longer flat, each cut will slice through several layers, revealing striations the way a road cut reveals underlying layers of earth and stone or a wood carver reveals the grain of a block of wood. Often these irregular slices are flipped over, laid on another sheet of clay, and rolled down to create a variegated sheet. This can be used as is or made into a veneer to cover an object. Depending on which clays are originally selected and whether other materials such as glitter or metal leaf are included, the effects can be very different.

Using Armatures, Inside and Out

Polymer clay is malleable until cured, and it becomes even softer for a short time during baking. Small objects usually aren't heavy enough to go out of shape during baking, but heat and gravity will make sheets and large items sag unless they're supported.

Heavy paper and cardboard can be used externally—for example, a stiff paper cone can be wrapped in a floppy sheet of clay, which will be sturdy once it has been baked. Heat-resistant materials can be used internally as armatures. Glass and most metals are suitable. Crushed aluminum foil makes a good core for sculptures and beads. Metal screening can be used to reinforce thin sheets.

With successive bakings, clay itself can become a kind of armature. After the foundation layer is baked, it becomes stiff and easy to handle; later layers can be added and baked, permitting the construction of elaborate objects. A tiny dab of translucent liquid clay on points that may be stressed later will help ensure a solid bond.

Covering Forms

When a sheet of clay is wrapped or draped over a glass, metal, wood, or cardboard form and then baked, the clay takes on that shape. You can use found objects such as bottles, bowls, boxes, lighting fixtures, switch plates, or tins as forms, or you can build your own with tape and cardboard. Keep in mind that manipulating decorated sheets of clay over a form can distort or destroy the surface treatment. Minimize this by applying decorated clay to simple forms or apply decorated clay as individual tiles. You may bake between each tile's application to ensure that the decoration is preserved.

If you don't want the clay and the form to stick together after baking, use a release agent between them. Pull the clay and form apart while they're still hot from baking; clay expands very little when hot, but that little can be helpful in separating tightly fitted pieces. If you're willing to leave the form in place, simple enclosure will hold them together. If you don't want to leave it in, you can cut the clay (preferably an angled cut), pull out the form, and then use glue or translucent liquid clay to reunite the cuts. Don't use varnished or painted metal as a form without a lot of release agent; the clay will stick to the varnish. Conversely, painted tins can easily be permanently covered with clay because it sticks to the paint.

Finishing Touches

Carving, Drilling, and Filing

Once fully baked, polymer clay can be easily carved, incised, filed, sawed, or drilled. Underbaked clay is usually too brittle to withstand this treatment. Experiment with wood-carving tools, sculpting tools, and any other kind of implement you can find at art- and craft-supply stores. Once carved, try rubbing paint into the grooves to accentuate them.

To drill a thin or small piece of polymer clay, mark the area first, and use a needle tool to gently dent the area. Then, simply hand-twist a drill bit into the dent to enlarge it. For thicker or larger pieces of clay, use a small hobby drill.

Artist's Tip: Incised or cut areas will likely appear white, but this residue can be removed by rebaking the piece. Alternately, the incised areas could be back-filled with clay or tube acrylic paint. You should rebake after back-filling with either clay or paint.

Artist: Gwen Gibson

Polishing

Polishing translucent clay is especially effective, because the transparency is greatly enhanced. When transparent liquid clay is applied over a surface treatment, the resulting baked surface may be sanded and buffed to a polished finish. But consider this step carefully, as the coating of liquid clay is thin and you don't want to sand away any of your decorative finish. You can apply more liquid clay to the piece and bake it again.

If you choose to sand and buff your piece, here are the general directions for doing so. When working with wet/dry sandpaper, always use it in water (a full bowl will do it) to keep the clay cool and the dust in the water, so you don't inhale it. If you want to remove a lot of clay, start at 180 grit (fairly coarse), then progress to 320, 400, and 600 grit; if you want a real shine, get superfine paper (800 grit and higher) at an auto-supply shop. Finally, buff it on your jeans or other cotton cloth until glossy. Aficionados may want to use

a bench grinder with an unstitched cotton wheel or even a variable speed buffer made for jewelers. Buffing attachments are available for hobby drills.

Artist's Tip: Keep the clay object moving at all times. If you let it linger too long in one spot on the buffing wheel, the friction could damage the clay.

Artist: Gwen Gibson

The decorated clay on this pin (left) and wearable box pendant (above) was created with handmade silk screens and acrylic paint.

What Is Polymer Clay?

Polymer clay is a synthetic modeling material that you can bake, or cure, in an oven. It comes in different brands and colors and can be sculpted, carved, textured, sanded, and painted. Polymer clay does not create a mess and does not require any special setup or equipment. These properties make this versatile medium very accessible to beginners, as well as a first choice for sculpting small characters. Polymer clay is easy to work with and allows you to concentrate on the process of creation rather than on struggling with the material.

Finding Polymer Clay Tools and Supplies

You can find polymer clay tools and supplies in arts and crafts stores, or you can order them online.

Please see the Resources section at the back of this book for more information.

The Wrong Tool for the Right Job

The philosophy of this book is that you shouldn't let a shortage of the *right* polymer clay or the *right* tools stop you. To illustrate this point, I have used polymer clays ranging from Fimo Soft to Super Sculpey and everything from a safety pin to a clay shaper as tools for the projects in this book. You should feel free to improvise. Personally, I prefer, and recommend, the Premo Sculpey brand of clay for its nice finish and sturdiness after baking. As a rule of thumb, try to avoid clays that are too soft or sticky for your taste. The brand of clay, its color, and its quantity should not be obstacles to sculpting success. The color schemes in the projects are only a suggestion, and it is up to you whether a Little Red Riding Hood will wear a bright yellow hat or not.

The quantities of clay needed, which are stated in the beginning of each project, are a rough estimate and always give you the maximum amount you would need. This method avoids impractical measurement units, such as $1/231$ block of clay, and helps you develop a sense of proportion.

As for tools, I recommend the use of *clay shapers*, because their rubbery tips are excellent for manipulating the clay. The tapered-point and the cup-round clay shapers in particular are used for most of the projects in this book. Alternatively, you can use a *cuticle pusher*, a common manicure tool, instead of a clay shaper. This tool is also the best choice for hard clays (or older clays), for which the soft tip of the shaper does not work well. Do not hesitate to experiment with other tools that seem to fulfill the same function as a clay shaper or a cuticle pusher; there is no tool that cannot be switched for something else—except for your hands, of course.

All the previously mentioned standard tools and supplies can be found online or in arts and crafts stores. For more information, see the Resources section in the back of this book.

How to Read the Instructions

The project instructions in this book are designed to first and foremost give you a *visual* idea of how a critter is made. While working, keep in mind that each step is not an isolated move, but comes in the continuity of what has already been done in the previous step and what will be done in the next one. To make the most out of the visual instructions for each step, try to take a quick look at the one before it and the one after it. That way you do not run risks such as making an excessively large earlobe that blocks a sideburn that needs to make its way onto the cheek of an Elvis impersonator.

How to Hold a Critter

Many of the pictures in this book do not show how you should hold a critter while working on it. A goofy head sitting by itself in the middle of a light blue desert with a clay shaper stuck in its ear will not be an uncommon sight. However, you will often need to exert counterpressure to a certain manipulation or simply hold a bit of clay to have better access to the surface on which you are working.

Generally, you should hold a critter like you would hold a baby—you have to support the bottom (the heavier part that is dragging down the whole) and you have to make sure its head doesn't come off. The easiest way to do this is to keep your thumb on the bottom and your fingers or fingertips on the back (which is usually plain and where there is nothing to ruin).

Baking

The last and often most important step of making a polymer clay character is baking. You can use either an electric or a gas oven to bake polymer clay. A convection oven is best because the fan inside helps the hot air circulate evenly around the critter. When baking, always follow the specific clay manufacturer's instructions on the package—they will provide the basics. The following tips are additional hints that may save you some trial and error:

- One of the main objectives when baking is to preserve the shapes you have created. Often when you put a character in the oven, it might lean to one side (or stick its nose to the baking tray, just out of curiosity). To avoid this problem, make tin foil props.

- Also use tin foil to cover your creatures so that they don't change color too much—prolonged, unprotected exposure of a critter to oven heat may lead to crisp, caramel-colored formations on their soft polymer-clay skin.

- Do not exceed the baking temperature indicated for the brand of clay you are using. As long as you bake at the right temperature, the critter will get stronger and stronger with every additional minute of baking and won't burn. Generally, bigger critters like to spend more time in the oven.

- Keep in mind that when you turn the oven dial to 275°F (135°C), the temperature inside the oven is not necessarily 275°F. Ovens are not exactly the sharpest NASA gear. Ideally, try to find an oven thermometer to measure the actual temperature, thus ensuring the safety of your critters. If you don't have a thermometer or if you are baking for the first time in an oven, it is always a good idea to give a small chunk of clay a test ride before baking your day's work. Check on the critter every now and then to make sure everything is all right.

- Be careful when you take critters out of the oven—they will be quite fragile until they cool. If you overbake a critter, do not inhale the fumes and immediately air out the room. Remember, you can always make a better one.

- You can bake an underbaked critter over and over again without damaging the clay as long as you bake at the right temperature. This is very useful for fixing critters—you can just attach a missing arm and cure the whole critter one more time.

- When making a more complicated character, you might find it helpful to bake the critter midway through the process and then continue working on a more solid structure.

You will be referred back to this basic "baking" section at the end of each lesson, so keep this section handy until you have become experienced with your baking methods.

Chapter 2
Surface Techniques and Applications

If you're one to dive into new projects, then you've come to the right place. This chapter will guide you through familiar surface techniques that are created with some innovative twists, such as using a kitchen scrubbing sponge to stipple layers of oil pastel (below left) or monoprinting with facial tissue (below right).

Stamping, a popular technique in general, is especially versatile when combined with polymer clay because not only color, but also texture come into play. Monoprinting, brayering, and masking are among the techniques for achieving different looks with paint or ink applications. Spraying, splattering, and sponging takes paint or ink in still another direction. Techniques involving powders, pastel crayons, and pens are also featured in conjunction with paint and ink methods as well as independently.

Note: White clay is the base for all tile swatches except where indicated. All clay is conditioned and rolled out to a medium thickness.

Surface techniques involving acrylic media can yield dramatic results. The techniques presented here introduce you to several acrylic products and faux surfaces that can be created with them. Imagine making faux suede or paste-paper ornaments! Clay as Surface Media (page 54) demonstrates that surface design on clay isn't only about applying *other* substances on clay.

The collection of Surface Technique Intensives (pages 60-81) gives you an opportunity to design surfaces using a combination of techniques. You can create either complex or subtle designs working this way. The choice is yours.

Whether you try the techniques in succession or work with them randomly, you'll gain a greater appreciation for the art of surface design.

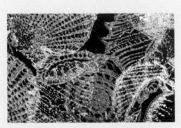
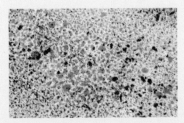

Basic Surface Recipes

Stamping to Add Images and Designs

Combining and applying stamps with various media allows for a wide array of effects.

Stamp credit: Stampendous

Materials

- beige or ecru clay
- opaque bronze metallic acrylic paint (shown: Lumiere)
- opaque copper metallic acrylic paint (shown: Lumiere)
- black acrylic gesso (shown: Golden)
- aluminum foil
- rubber stamp
- piece of a foam pad or a fine-textured cosmetic sponge

1. To prepare the background, use a piece of crumpled aluminum foil to stipple on a layer of bronze metallic paint. Let the paint dry. Repeat this step to apply another layer of copper metallic paint, and let it dry again.

2. Create a foam ink pad by applying black acrylic gesso to a section of foam pad.

3. Press the rubber stamp against the custom-made ink pad.

4. Stamp your design onto the stippled background of the polymer clay. Be sure to clean the stamp immediately.

> **Note:** A fine-textured sponge is used predominately throughout this book except where indicated. You can use a sponge with different texture, but your results may vary.

Variations

1   Apply acrylic craft paint to plastic grids (found in the embroidery section of craft stores), coarse-weave embroidery-type cloth, and the prongs of a furniture coaster to create this collage of abstract images.

2   For extra contrast, use opaque metallic acrylic paints, such as any of the Stewart Gill lines or Jacquard's Lumiere, to stamp onto a background of black clay.

3   Smooth a light layer of mica powder onto the clay. Sponge an acrylic media, such as acrylic gel media or silk-screen media, onto a rubber stamp. After stamping, spray water on the stamp to keep the acrylic media from drying until the stamp can be cleaned. Smooth mica over the clay again to reveal the invisible images. Sponge Kato liquid translucent clay over the clay to seal the mica powder.

Shadow and Bold Image Stamps

A dramatic overall image can be created with shadow and bold image stamps.

Stamp credits: Hero Arts; Hot Potatoes

Materials

- pigment ink palette set (shown: Clearsnap's ColorBox Fluid Chalk ink pad because of its ability to dry on polymer clay; Tsukineko's Brilliance is another pigment ink that similarly dries on clay)
- assortment of shadow and bold image stamps
- scrap of plain paper or paper towel

1. Lightly ink the shadow stamps (the squares) and a bold image stamp (the leaf) with colors from pigment ink palette set.

2. Stamp onto the clay, then gently blot the image with paper or a paper towel to remove excess ink and hasten the ink's drying. If you blot with a textured paper towel, a bit of the towel's texture will transfer.

Tip: The stamp may not adhere evenly on the clay and, as a result, the image may come out splotchy. You may like the look. If not, simply touch your finger to the ink pad and dab on more ink to fill in the splotches as desired.

Variations

1 Ink a bold image stamp with various colors of metallic acrylic paint, then stamp on the clay and smooth on mica powder. Create the border pattern by sponging on metallic paint. Use liquid translucent clay to seal the powder.

2 Here, preserve the detail of an intricate stamp by using Clearsnap's ColorBox Fluid Chalk ink pad.

3 Stamp this tile using acrylic ink (shown Dr. Ph. Martin's iridescent ink). Inks of this type cover the stamp and adhere to the clay differently than pigment inks or acrylic paints. As a result, this medium leaves lacelike images.

Stamp credit: Hot Potatoes

Stamp credit: Hero Arts

Stamp credits: Hero Arts, Magenta, Hampton Art, Judikins

Basic Surface Recipes

Stamps and Texture Tools

Stamps and texture tools provide dimensional interest to clay surfaces.

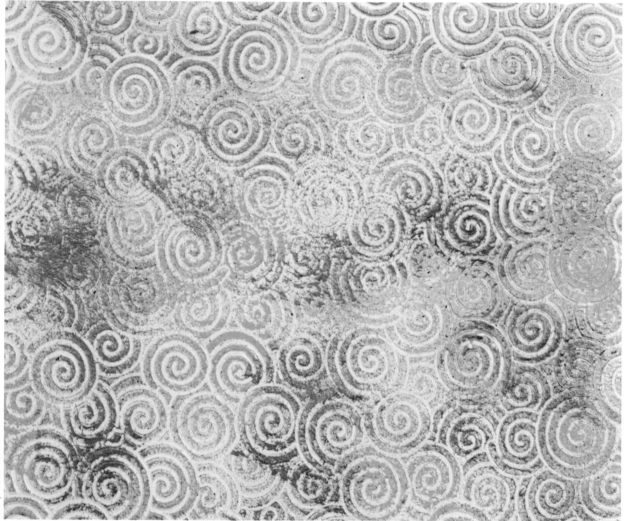

Stamp Credit: Judikins

Materials

- assortment of metallic and nonmetallic acrylic paints (shown: Jacquard's Textile Color)
- background or overall-pattern rubber stamp
- Armorall or spray bottle with water
- piece of a foam pad or a cosmetic sponge

1. Spritz the stamp with Armorall (car protectant finish) or water. This keeps the clay from sticking to the stamp.

2. Press the stamp into the clay to make an even impression.

3. Use the foam pad to lightly dab on one color of paint over the clay. Let the paint dry.

4. Apply additional layers of paint in a similar manner letting the paint dry after each layer.

Variations

1 Impress a texture sheet (shown: Shade-Tex) into brown clay to create a design. Sponge beige acrylic craft paint over the clay. Apply green, violet, and magenta metallic acrylic paint with a paintbrush and apply the magenta paint with small round sponge daubers.

2 Impress a daisy-patterned rubber stamp into a custom color of green clay. Sponge assorted acrylic paints onto the textured clay.

3 Sponge one color of acrylic paint over clay texturized with a rubber stamp.

Stamp Credit: Embossing Arts

Stamp credit: Just for Fun

Basic Surface Recipes

Monoprinting

Monoprinting emphasizes the interplay among paint or ink colors. Apply a minimum of colors to avoid creating a muddy mixture of paint or ink.

Materials

- metallic acrylic paint (shown: Stewart Gill's Pearlise and Byzantia)
- plastic sheet protector (found in craft and office supply stores)

1. Cut open a plastic sheet protector so it opens like a book.

2. Place a few dollops of metallic acrylic paint between the plastic pages. If you are using multiple colors, space each color widely because as the paints spread, some colors can be obscured.

3. Close the sheet protector and smooth your fingers over the plastic to spread the paint between the sheets.

4. Open the sheet protector and lay a sheet of clay over one or both sides of the protector.

5. Press your fingers over the clay to ensure the paint is picked up by the clay.

Variations

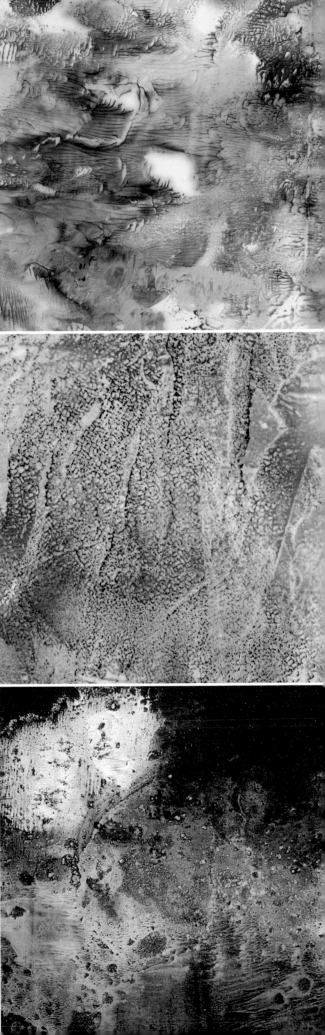

1 Spread dots of tube acrylic paint between the pages of a sheet protector. Lay the clay over the paint to apply.

Tip: Spray a light mist of water over any acrylic paint or ink that starts drying on the sheet protector as you are working.

2 Place facial tissue between the pages of a sheet protector, then dot liquid acrylic paint or ink onto the tissue. (This is done so that if the liquid acrylic beads up on plastic, it would be absorbed by the tissue paper instead.) Lightly spray water over the tissue to help spread the liquid acrylic. Note how the folds in the tissue transfer as impressions in the color.

Stamp credit: Judikins

3 Dot Magic Color liquid acrylic directly onto the pages of a sheet protector. Fold the sheet protector and spread the liquid acrylic inside it. (This liquid acrylic does not bead up on the plastic.) Sprinkle a metallic powder (shown: Angelwing's Polished Pigments) over the spread of liquid acrylic, then layer the clay over the combination of media. The powder that adheres to the liquid acrylic will also adhere to the polymer clay.

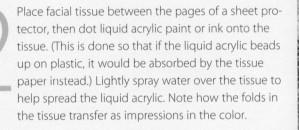

Basic Surface Recipes

Masking

Masking on clay can be done with a variety of materials: paper, plastic film, metal wire, and low-tack or Post-it tape. If the masking material is impressed in the clay, you can create the look of dry embossing similar to paper with impressed images.

Materials

- assortment of acrylic craft paint (shown: Anita's)
- stencil plastic, acetate, or overhead projector sheet (shown: E-Z Cut plastic stencil)
- piece of a foam pad or cosmetic sponge
- jewelry tweezer
- scissors, regular or decorative cutting edge

1. Cut a piece of plastic into small sections. Place the plastic sections over the clay, leaving space between each section.

2. Sponge one of the colors all over the clay. You do not need to cover the clay entirely.

3. Let the paint layer dry.

4. Carefully pick up and reposition the plastic sections. Sponge another paint color over the clay. Let it dry.

5. Reposition the plastic sections and sponge on another layer of paint. Let it dry.

Variations

1 Make a mask of any shape out of artist vellum paper cut with decorative-edge scissors and apply D'uva ChromaCoal Sticks with the back of a section of foam. D'uva pastels can be slightly sticky on raw clay, but they fix permanently after the clay is baked.

2 Apply acrylic gloss gel media on black clay and let it dry. Place artist vellum paper masks cut with scissors and a spiral punch on the clay, and smooth the masks over the clay to secure them. Apply mica or pigment powders (shown: Angelwings' Polished Pigments, which are a combination of mica and pigment powders). Remove the stencils and bake the tile. Apply liquid clay to seal the powders and bake the tile again.

3 Layer Post-it tape onto the clay. Apply Crayola Portfolio water-soluble oil pastels with the abrasive side of a kitchen scrubbing sponge. Apply translucent liquid clay and bake.

> **Tip:** Avoid leaving small clumps of the oil pastels on the clay. These might not get sealed under the liquid clay and will rub off.

Basic Surface Recipes

Brayering

Ink or paint can be applied with brayers to a smooth or textured finish.

Materials

- assortment of liquid acrylic paints (shown: Golden)
- rubber brayer

1. Place a few drops of the acrylic paints on the clay. Be careful not to use too many colors. They may become muddy when mixed.

2. Roll the brayer over part of the tile. Lift the brayer and roll it over another section of the tile.

3. Repeat this process to create a look you like.

Variations

1 Smooth a metallic powder onto clay. Roll a textured brayer in acrylic paint, then roll the brayer over the tile.

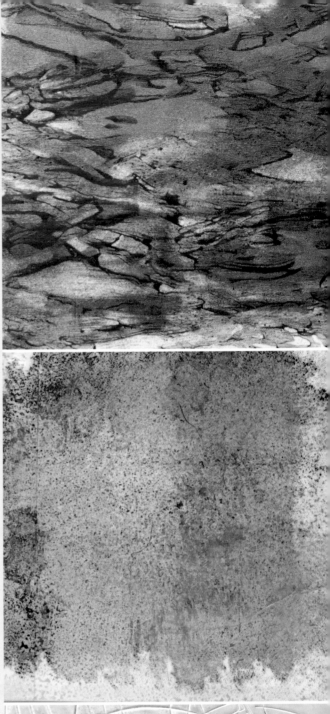

2 Apply Dye Na Flow fabric inks to a foam pad. Roll a rubber brayer over the pad, then roll it once over clay. Turn the clay 90 degrees, and roll the brayer once again.

Stamp credit: Stamps Happen, Inc.

3 Press a rubber stamp into clay. Roll a rubber brayer over a foam pad inked with Dye Na Flow fabric ink. Roll the brayer over the stamped clay several times to smooth the ink onto the clay. If you are using a rainbow of colors, be sure to keep the brayer aligned with the color stripes.

Basic Surface Recipes

Paste Paper

There are several acrylic gels and liquids available to try on polymer clay. Use acrylic media to create designs reminiscent of classic paste papers.

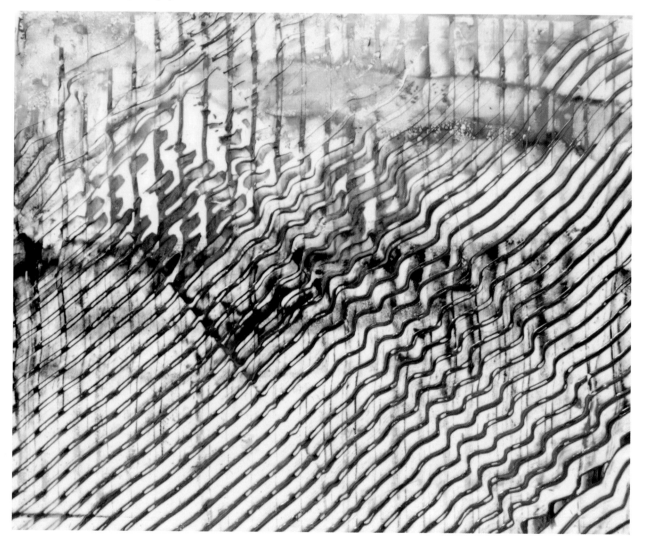

Materials

- assortment of liquid acrylic paints
- metal wood-graining combs
- small artist palette

1. Place lines of paint across the clay. The paint lines can touch or not.

2. Run a medium-tooth comb across the painted clay to spread the paint and to create classic paste-paper design.

3. Turn the clay diagonally and run a thin-tooth comb across it.

Variations

1 Mix drops of silk dye into a fluid acrylic medium. The amount varies according to how much mixture you need and how much color you want (shown: Colorhue dyes and Golden silk-screen medium). Smooth the mixture over clay. Comb a decorative pattern through the layer with a Coit multiline calligraphy pen.

2 Layer a mixture of liquid acrylic paint and acrylic gel medium over clay. Comb a decorative pattern through the layer with a wood-graining comb.

3 Smooth various colors of D'uva ChromaCoal pastel on clay. Layer on a mixture of liquid acrylic paint and acrylic gel medium, and comb through with two sizes of wood-graining combs.

Basic Surface Recipes

Acrylic Media

In "Paste Paper" acrylic gel effectively substitutes for the starch paste traditionally used to comb on paper. Here, two other acrylic compounds are used to affect the distribution of color.

Materials

- Golden Micaceous Iron Oxide acrylic medium (Linda Twohill coined the term "raku sauce" for this product.)
- oil pastels (used here: Crayola Portfolio)
- metallic powders
- palette knife or dinner knife
- small brush

1. Smooth the medium onto the clay with a knife and let it dry.

2. Brush metallic powders over the layer.

3. Rub oil pastels selectively over the surface. Smooth and blend the oil pastels as you apply them to complete the raku look.

Variations

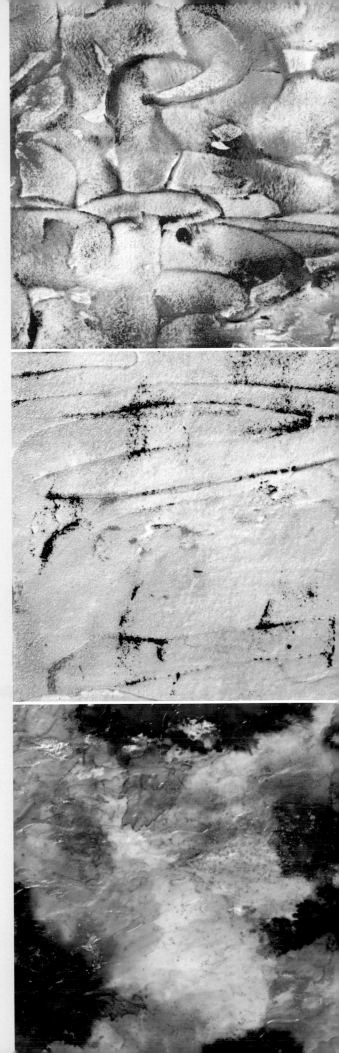

1 Apply acrylic modeling paste on clay and let it dry. (shown: US ArtQuest 101 Light Artist's Medium. You could also use Golden modeling paste.) Sponge on various colors of acrylic craft paint.

2 For a different look, apply an opaque acrylic medium, such as US ArtQuest 101 Light Artist's Medium, leaving less texture, then let it dry. Paint all over with one color of craft paint and apply additional colors sparingly.

3 Apply US ArtQuest 101 Heavy Artist's Medium (or Golden white gesso) on clay and let it dry. Dab on alcohol-based inks with cotton swabs or cosmetic applicators. Alcohol-based inks are fast-drying, yield dramatic blending effects, and have vibrant color (we used Ranger Crafts' Adirondack alcohol inks). Spritz on Adirondack alcohol blender solution, and while the surface is wet, sprinkle on metallic powders or dab with a metallic marker, such as Krylon, Sharpie, or Posh Impression markers.

Basic Surface Recipes

Silk-screening

Silk-screening is another way to transfer images—especially fine-lined or intricate ones—onto clay. Silk-screening results in a brocadelike finish on clay.

Materials

- fabric dye (shown: Colorhue)
- carrier medium (shown: Golden silk-screen medium, but a heavy hair gel containing alcohol can also be used)
- silk-screen stencil (used here: a stencil from the African series from Gwen Gibson)
- squeegee tool (used here: a wide Colour Shaper, but an old credit card or small rubber spatula can also be used)
- palette knife or a dinner knife
- foam plate or tray
- small spoon
- pan of cool water

1. Use a spoon to mix a few drops of the dye with a small amount of medium on a foam plate. Apply this mixture to the clay with a palette knife. Let it dry. Make a second color mixture.

2. Lay the stencil, shiny side down, onto the clay. Squeegee a small amount of the color mixture over the stencil. Lift the stencil and place it in the pan until you are ready to clean it.

Variations

1 Stencil metallic paint onto black clay (shown: Stewart Gill's Byzantia, which doesn't dry fully on the clay, but dries sufficiently for this application). When the first layer is dry, place a second stencil on the decorated clay. Spread tube acrylic paint across the second stencil. The opaque tube paint contrasts nicely with the more transparent metallic paint.

2 Spoon out small amounts of silk-screen medium on the plate. (Make a dollop for each color you are using; we used four colors.) Mix drops of the dye into the silk-screen medium, making individual color mixtures. Lay the stencil, shiny side down, onto the clay. Pick up a bit of one color mixture with a spoon and place bits of it on the stencil. Repeat with the remaining colors. Run the squeegee along the stencil, smoothing all the colors along the way. If there were sections of the clay left without color, clean off the squeegee and pick up color from the plate to correct this. This will keep your colors from getting muddy.

3 Sponge alcohol-based inks onto the clay with a cosmetic sponge. Lay the stencil over the clay, and squeegee tube acrylic paint across the stencil.

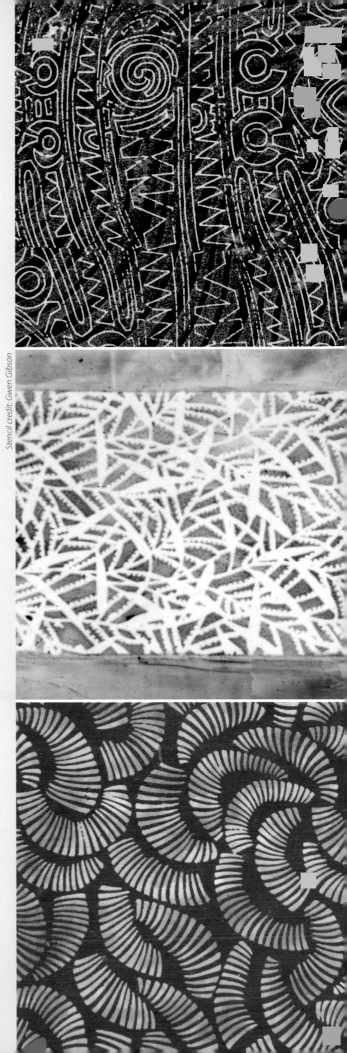

Stencil credit: Gwen Gibson

Basic Surface Recipes

Alcohol Inks

Alcohol inks blend like watercolors on polymer clay.

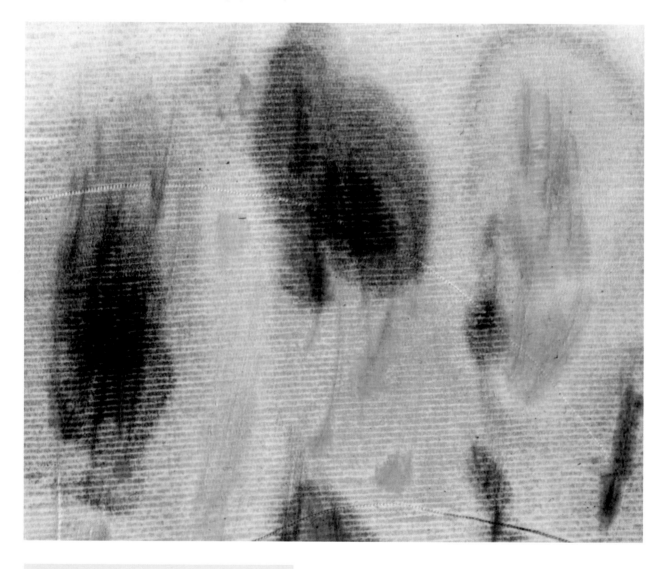

Materials

- alcohol-based inks, such as Ranger Crafts' Adirondack alcohol inks and Jacquard Piñata Colors
- swatch of fabric with a texture
- wax paper
- spray bottle containing rubbing alcohol
- brayer

1. Place the fabric on wax paper and spritz it lightly with alcohol.

2. Drop various colors of ink onto the fabric, allowing the colors to bleed into one another.

3. Pick up the fabric and wax paper together and place the fabric side on clay.

4. Roll the brayer over the wax paper, applying pressure to transfer both the ink and the fabric texture.

Note: In this example, some colors were applied by rubbing the bottle tip on the fabric. This translated as scribble lines in the design. You might exploit this to create a look of writing. Also, the thin lines across the tile were the result of a happy accident. Some fabric threads were caught between the clay and fabric. The threads were colored and impressed in the clay.

Variations

1   Moisten a swatch of fabric with rubbing alcohol and drop colors of alcohol ink on it. Brayer the inked fabric on clay.

2   Drop alcohol ink all over clay. Follow with a spritz of rubbing alcohol.

3   Moisten a small piece of felt that is attached to a die or miniature building block with the hook-side of a piece of Velcro tape. Ink the felt with a light color, and stamp the felt on clay in an all over pattern. Fill in any spaces with other ink colors, changing the felt pads between each new color.

Basic Surface Recipes

Acrylic Floor Finish

Acrylic floor finish can be used to create a glossy "paint" or veneer for polymer clay. This technique was contributed by Mona Kissel.

Materials

- acrylic floor finish, such as Future
- metallic powder, such as Pearl Ex
- acrylic paint
- soft craft brush
- pasta machine

1. Mix metallic powder with acrylic floor finish and use a soft craft brush to paint this mixture onto clay.

2. When the surface is dry, roll the decorated clay carefully through a pasta machine to "craze" or crackle the acrylic finish.

Variations

1 Mix both metallic and embossing powders with acrylic floor finish, and apply to clay. When the clay is dry, crackle the finish by rolling through a pasta machine.

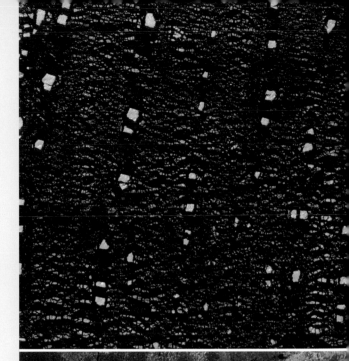

2 Use a soft craft brush to brush on acrylic floor finish over acrylic paint to minimize finger marks or to intensify the color.

3 Brush on acrylic floor finish with a soft craft brush over silk-screened patterns for a glossy shine.

Basic Surface Recipes

Stenciling

Stenciling is the opposite of masking. In masking, color is applied around a barrier; in stenciling, color is applied through selected openings of a barrier. You can purchase craft stencils or make your own using punch cutters or a craft knife. Save the cut-out pieces to use as masks. Silk-screening, which can be found on page 46, is a form of stenciling.

Materials

- assorted tube acrylic paints
- liquid translucent clay
- purchased craft stencil
- squeegee tool
- pan of water

1. Wipe a thin application of liquid translucent clay onto the stencil using a squeegee tool. Lay this treated side on clay, then smooth over the stencil with your fingers to ensure that it is completely in contact with the clay.

2. Using a squeegee tool, apply paint over the stencil. Put the decorated clay aside to let the paint dry. Use the pan to wash paint off of the stencil and squeegee. Dry the stencil and tool.

3. Stencil on three additional paint layers, letting each layer of paint dry before another is added. Applying liquid clay to the stencil helps keep the stencil from pulling up previous layers of paint.

Variations

1 Use stencil plastic and a craft punch to make a custom stencil. Lay the stencil on clay, and apply Crayola Portfolio oil pastels on the stencil around the design. Use a soft, dense sponge to wipe the oil pastel over the stencil and create a design.

2 Use your finger to press embossing powder through the designs of a purchased or custom-made stencil. Keep a wide, soft-bristle brush handy to sweep away excess powder.

3 Apply acrylic gel media to clay with a palette knife and let it dry. Brush on an acrylic ink, then let it dry (shown: Dr. Ph. Martin's Spectralite with Spectralite extender added). The ink brushes on smoothly over the gel, but beads up when applied to clay directly. Note the beading where the end of the violet stripe is applied directly onto clay. Lay the stencil on clay. Apply some gel media over the open design. Apply metallic powder over the gel. Let the clay surface dry, then go over it with liquid translucent clay.

Basic Surface Recipes

Clay as Surface Media

The applications shown are with unbaked clay only, but baked clay can be added to raw clay to create mosaics. Raw or baked pieces can be applied to baked clay to add ornamentation. Adhere raw or baked pieces to baked clay using liquid translucent clay or Poly Bonder and bake again.

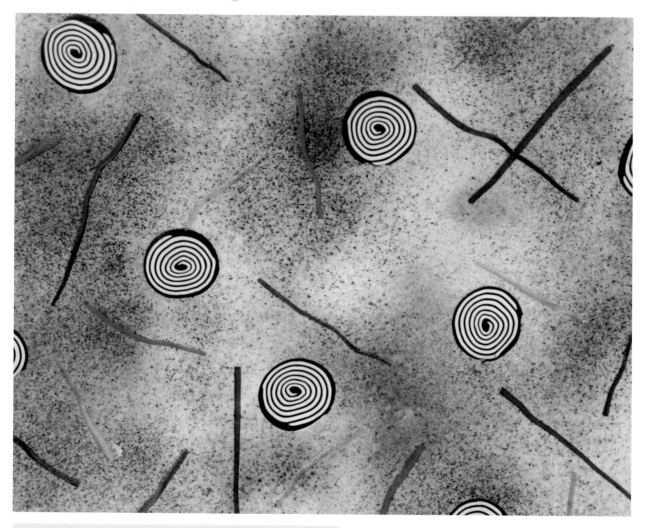

Materials

- white polymer clay (for the base layer)
- small pieces of four colors of polymer clay (shown: violet, magenta, yellow-green, and yellow)
- small black-and-white spiral cane of polymer clay
- assortment of alcohol markers and their airbrush attachment (shown: Letraset Promakers)
- air compressor or can of compressed air for airbrushing
- wax paper
- pasta machine

1. Assemble the airbrush attachment, air source, and a marker.

2. Spray ink from an assortment of markers onto the white clay.

3. Run each of the four colored clay pieces through the pasta machine on a thin setting.

4. Cut and apply thin strips of the colored clays.

5. Cut and apply thin slices of the spiral cane.

6. Cover the decorated layer with wax paper and smooth the applied clay and cane slices with a roller or brayer. Be sure to smooth the layer in various directions to avoid distorting the applied clay and cane slices.

Variations

1 Apply ink from alcohol markers on a very thin layer of translucent clay. Cut out blocks of the inked clay and apply them to a medium-thick base layer of white clay. Roll the resulting sheet through the pasta machine to a desired thinness and level of distortion.

2 Cut thin slices from a mokumé gané block of metallic clay with impressions from cookie cutters and layers of acrylic paint through it. (For more on mokumé gané, see page 24; shown: Stewart Gill's Byzantia metallic paint.) Cut out small shapes from the slices with miniature cookie or hors d'oeuvres cutters and apply them to black clay. Thin out the sheet through the pasta machine.

3 Decorate a sheet of clay with thin canes in a scattered (shown here) or allover pattern.

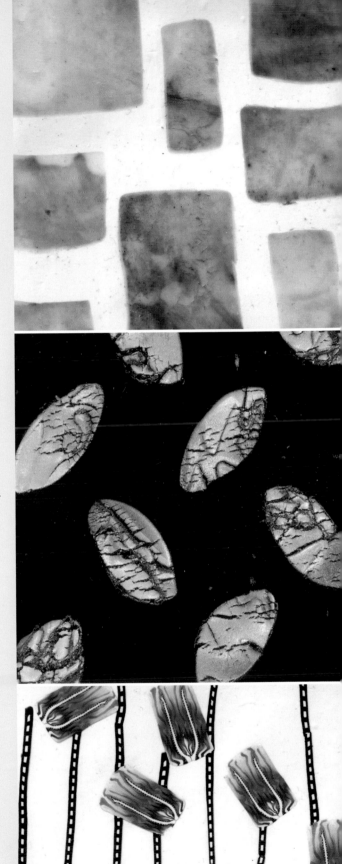

Basic Surface Recipes

Writing on Clay

When the surface design is not enough, you can write, scribble, or carve on it. Several methods are described here. You may need to practice a bit with either of these methods to get the results you like.

Materials

- rubber stamp with a background design
- acrylic paint (shown: Lumiere)
- acrylic ink (shown: Dr. Ph. Martin's Spectralite)
- assortment of markers (shown: Sharpie oil paint and Marvy DecoColor opaque paint markers)
- artist-grade tissue paper
- detail paintbrush
- ruling pen or Coit single line calligraphy pen
- piece of foam pad or cosmetic sponge

1. Texture a clay sheet using the rubber stamp. (Texturing clay will make writing a little more challenging, so this step is optional.)

2. Lightly sponge on acrylic paint to reveal the stamped design. Let the paint dry.

3. Write on the decorated clay using any of the following methods:

  • Add ink to the ruling or calligraphy pen. Write initially on a sheet of scrap clay to test the ink flow. Write on the decorated layer (as shown in the words "dream" and "play" above), being careful not to scratch into the clay. Re-ink as needed.

  • Write directly on the clay with the oil-paint marker (as shown in the words "art" and "color" above).

  • Lay a piece of tissue paper where you want to write on the clay. Write on the clay through the paper (as shown in the words "create" and "beauty" above).

  • Write on the clay with the detail brush charged with ink (as shown in the word "imagine" above).

Variations

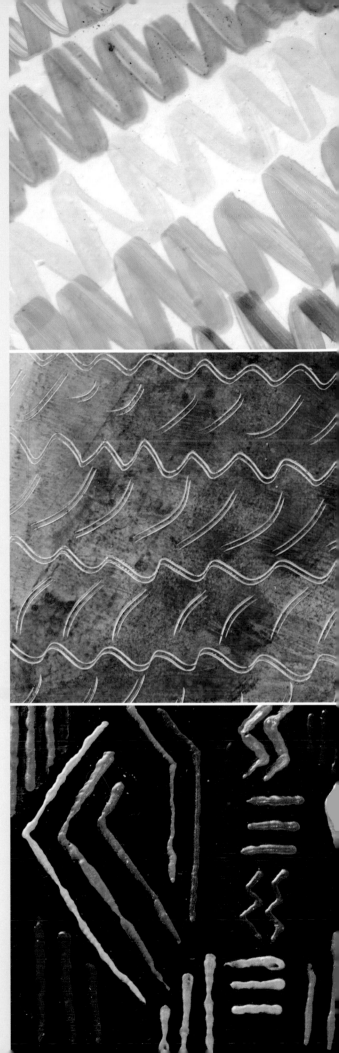

1 The broad tips of dual-point alcohol markers make brushlike strokes on clay. Dip the marker in a drop of rubbing alcohol to wet its tip.

2 Sponge on various colors of dye, paint, or ink (shown: Colorhue dye) and let it dry. Lightly carve into the decorated clay sheet with a needle or carving tool (used here: a Kemper needle tool).

3 Writing with Ranger Crafts' Adirondack acrylic paints doesn't require any additional tools because these paints come in fine-tipped bottles.

Basic Surface Recipes

Spray, Splatter, and Sponge

You can create spray effects on clay through both direct (spray bottle, airbrushing, toothbrush) or indirect (sponge, sprinkled powder) means. The design possibilities are endless.

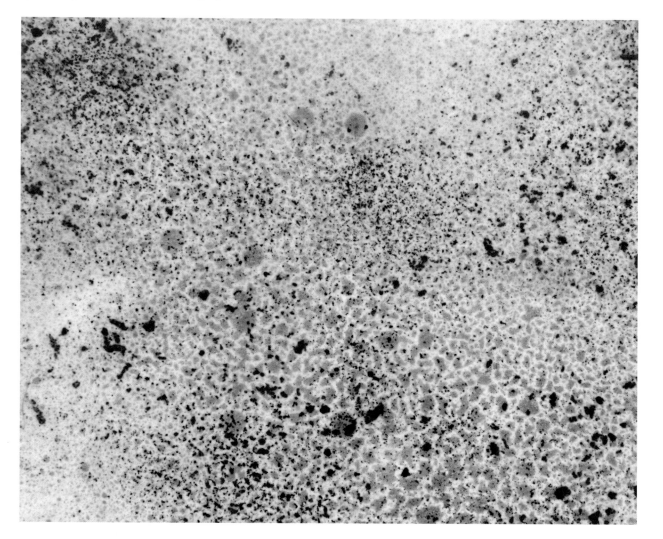

Materials

- fabric dye (shown: Colorhue)
- airbrush medium (shown: Golden)
- chalk pastel sticks
- translucent liquid clay
- small spray bottle
- tissue blade or craft knife
- craft sponge brush

1. Add a few drops of dye to the spray bottle and dilute it with about twice that amount of airbrush medium.

> **Tip:** Colorhue can be diluted with water, but a watery liquid would run off the clay. We diluted the dye with acrylic airbrush medium because it adheres to clay. You can also dilute the dye with denatured alcohol, which will also adhere.

2. Spray across a clay sheet, creating a pattern you like.

3. While the dye is wet, use a tissue blade or craft knife to scrape a fine powder of various colors of pastel sticks over the inked clay sheet. Let it dry.

4. Sponge on the liquid clay before or after baking to seal the pastel. Be sure to apply liquid clay with careful dabbing motions to minimize disruption of the pastel.

Variations

1 With a sponge with a very open mesh, lightly apply various colors of craft acrylic paint. You can achieve a similar look by applying paint with a piece of crumpled aluminum foil.

2 Splatter acrylic ink or dye (shown: Ranger's Posh Impressions metallics) onto clay by scraping a tooth-brush with a palette knife. Mask the clay sheet with palette or wax paper to create a pattern of colors. Let it dry. Use alphabet cookie cutters dipped in acrylic paint to stamp a design of letters on the painted sheet.

3 Airbrush a base color of acrylic airbrush paint on clay, then let it dry (shown: Golden opaque airbrush color). Use a craft punch to make masks out of palette paper, and apply the masks to the painted clay. Airbrush other colors over the clay. Remove the masks. Note: Golden airbrush color will remain slightly tacky on clay, especially if it is applied heavily; however, it dries completely on clay when baked.

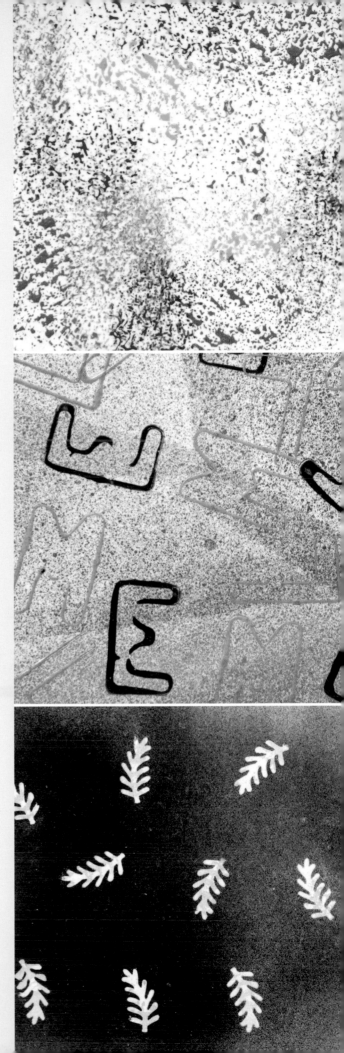

Surface Technique Intensives

Once you are familiar with polymer clay, understand how various materials work on it, and are comfortable with some basic surface techniques, you may want to try more elaborate combinations. Here are ten "intensives" to guide and encourage you.

Airbrushing

With airbrushing, fine droplets of paint are applied to clay. In this example, the underlying design in orange paint isn't disturbed by the layer of blue paint airbrushed over it.

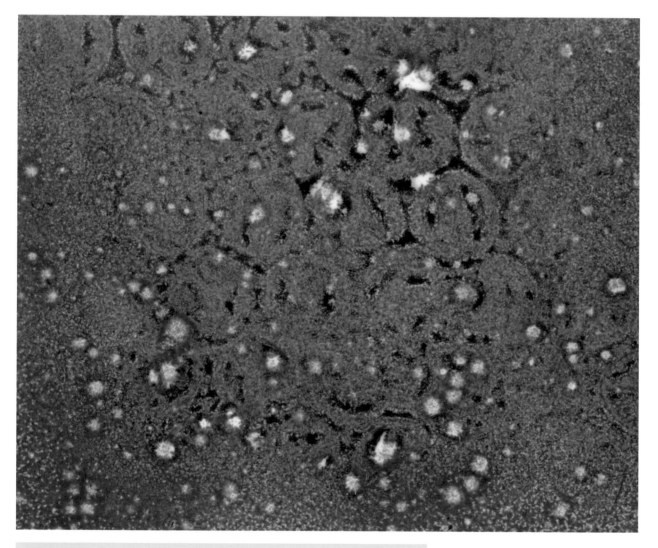

Materials

- yellow, orange, and blue airbrush paint (shown: Golden; you may need to thin other brands with airbrush medium if you are using a compressor with a maximum pressure of 40 PSI or less.)
- airbrushing kit that includes a can of compressed air
- bubble wrap

1. Condition the clay and roll out a medium thin layer.

2. Spray a thin layer of yellow paint evenly over the clay.

3. Spray orange paint randomly over the painted clay. Let the paints dry slightly.

4. Press bubble wrap over the painted clay to create impressions in the orange paint **(a)**.

5. Spray blue all over the decorated clay. The bubble wrap impressions will be revealed as the blue and orange paint mix **(b)**.

Notes on airbrushing: The paint can mist a bit in the air while brushing, so airbrush in a well-ventilated room. You may also want to use a painting box or hood made out of a cardboard box. One of the best ways to keep your airbrush in good working condition is to run airbrush cleaning fluid through the brush at the end of every painting session.

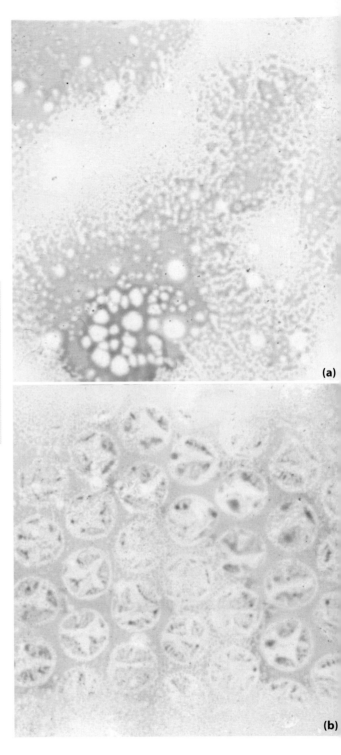

(a)

(b)

Brocade

Paint and a stamped design combine to create either a course or a fine brocade, depending on whether the decorated clay sheet is rolled through the pasta machine or not. Note the variation swatch to compare the results of this approach when using a thin layer of the original blue paint.

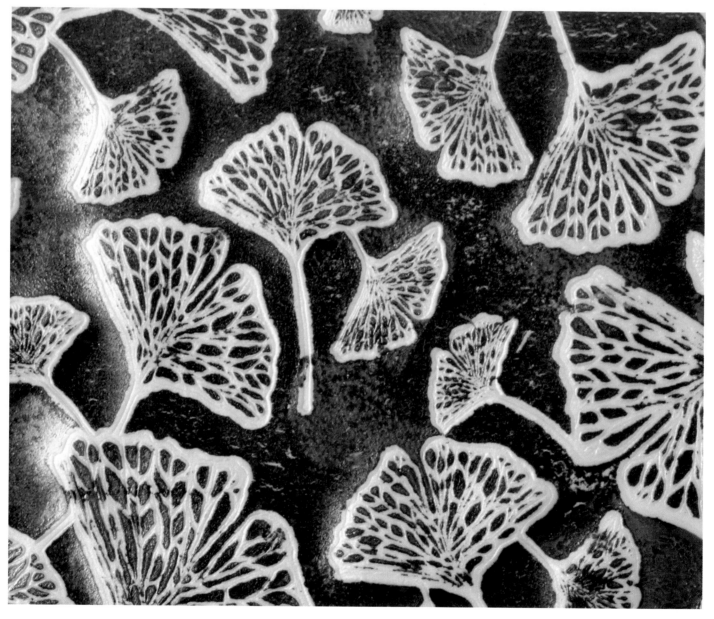

Stamp credit: US ArtQuest

Materials

- pearl metallic polymer clay (shown: Kato)
- metallic acrylic paint (shown: Lumiere)
- texture stamp
- pasta machine

1. To make this tile look somewhat aged, we used pearl, rather than white clay, and change the main paint color. We added a small amount of metallic orange Jacquard Textile Color to blue pearl Lumiere **(a)**.

2. Press the texture stamp into the clay sheet.

3. Sponge or brayer the new color of blue paint over the textured clay sheet **(b)**.

4. Sponge gold paint on sections of the decorated clay sheet. Let all the paint dry **(c)**.

5. Roll the sheet through the pasta machine to thin it. Be sure to rotate the sheet 90 degrees and roll through again to minimize distortion of the texture pattern.

Variation

Here is a sheet done with a lighter application of unaltered blue paint.

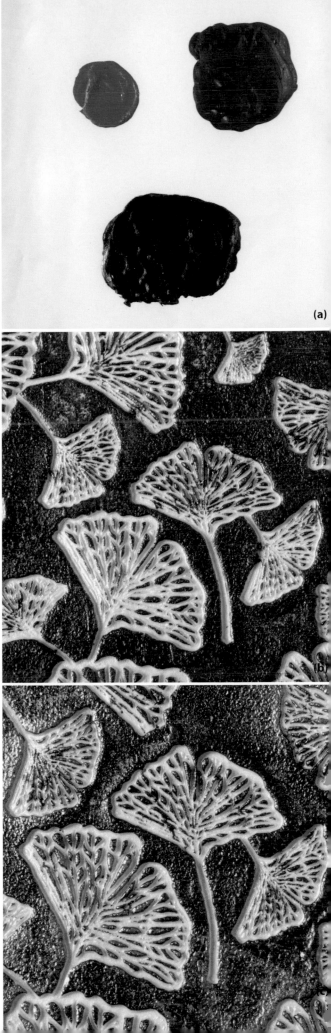

(a)

(b)

A Hint of Pearl

Metallic clay alone or in combination with nonmetallic clay offers an array of design options.

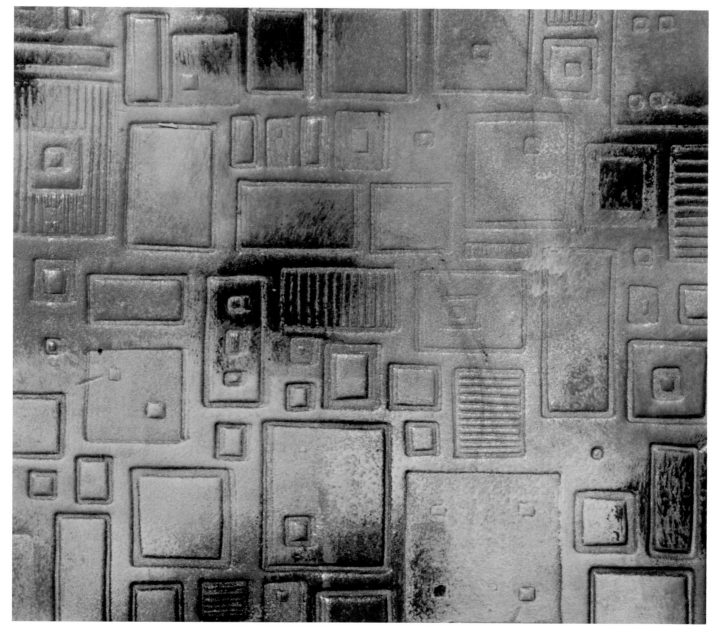

Stamp credit: Judikins

Materials

- pearl metallic and black polymer clay
- assortment of opaque and metallic acrylic paints
- background stamp or texture sheet
- cookie cutters
- pasta machine

1. Make a metallic mokumé gané loaf of pearl clay, and place thin slices of it on a layer of black clay **(a)**. (For more on mokumé gané, see page 24.)

2. Stretch the resulting layer by rolling it through a pasta machine **(b)**.

3. Impress the stamp or texture sheet into the stretched clay sheet **(c)**.

4. Lightly sponge on various colors of paint. Be sure to leave areas of the pearl clay showing **(d)**.

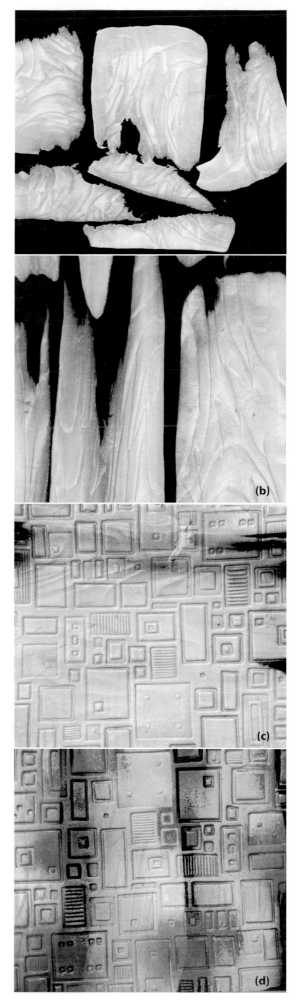

(b)

(c)

(d)

Surface Technique Intensives

Masking with Wire

When masking with wire in clay, or any even paper, you have the option of retaining or removing the impressions made by the mask. Visual interest was created on this tile by varying the gauges of the wire and size of the wire masks.

Materials

- black polymer clay
- acrylic craft paint
- opaque fine-tipped marker
- various gauges of craft wire
- square paper clips
- cardstock

- ball stylus
- round- and flat-nose pliers
- wire cutter
- pasta machine
- acrylic brayer

1. Use the pliers to bend and shape the wire pieces as you desire.

2. Lay the wire pieces and paper clips on a sheet of black clay.

3. Cover the sheet with cardstock, and roll over it with brayer to impress the wire and clips into the clay.

4. Remove the cardstock, wire, and clips, and impress the ball stylus over the sheet to add a dot pattern.

5. Sponge or brayer on craft paint **(a)**. Let dry.

6. Dab on a second paint color **(b)**. Let dry

7. Add other colored dots with an opaque marker **(c)**.

8. Stretch the decorated sheet using the pasta machine.

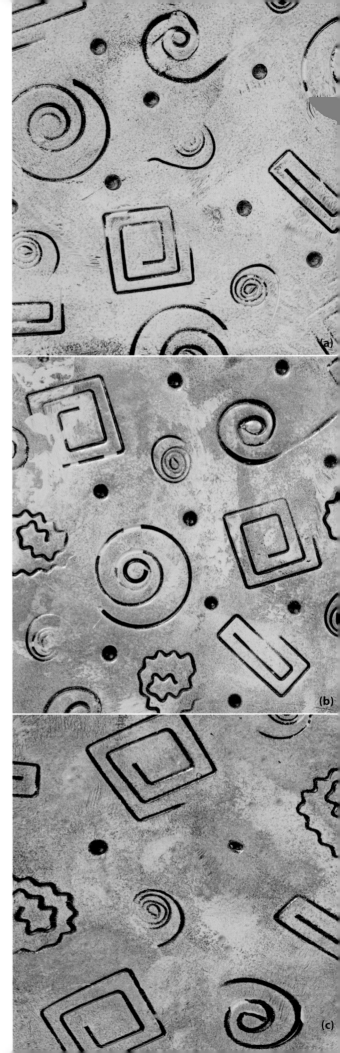

(a)

(b)

(c)

Impressions with Paint and Texture

When working with coarsely textured clay, expect that some of the clay will show through the surface application at least minimally. Here the texture pattern and brush strokes complement each other.

Materials

- acrylic craft and metallic paint
- texture sheet (shown: a Shade-Tex texture sheet)
- fan brush

1. Impress the texture sheet into a layer of clay. Paint the resulting clay layer with metallic paint **(a)**.

2. Apply additional metallic and opaque paint colors. We applied blue metallic paint with a fan brush and the gold and periwinkle paints with the straight edge of a sponge **(b** and **c)**.

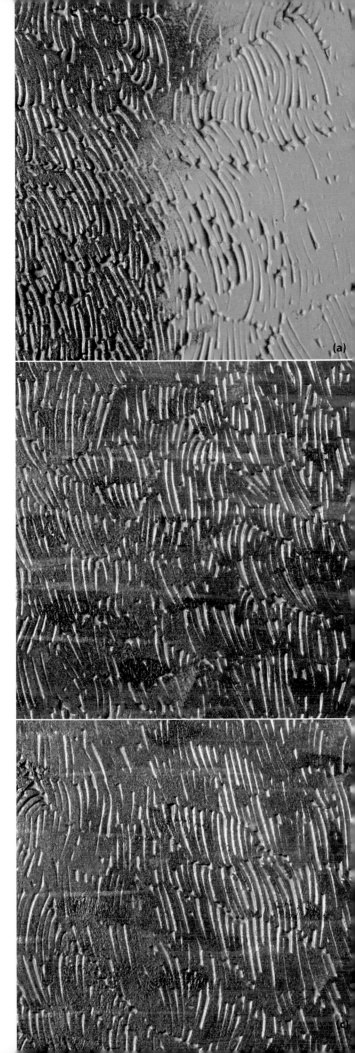

(a)

Surface Technique Intensives

Pastel Collage

Sometimes mixtures of clay colors look interesting before they are fully combined. Adding surface design judiciously, so as not to obscure the marbled clay layer, results in a decorated sheet with a bit of mystery and depth.

Stamp credit: Embossing Arts (background); Hero Arts (design stamps)

Materials

- brown, red, magenta, gold, and black polymer clay
- opaque acrylic paint in pastel colors (shown: Sherrill's Sorbets paints by Jacquard)
- background rubber stamp and an assortment of design stamps
- spray bottle with water
- pasta machine

1. Mix small amounts of red, magenta, gold, and black clay with a larger quantity of brown clay.

2. Run the mixture of clay through the pasta machine to achieve a marbled look. See top image **(a)**.

3. Sponge or brayer pastel paint on a background stamp, then press the stamp into the clay. Be sure to press the stamp evenly to achieve good coverage, but try not to impress the stamp in the clay. See image at right **(b)**. Clean the stamp immediately or spritz it with water to prevent paint from drying.

4. When the paint dries, add another stamped image to create a layered design **(c)**.

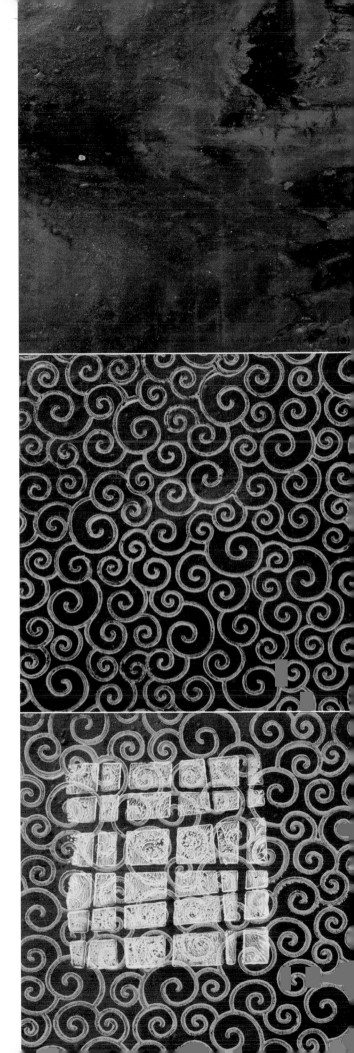

Gossamer Color

It can be difficult to control the intensity of alcohol inks when applied directly to clay. You can avoid this frustration by applying the ink to translucent clay first and then layering this ink on to opaque clay. When inked translucent clay is left to leach a bit, a nice crackling may result when the translucent and opaque clays are rolled out together. You can combine sections of one inked layer with different compatible colors of opaque clay.

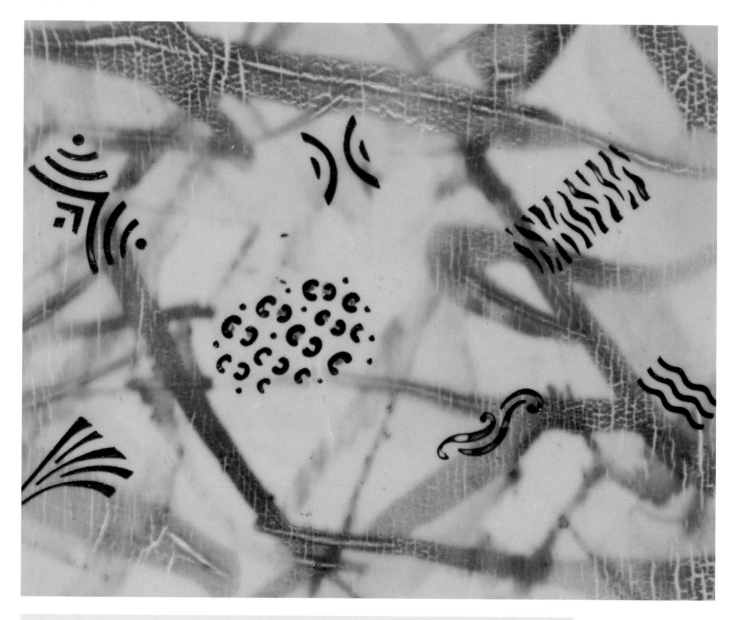

Materials

- beige or ecru and translucent polymer clay (shown: Premo)
- assortment of alcohol-based inks (shown: Ranger Crafts' Adirondack alcohol inks)
- stencils (shown: Createx fingernail stencils, animal prints set)
- tube acrylic paint
- pasta machine

1. Roll out ecru clay on the thickest setting of your pasta machine, then set the clay sheet aside **(a)**.

2. Roll out translucent clay on the thinnest pasta machine setting.

3. Apply alcohol inks to the translucent clay. Let the ink dry **(b)**.

4. Place the inked translucent clay (with the inked side down) on the ecru clay **(c)**.

5. Roll the two clay layers through the pasta machine until the ink is thinned to your liking **(d)**.

6. Stencil designs using tube acrylic paint on the resulting clay sheet.

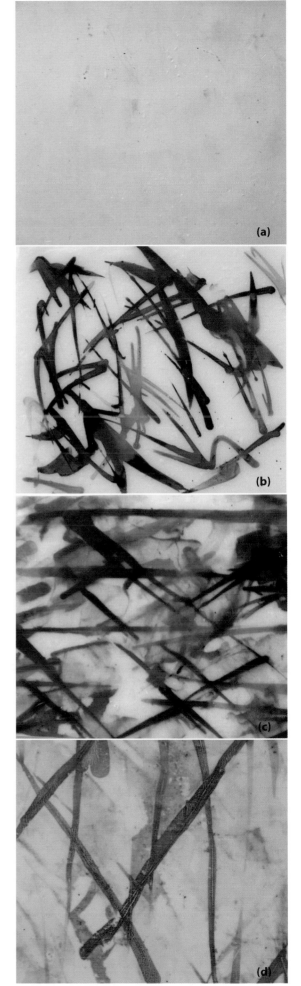

(a)

(b)

(c)

(d)

Surface Technique Intensives

Ikat Color Blend

Ikat, a form of textile weaving, was mentioned in Polymer Clay Basics (page 15). Here are techniques for creating and using this design. The resulting ikat sheet is embellished with a silk-screened graphic.

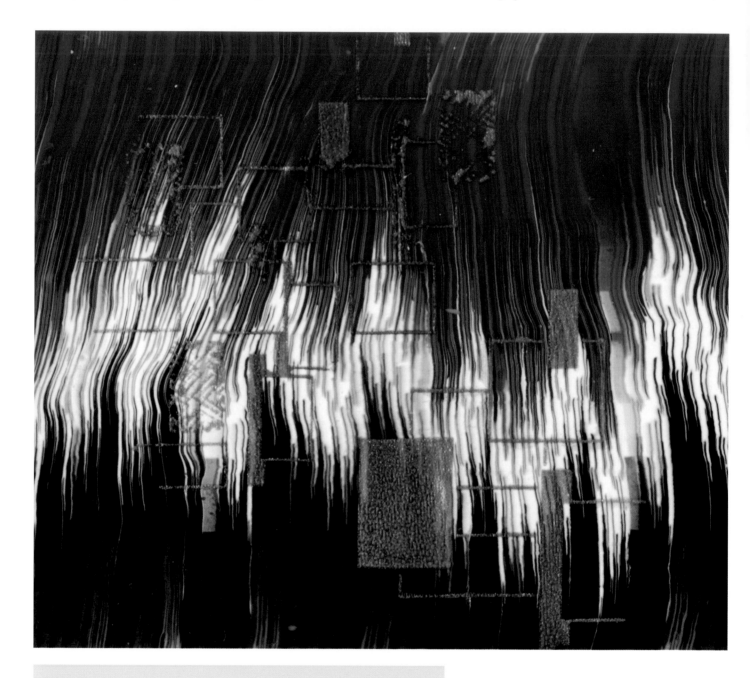

Materials

- 8 oz (227 gm) each of white, cadmium red, cadmium yellow, violet, magenta, ultramarine blue, and scrap polymer clay (shown: Premo)
- metallic acrylic paint
- silk-screen stencil (The stencil used here was designed with Photo-EZ.)

1. Set the scrap clay aside.

2. Partially mix magenta and violet clay in a two-to-one ratio.

3. Roll the combined clay and each of the individual colors out on the thickest setting of the pasta machine.

4. Prepare a sheet for blending using the Skinner blend method (see page 23 for more on Skinner blends), with each of the triangles two layers thick.

5. Arrange the colors in this order: yellow, blue, violet, white, magenta-violet, red, yellow **(a)**.

6. Roll the colored layers through the pasta machine according to the Skinner blend method until the colors partially blend **(b)**.

7. Cut the resulting layer across the colors into three equal sections.

8. Stack the sections, staggering the color blend as seen on the cross-section. Cut the resulting loaf in half and restack **(c)**.

9. Roll out scrap clay on a thin but workable setting. Cut slices of the loaf along the cross-section and layer them on the scrap clay **(d)**.

10. Smooth the resulting sheet with a roller, and roll the sheet carefully through the pasta machine, if you choose.

11. Stencil over the smoothed clay sheet.

(a)

(b)

(c)

(d)

Ghost Printing and Batik Effect

With this technique you will be effectively mixing paint colors, so keep color mixing principles in mind. Lascaux Aquarcyl paint is especially suitable for the technique demonstrated here. Other liquid acrylic paints may yield different results.

Materials

- liquid acrylic paint (shown: Lascaux Aquarcryl permanent blue, yellow, magenta, and orange transoxide)
- rubber brayer
- rubber stamps (shown: our own hand-carved stamps)
- needle tool
- spray bottle of water

1. Brayer on blue paint, leaving subtle gradations as shown. Let it dry. Clean the brayer. See image top right **(a)**.

2. Sponge magenta paint along a section of the painted clay. Be careful not to lift too much of the blue paint.

3. While the magenta paint is wet, place a stamp in it. Press lightly to ensure full contact, but do not impress the clay. Lift the stamp. Spritz the stamp with water to keep the paint moist until you are ready to clean the stamp **(b)**.

4. Repeat step three using the yellow and orange paints **(c)**.

5. Write into the clay with the needle tool, tracing around the stamp images.

(a)

(b)

(c)

Surface Technique Intensives

Putting It All Together

Manipulating the surface of polymer clay is one of the many ways to transform the material. With a variety of surface techniques at your disposal, you can transform your clay by applying techniques individually or by combining them as demonstrated here. Whichever you choose, don't be afraid to go further by cutting your finely decorated clay sheet and reforming it or adding pieces of it to pieces from other sheets.

Stamp credit: Earthtone Stamps

Materials

- translucent liquid clay
- assortment of acrylic paints and inks
- chalk pastel
- wire tool
- flea comb
- rubber stamps

1. This decorated sheet was inspired by trying out some initial techniques with a scrap of clay. It became a way to start the tile **(a)**.

2. Texture neutral-colored clay with a flea comb **(b)**.

3. Start applying horizontal lines of acrylic paint and/or ink. Think about adding a combination of dark, medium-light, and light colors. In other words, vary the color (hue) and value (lightness and darkness). Note that there was no attempt to keep distinct lines of color or prevent colors from blending. Also, note that the sheet may not look particularly interesting at this point **(c)**.

(a)

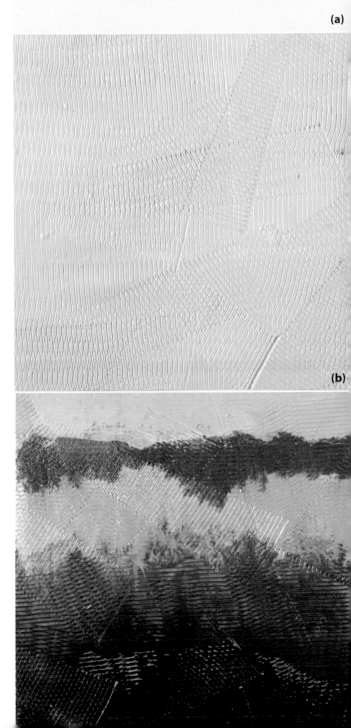

(b)

4. Start adding decoration to each of the paint/ink lines. Add pastel shaved from a pastel stick to moist paint. Add other decoration when the paint/ink lines are dry **(d)**.

5. Completed sheets such as this one could be used as a small wall decoration, on the cover of a book, as part of an altered book page, or as decoration on a box. The sheet (as a whole or cut into sections) could also be used as embellishment for a quilt **(e)**.

6. You can present a decorated sheet in another way entirely by cutting it and reforming the sections. We cut the sheet into strips, but you might try other variations **(f)**.

(f)

In time, as you explore surface design on clay, you may amass a collection of decorated clay sheets. You can create new work with tiles made by reassembling strips from previously decorated sheets.

Tip: Store your decorated sheets between sheets of waxed paper. This helps keep the clay from drying too quickly.

Projects

This book is primarily about technique and design. While it is great fun to make sumptuously decorated clay sheets, what would you do with them all? The projects in this chapter begin to answer that question.

Offered here are a variety of projects that can be successfully executed by either a dedicated crafter or an occasional one. All of them are very functional and they make terrific gifts (to yourself as well). If you're interested in paper or fiber arts, then you might make the Mosaic Card, Painted and Stamped Photo Journal Cover, or the Arts and Crafts Notepad. If you like to cook or entertain, try the Creative Utensil Handle. You may want to cover other utensils as well. Imagine place settings with decorated flatware! Last, if you like to wear your art, then the Faux Paper Bead Necklace and Tile Bracelet are for you. Both projects are distinctive designs that are almost certain to win you notice.

The projects are useful as learning opportunities because they employ a variety of skills and methods. The utensil handle and necklace projects illustrate how decorated clay can be manipulated to make dimensional objects. The photo journal and card projects highlight decorated clay as ornaments. The jewelry projects are as much about jewelry design and construction as they are about surface treatments on clay.

We hope making these items will fuel your creative energy. For further inspiration, see the gallery section, containing other exemplary uses of surface design on polymer clay.

Project: Mosaic Card

Cut unique shapes from decorated clay sheets and use them to embellish
items such as note cards and book covers.

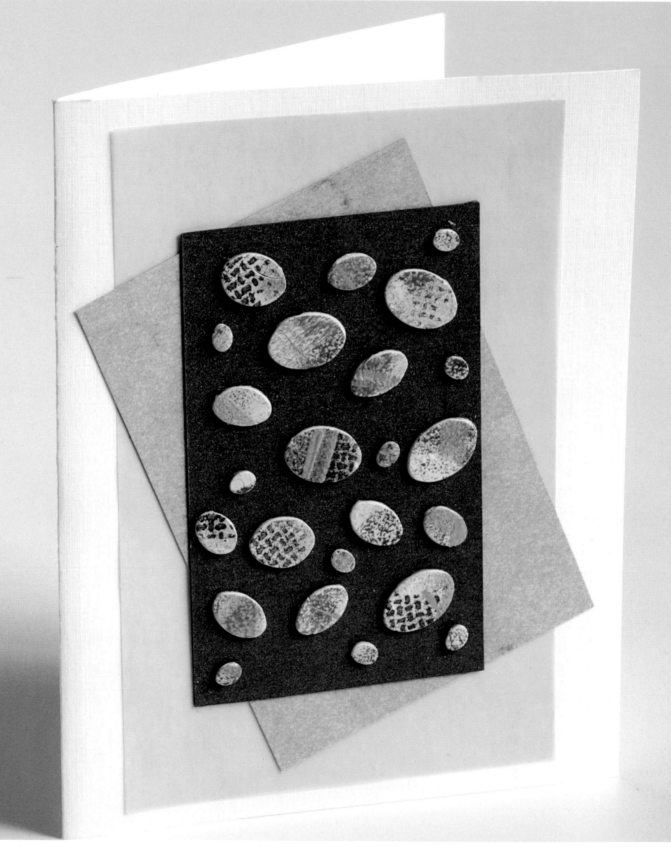

Artist: Ellen Marshall

Materials

- 2 oz (56.5 gm) of white polymer clay

- assortment of acrylic paints (shown: Anita's in lily pad, olive green, kelly green, rust red, and moccasin brown and Lumiere pearl blue and metallic gold)

- section of embroidery or coarsely woven fabric

- archival craft glue (used here: Crafter's Pic Memory Mount)

- one 8 ½" × 11" (21.5 × 28 cm) sheet of white or cream linen card-stock, dark olive green cardstock with metal-lic veneer, light brown cardstock with brown marbling, and light olive green vellum

- glue stick

- flat craft or artist's brush

- piece of a foam pad or cosmetic sponge

- rubber-tipped craft tool, such as a Colour Shaper

- ruler

- paper trimmer

- bone folder

- micro cutters (used here: Kemper Ovals set)

- pasta machine

Preparing the Card

1. Cut a strip of the linen cardstock to 8 ½" × 5 ¼" (21.5 × 13 cm).

2. Score the center of the strip with a bone folder, then fold the cardstock in half using the bone folder to make the fold crisp.

3. Using a ruler and a paper trimmer, trim the dark olive green cardstock to measure 3 ¼" × 4 ¼" (8 × 11 cm). Trim the light brown piece of cardstock to measure 3 ½" × 4 ½" (9 × 11.5 cm). Trim the light olive vellum paper to measure 3 ¾" × 4 ⅛" (9.5 × 10.5 cm).

4. Set all paper aside.

Preparing the Polymer Clay Tiles

1. Condition the polymer clay and roll out a thin sheet of clay (number five setting on the pasta machine or ¹⁄₁₆" [1.5 mm]).

2. Decorate the clay by sponging on some paint colors, smoothing paint on the cloth, then pressing the sections of the cloth onto the clay **(a)**

3. Add more layers of paint colors with the brush. Let each layer of paint dry fully **(b)**.

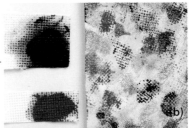

4. Choose three distinctly different sizes of the cutters and use them to cut an assortment of tiles out of the decorated clay sheet **(c)**.

Constructing the Card

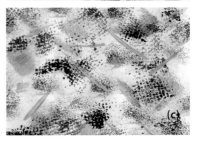

1. Use the rubber craft tool to add a thin layer of glue to the back of the clay tiles as you apply them to the dark olive rectangle. First apply a few of the largest ovals in an allover pattern on the card-stock. Next, fill in the spaces with the medium, and then the smallest ovals.

2. Bake the decorated cardstock for 20 minutes at 275°F (135°C). When the baking is done, let this cardstock and clay cool.

3. Try out arrangements of the green-gold and light brown cardstock and light olive vellum on the front of the folded card until you like the positioning.

4. When you've chosen a pleasing design, glue the layers, starting with the vellum, to the front of the card.

Project: Creative Utensil Handle

Use decorated sheets of clay, either one piece or several spliced together in a pleasing way, to easily cover utensil handles. Cylindrical handles are the easiest to cover with a rectangular sheet trimmed to fit. A total sheet thickness equal to the thickest setting on the pasta machine works best for most applications.

Artist: Mona Kissel

Materials

- decorated polymer clay sheets
- ice cream scoop
- wax paper
- pencil or pen
- tissue blade
- large knitting needle
- cardboard baking surface
- pasta machine

Note: Use only solid metal utensils with no plastic components. If there is doubt about whether a tool is solid metal, or whether any plastic plugs were used inside the tool you can test it by baking the tool at 275°F (135°C) for ten to fifteen minutes. The utensil must be carefully watched as the oven gets warm. If plastic was used in the assembly of the tool, the heated plastic will swell and become very visible. This will ruin the utensil, so it is best to work with solid metal utensils.

1. Prepare decorated sheets of clay.

2. Make a template by cutting a piece of wax paper to the length of the handle. Wrap the wax paper around the cylindrical handle, and use a pen or pencil to mark where the paper meets. Extend the line across the paper. This will be the template for the size of the clay sheet needed to wrap the handle **(a)**.

(a)

3. Using a tissue blade, trim the decorated sheet to size using the template. Note: Using this method will result in a clay sheet that seems a bit short at the seam, which is intentional. The tight fit is the most important part of wrapping the handle **(b)**.

4. Lay the decorated, trimmed clay sheet upside-down on wax paper, and bevel all the (inside) edges with the tissue blade. Beveling ensures an almost invisible seam at the joint and allows for smooth edges **(c)**.

(b)

5. Place the clay sheet (decorated side out, beveled side in) on the handle, centering it on the front. This will position the seam at the back of the handle. Place the wax paper between your hand and the clay sheet, and wrap the sheet around the handle, gently shaping the clay sheet to fit.

6. Remove the wax paper, and use a large knitting needle to roll the clay sheet toward the seam so that the two edges meet. Gently "persuade" the clay sheet to wrap more tightly around the handle. If you are covering an ice-cream scoop handle, as in this example, you can firmly hold the scoop with one hand as you finesse the wrap with the other hand. Smooth the seam by rolling the knitting needle along it.

(c)

7. At the ends, use your fingers to taper the ends and press the clay into shape. Gently roll the knitting needle over the edge of the clay to finish shaping the ends and smooth out any finger marks.

8. Finally, examine the clay covering. If the covering is uneven or irregular, very gently roll the entire handle between your flattened hand and a smooth work surface, applying only very light pressure. Pressing too hard will stretch the clay covering and cause air pockets to form during baking. A tight fit is essential.

9. Place the tool on the cardboard with the seam-side down and bake for one hour at 275°F (135°C) in a convection oven. Let the utensil cool thoroughly before handling. To clean the clay-covered utensil, hand wash it with dish soap and towel dry.

Project: Faux Paper-Bead Necklace

These jewel-toned beads with their glass seed beads and metal wire embellishment are opulent and fun to wear. They are reminiscent of the paper beads we made in summer camp, but with a sophisticated twist.

Artist: Ellen Marshall

Materials

- 6 oz (170 gm) of white, pearl, or light neutral-colored polymer clay
- assorted colors of fabric dye (shown: Colorhue silk dyes)
- metallic acrylic paint, such as Lumiere or Stewart Gill's Byzantia
- 22-gauge craft wire (shown: Artistic Wire)
- seed beads, size 8/0
- 2 ½" (1 m) silver-toned chain
- silver-toned clasp and jump rings
- steel mandrels, 1 1/16" (3 cm), or other thin metal rod
- wax paper
- shaving cream
- small container of water
- eyedropper
- foam plate, any size
- paper towels
- block of flower foam, about the size of a building brick
- disposable aluminum baking pan
- cutting mat
- tissue blade
- wire cutter
- needle-nose pliers
- narrow flat-nose or curved flat pliers
- pasta machine

1. Condition the clay and roll it out to be 1/16" (1.5 mm) thin (or use setting five on the pasta machine). Place the sheet on wax paper.

2. Trim the sheet lengthwise. Cut the clay sheet width-wise into long, narrow, equilateral triangles. The longer the base, or shortest side of the triangle, the longer the resulting bead. You can create beads of varying length for this necklace. Set the cut sheet of clay aside **(a)**.

3. Roll the clay triangles, starting at the base of the triangle, on the steel mandrel. Roll all the clay triangles, leaving the resulting beads on the mandrel, and lay them aside on wax paper. The beads stay on the mandrel until after they are baked.

4. Turn the foam plate over so the underside is up and smooth on it a ½" (1 cm) layer of shaving cream. It will be easier to dip the beads this way.

5. Using the eyedropper, deposit a few drops of the dye all around the shaving cream. Start with the lightest color. Repeat with other colors of the dye, rinsing the eyedropper between each color. Drizzle metallic paint over the shaving cream and dye.

6. Roll a clay bead in the shaving cream mixture. Stick the mandrel in the craft foam with the dyed bead sticking up. Repeat with all the beads.

7. Arrange the mandrels in the aluminum pan so the beads do not touch each other. Bake the beads for 45 minutes at 275°F (135°C).

8. Cut lengths of wire that are about two-and-a-half times the length of your beads. String on three seed beads and pull up and twist the wire to secure the beads as a loop at the end **(b)**.

9. Cut the chain to the length you desire, adding in the length of the clasp.

10. Lay out the clay beads and choose the clay bead you want to be in the center of your necklace. String it on to a piece of the wire you prepared. Add a seed bead at the top of the clay bead.

11. Find the center of your chain and attach your first full bead to the center link of your chain. Attach your first bead by using the round-nose pliers to make a wire loop at the top of the bead. Leave a 1/16" to 1/8" (1.5 to 3.5 mm) space at the base of the loop for wrapping wire later. Don't close the loop—leave the wire extended. Thread the extended wire through the chain link until the chain link rests in the wire loop. Wrap the wire closing the loop around the base of the wire at the top of the bead using the flat pliers. Attach all other beads in this manner **(c)**.

12. Construct the necklace by adding the wired beads, one at a time, alternating from one side of the center bead to the other. This way you will see how your necklace is forming.

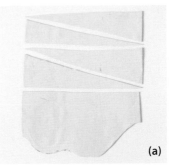

(a)

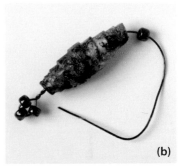

(b)

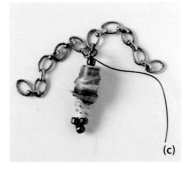

(c)

Note: The shaving cream method was adapted for polymer clay by Gwen Gibson. The author chose to apply the method to the faux paper beads.

Project: Painted and Stamped Photo-Album Cover

This is a great low-cost project in which polymer clay tiles are added to the cover or spine of an inexpensive photo album to achieve a sophisticated design. The amount of fabric required is quite small, so you can splurge on silk and still stay within budget.

Materials

- approximately 8 oz (227 gm) of polymer clay in a color that coordinates with the painted fabric colors (shown: a mix of blue, yellow, and white Kato Polyclay to create a soft green shade)
- various fabric and acrylic paints, dyes, pens, and markers for use on fabric and clay (shown: Jacquard Textile Color, Jacquard Lumiere, and Daler Rowney's Pearlescent Liquid Acrylic)
- three-ring-binder photo album, any size (the album shown is 8" × 10" [20 × 25.5 cm] with a 1" [2.5 cm] spine)
- fabric suitable for painting, such as 100% tight-weave cotton, silk, or rayon (shown: dupioni silk; the fabric should be at least 2" [5 cm] wider on all sides than the combined measurement of the front, back, and spine of the album)
- two sheets of paper for the interior of the album covers, such as cardstock, predecorated scrapbook papers, or your own decorated paper
- 2" (5 cm) tassel with a cord that measures 2" (5 cm) longer than the spine of the album (optional)
- rubber stamps, if desired
- 1" (2.5 cm)-wide foam paintbrush
- tissue blade
- spray adhesive (used here: Super 77)
- hot-glue gun or craft glue
- pasta machine

1. Prewash the fabric. Decorate your fabric by painting, stamping, and embellishing it. In the finished project shown, various shades of diluted blue, green, and yellow fabric paints were painted in 2" (5 cm) freeform waves. Pearlescent paint was added last in arcs of blue. Add any beadwork or embroidery you wish at this stage **(a)**.

2. Heat-set the fabric dye according to the manufacturer's instructions, usually by ironing at the highest tolerated setting, first on the back, then on the front.

3. Lay the fabric, decorated side down, on your work surface. Lay the album faceup and open on the painted fabric. Trim the fabric to create a 1" (2.5 cm) border all around. Miter the corners on an angle, leaving ½" (1 cm) of fabric extending at each corner.

4. If you plan to use a decorative tassel as a bookmark, insert 2" (5 cm) of the tassel cord between the spine and the fabric.

5. Remove the album, and apply two fine coats of spray adhesive to the unfinished side of the painted fabric, following manufacturer instructions. Allow the adhesive to air dry a bit until it is tacky. Carefully reposition the open album on the sticky fabric, smoothing away any air bubbles from the center out. Fold over the long sides to adhere them to the inside of the cover, trimming at the spine where necessary. Tuck in the corners and fold over the short sides

6. Trim your sheets of interior paper so they will cover all of the raw fabric edges on the inside of the front and back covers, generally leaving ¼" (6 mm) around all exterior edges.

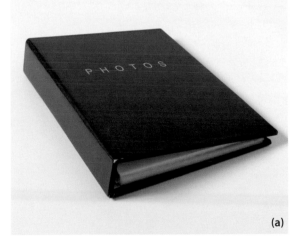

(a)

The undecorated album

7. Condition and mix polymer clay in colors to coordinate with painted fabric. Here, we created a medium green by combining white, yellow, and blue clays. Roll out an approximately 5" × 10" (13 × 25.5 cm) sheet of clay using the number three setting on the pasta machine. Fold this in half and smooth out any air bubbles. Roll a second sheet of the same color approximately 5" × 5" (13 × 13 cm) using the number five setting. Paint, stamp, and embellish this sheet of polymer clay to coordinate with the painted fabric **(c)**.

8. Adhere the thin, painted polymer clay sheet to the other folded sheet of clay, smoothing out any air bubbles that may be trapped. Use your craft knife, tissue blade, or shape templates to cut out decorative "tiles" from this decorated sheet of clay. Bake the tiles according to the manufacturer's instructions.

9. The polymer clay tiles can be used as is, or a coordinating border can be applied to the tiles, as shown. A simple striped pattern was cut into strips and applied around the edge of each tile, using liquid polymer clay as an adhesive. Edges were trimmed neatly with a tissue blade before a second baking.

10. Adhere the tiles to the front cover of the album. We used hot glue, but white craft glue also works well **(d)**.

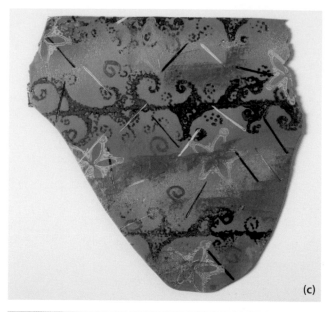

(c)

(d)

Stamp credit: Artist-designed stamps produced by Ready Stamp

Variation

This is another example of this album, using yellows, oranges, and reds. An old credit card was dipped in paint and then dragged over the fabric to create the lines.

Project: Arts and Crafts Notepad

You can make a collection of these notepads for gifts or various purposes of your own. But do keep one handy to jot down project ideas and inspirations, and your list of must-have craft supplies.

Artist: Valerie Wright

Materials

- 3" × 5" (7.5 × 13 cm) spiral notepad
- one block of pearl white polymer clay
- liquid polymer clay (we used Kato brand)
- alcohol-based inks (we used Jacquard's Piñata Colors in sunbright yellow, lime green, rainforest green, and Havana brown)
- Polymer-compatible gloss varnish
- acrylic roller or pasta machine
- pliers
- tissue blade
- small cutter or hollow plastic coffee stirrer
- release agent (cornstarch can be applied with a soft-bristle brush, such as a cosmetic brush, or a mixture of water and Amorall can be applied with a spray bottle to prevent clay from sticking to the texture sheet)
- ½" (1 cm)-wide flat paintbrush
- 5" × 7" (13 × 18 cm) piece of glass
- texture sheet
- nonporous flat surface, such as a glass dish or wax paper

1. Use the pliers to straighten the bent wire end on one side of the spiral notepad. Remove the wire by twisting it out of the holes. Set the wire aside **(a)**.

2. Condition the entire block of white pearl clay. Roll the clay to a thickness of ¹⁄₁₆" (1.5 mm), using the pasta machine or acrylic roller. The clay should be roughly the size of the notepad. Place the sheet of clay onto the piece of glass **(b)**.

3. Apply release agent to the clay sheet. Place the texture sheet on top of the clay and press firmly to impress the pattern onto the clay. (The best texture sheet is one that has a very deep design.) Remove the texture sheet **(c)**.

(a)

(b)

(c)

4. Lay the cardboard backing from the notepad onto the area of the clay with the desired pattern. Use the coffee stirrer to punch out the holes along the top of the cardboard **(d)**. (Trim off the end of the coffee stirrer as it fills with clay.) Use the tissue blade to trim the clay around the cardboard, leaving a 1/16" (1.5 mm)-wide margin around the sides and the bottom of the cardboard. Trim the top of the clay sheet flush with the cardboard. Remove the cardboard from the clay.

5. Place four quarter-size drops of liquid clay onto the nonporous surface, arranged in a circle. Place three drops of sunbright yellow ink onto one circle, then mix the ink into the liquid clay. Place three drops of lime green ink onto the next circle and mix. Place three drops of rainforest green onto the next circle, then mix. Place three drops of Havana brown onto the fourth circle, and mix it into the liquid clay.

6. For this design, begin by painting the outside of the design with the brown liquid clay. Apply a fairly heavy coat so the impressions made by the texture sheet will fill with the liquid but won't overflow.

7. Use the remaining three colors of liquid clay to fill in the rest of the design. The three colors can be placed on the sheet of clay and blended together to mimic the style of glazing found in Arts and Crafts ceramic tiles **(e)**.

8. Keep the sheet of clay on the glass, and place it in the oven to bake. Bake for thirty minutes at the manufacturer's recommended temperature. Remove it, and allow it to cool.

9. Once cooled, apply three thin coats of gloss varnish, allowing the piece to dry between coats.

10. See image below right. Remove the clay from the glass, and place it on top of the notepad pages and backing cardboard. Carefully twist the wire back onto the notepad by twisting it through the holes of the paper and the clay. Bend the end of the wire so it will not twist out of the notepad.

(d)

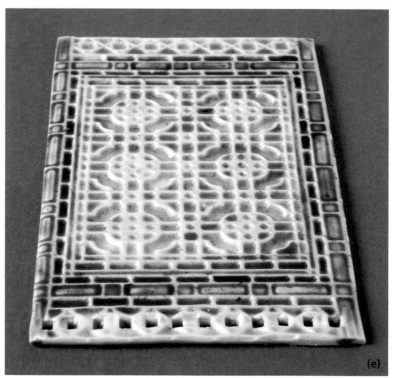

(e)

Note: The cover is reusable. When all the notepad pages are full, simply untwist the wire, place the clay cover onto a new pad, and twist the wire back on.

Project: Triangle Bracelet

This bracelet could easily become one of your favorites. You may have to remind yourself to glance at it less often. The basic design could be adapted to numerous color palettes.

Artist: Sue Springer

Materials

- one block each of black, copper metallic, red, and yellow polymer clay
- two blocks of translucent polymer clay (we used Fimo Soft)
- black elastic cord
- cardstock
- black-and-white copy of template (page 120)
- cyanoacrylate glue, such as SuperGlue or Krazy Glue
- tissue blade
- wax paper
- brayer or acrylic rod
- needle tool
- ruler
- bamboo skewer
- stenciling brush
- 400, 600, 800, and 1,000 grit wet sand paper
- polishing wheel or soft cloth
- pasta machine

1. Condition black clay by running it through the pasta machine on the number one setting, six to eight times, folding in half each time. Insert the crease first to avoid air pockets. Roll on setting number two, then cut two pieces approximately 2" × 7" (5 × 18 cm) and set aside on wax paper. Condition half of the copper clay, roll on number two, cut into ½" (1 cm) strips, and set aside on wax paper.

2. Combine the following by conditioning until uniform:

¼ block of translucent to ⅛ block of red
¼ block of translucent to 1/16 block of red and 1/16 block of yellow to make orange
¼ block of translucent to ⅛ block of yellow
¼ block of translucent to ½ block of copper metallic

3. Roll red, orange, and yellow mixes to form three 5" (13 cm) snakes, then set them aside. Roll copper mix through the pasta machine on setting number one to form a sheet. Roll translucent clay on setting number one to form a sheet. Cut each sheet to create 4" × 3" (10 × 7.5 cm) sections. Stack the copper and translucent sheets together and roll them through the pasta machine. Insert the 4" (10 cm) side into the pasta machine, first on setting number one, then number three, and then number four. Wrap each snake in a single combination translucent/copper sheet (translucent side touching the snake). Trim to fit, then form the canes **(a)**.

4. Place one sheet of black clay on wax paper, then put thin, diagonal slices of canes in a random design on it. Feel free to layer them or form a pattern. You may cover all or part of this sheet. Use the brayer to roll and secure them as you place them on the sheet. When you are satisfied with your design, roll it through the pasta machine on settings number one and number three. Place this sheet face up on cardstock **(b)**.

(a)

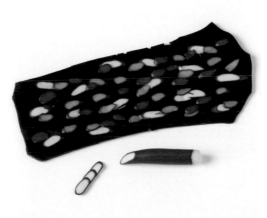

(b)

5. Cut around the paper template (page 120) and place the template on top of the sheet. Mark all the points by poking a needle tool directly into the clay at each point. Remove the pattern and cut the clay with a blade by connecting the dots and mimicking the pattern lines. Remove the scrap clay, and bake the triangles at 265ºF (129 ºC) for 10 minutes, then cool **(c)**.

6. Place the second sheet of black clay on wax paper. On the sheet of black, run the three strips of copper clay in parallel horizontal lines to form channels for the elastic cording. On this arrangement, place the triangle tiles vertically in opposing directions. Press the tiles firmly to the copper strips without distorting them. Carefully trim around each of them **(d)**.

(c)

(d)

7. Peel the three layer tiles from the wax paper and place them facedown on cardstock with the black side up. Place the needle tool in each channel for support, while using the stencil brush to texture the black side of the tiles **(e)**. Bake the tiles for 30 minutes at 265°F (129°C), then cool.

8. Make a snake of black clay approximately ¼" (6 mm) in diameter and 5" (13 cm) long. Measure at ¼" (6 mm) intervals and cut the clay at each mark. Roll the clay pieces into tiny balls by hand and push a bamboo skewer through the center to form 20 small beads **(f)**. Reshape by lightly rolling the beads again. Enlarge holes in two of the beads to later hide knots tied in the elastic. Bake the beads on cardstock for 20 minutes at 265°F (129°C), then cool.

9. Wet sand the front and sides of the tile with consecutive 320, 400, 600, 800, and 1,000 grit sand paper. Buff with a polishing wheel or soft cloth.

10. Put cyanoacrylate glue on the first 1" (2.5 cm) or so of elastic, and let it dry thoroughly. Then trim the end so it isn't frayed. This forms a needle. In two parallel lines, alternately string tiles (inverting every other one) and round beads, making sure the large-holed beads are at the end. Keeping a little tension, knot the string and place a drop of glue on each knot to permanently secure it. When the glue is dry, trim the stray ends close to the knot and tuck it into the bead.

> **Tips:** Make an extra tile for a matching pendant.
>
> If the backs of your tiles don't bake securely to the fronts, glue the layers together with cyanoacrylate glue prior to sanding.

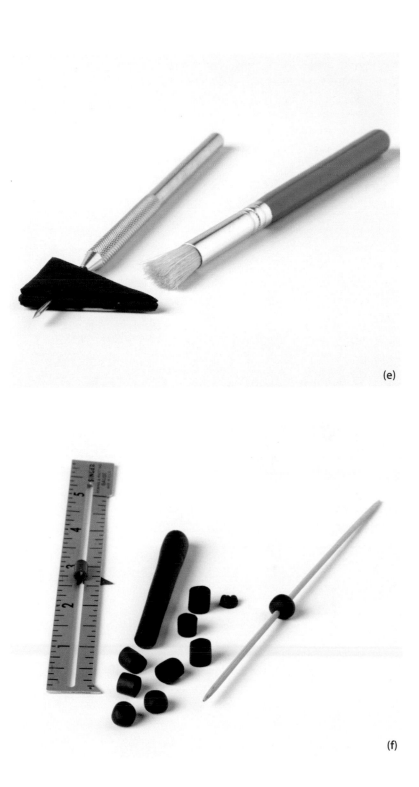

(e)

(f)

Chapter 3
Transforming the Clay

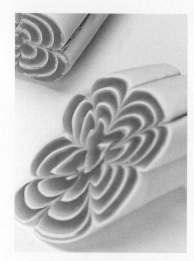

Polymer clay can be combined with many other materials, but there are so many special clays—glittery, pearly, opaque, transparent—that it can also be completely transformed without using anything other than the clay! In this chapter, we'll explore how to manipulate this medium with astounding effects.

One satisfying basic way to transform polymer clay is to stack many thin layers of contrasting colors and roll it into beautiful canes. The resulting "jelly-roll" canes can be further shaped, then sliced to create gorgeous veneers and beads. This technique can be varied in so many ways—and each one is sure to be original. It's a great introduction to caning.

You'll also discover the fascinating attributes of metallic clay, which contains particles of a shimmery mineral called mica. By simply rolling mica-rich clay repeatedly, you can actually change the alignment of the particles. We'll show you how to use this technique to create a stunning holographic "ghost" image.

Another basic technique is to blend clay colors. Clays can be blended to make smooth gradations from one hue to another, then stacked and recombined to create stripes, plaids, and other patterns. We'll teach you how to elaborate and expand on this technique to create visually intricate patterns using a pasta machine attachment and contrasting clay colors.

With the array of available colors, and more specialty clays arriving on the market all the time, there's no end to the effects you can create using only clay. Experiment—you're sure to get results no one else has ever seen.

Chrysanthemum Cane Heart Pendants

Artist: Elissa Powell

These heart-shaped pendants are covered with chrysanthemum-shaped slices of a beautiful, simple, and versatile translucent polymer clay cane. Transform a basic jelly-roll cane using a simple distortion technique, then use thin slices to decorate polymer clay heart pendants. Once you have mastered this technique, you can move on to cover other things—frames, light switch plates, sculptures, glassware, pottery. Don't worry about cutting the cane into perfectly even slices. Slight variations in thickness result in a more interesting, variegated effect. Slicing the cane diagonally helps to create an even greater illusion of depth.

Materials

- basic polymer clay equipment and supplies (see page 15)
- ½ block of white clay
- 1 block of pearl clay
- 1 block of translucent clay
- scrap clay for the core of the pendants
- ¼ block of brightly colored base clay to cover the core of the pendants
- screw eye
- varnish, if desired
- pasta machine
- credit card or similar stiff, thin object
- cellophane or plastic wrap
- small piece of cardstock or a matchbook cover
- soft cloth

Getting Started

Choose the base color of the pendant carefully. When slices from the same cane are applied over different colors, the final results can vary greatly.

1 Make the cane.

Roll the white clay through the pasta machine on the next-to-thinnest setting. Trim the clay so that the sheet is about 10" (25 cm) long and 4" to 5" (10 cm to 13 cm) wide. Roll the pearl clay through the pasta machine on the thickest setting, then do the same with the translucent clay. Trim both sheets so that they're the same size as the white sheet. Lay the pearl clay on top of the white clay, then lay the translucent clay on top of the pearl clay. Smooth the stack with a roller to get rid of any air bubbles. Trim one of the shorter edges to make it straight. Run the roller across the edge to bevel the layers, then roll the sheets up tightly. This creates a basic jelly roll cane.

Cover one edge of the credit card or similar stiff, thin object with cellophane or plastic wrap. Gently and evenly press the covered edge of the credit card into the cane lengthwise. Roll the cane a quarter turn, then press the credit card into the clay again. Repeat twice more so that the cane has four evenly spaced indentations. Repeat the process four more times, pressing the credit card into the clay between each of the four original indentations. The cane should have eight deep, evenly spaced indentations. Allow the clay to rest at least 30 minutes to firm up, then trim off the rough edges at a slight angle.

TIP

Distort the cane immediately after making the jelly roll while the clay is still soft, warm, and pliable.

2 Prepare the heart cores.

Form the scrap clay into two balls, each about 1" (3 cm) in diameter. The scrap clay should be well blended so that no lumps remain. Roll the brightly colored base clay through the pasta machine on a thin setting, then wrap it around the cores to create an attractive, uniform color. Remove any excess clay, and smooth the surface of the covered cores.

3 Decorate the cores.

Slice the end of the chrysanthemum cane at a slight angle, then cut several slices as thin as possible; however, don't worry about cutting the cane into perfectly even slices: Slight variations in thickness result in a more interesting, variegated effect. Roll a few slices through the pasta machine on medium-thin setting, then place them on the balls of clay, overlapping the edges. (This step enhances the visual depth created when translucent and opaque clays are used together.) When the balls are completely covered, roll them gently to smooth and round them out.

4 Shape and finish the hearts.

Examine the balls of cane-covered clay to choose the fronts and tops of the hearts. Form the point at the bottom of the heart by rolling an area of the clay ball tightly between your fingers. The clay should resemble an upside-down tear drop. Form the upper lobes of a heart by making an indentation in the middle of the rounded part of the tear drop. To deepen and accentuate the cleft, press a folded piece of cardstock, such as a business card, between the lobes, and rock it back and forth. Smooth and refine the shape as desired.

Now you're ready to insert the screw eye so you can hang the heart. Make a pilot hole about ½" (1 cm) deep exactly between the two lobes with a needle tool, then enlarge the hole slightly using a tiny circular motion. Insert the needle into the hole about ¼" (6 mm) deep, and press sideways with the end of the needle on each side of the pilot hole to create slits to accommodate the sides of the screw eye. (Creating side slits will prevent any distortion caused by pressing the screw eye downward.) Carefully insert the screw eye, making sure that it's perfectly parallel with the plane of the heart, and pinch closed the open spaces around it. If it's at all crooked, gently twist it into proper alignment with some tweezers or needle nose pliers. Bake following the clay manufacturer's directions.

To achieve the ultimate transparent effect, there are no shortcuts. Sand the baked hearts, first with 400-grit wet/dry sandpaper, then with 800-grit (or finer) sandpaper. Buff with a soft cloth until shiny. Finally, apply a coat of varnish, if desired.

Variations

Adding inclusions—such as glitter, sand, embossing powders, and dried herbs—into polymer clay is a simple and satisfying way to embellish a project. The technique produces especially striking effects when applied to translucent clay. You can use Fimo glitter clay for one of your layers, or you can make your own glitter clay: First pour some glitter into a bowl. Next, flatten conditioned clay into a pancake, and press it into the glitter. Then, fold the pancake in half, with the glitter on the inside; pinch the sides shut to keep the glitter from flying out, flatten the clay, and roll it into a log. Twist, flatten, fold, and roll the clay again. Repeat these steps until the glitter is evenly mixed throughout the clay. This technique can be used to mix other inclusions into clay, but make sure that all materials are completely dry. You can also use metal leaf as one of the layers in creating the cane, sprinkle multicolored shreds of clay on one of the layers to give a confetti look, or substitute a multicolored blend for the white layer.

Instead of distorting the spiral into the chrysanthemum form, use it as is or square it off. Try covering your cores with other decorative clay, such as mokumé gané (see page 118) or metallic "ghost image" clay (see page 108).

Textured Ikebana Vase

Ikebana, the elegant Japanese art of flower arranging, calls for an equally elegant vase. The beautiful finish on this one is created by imprinting a pearly or metallic clay slab with a textured surface, slicing off the top layer of the texture, rolling it smooth, and then polishing the baked piece to a high shine. This technique produces an almost holographic effect sometimes called a ghost image—that is, a pattern you can see but can't feel. One to three flowers can be displayed in this vase. Use it with a pin frog, which will support the flowers easily. Simply add water every other day, and the flowers can be enjoyed for up to two weeks. Pin frogs are available at craft and floral supply stores.

Artist: Mona Kissel

Materials

- basic polymer clay equipment and supplies (see page 15)
- 1 block of black clay, Premo
- 3 blocks of gold clay, Premo
- 1 ⅛" (about 3 cm) round floral pin frog
- 1 ¼" (3 cm) round biscuit or cookie cutter
- small square Plexiglas sheet
- pasta machine
- Shade Tex brand textured plastic sheets for imprinting, cut to 4" x 5" (10 cm x 13 cm)
- spray bottle
- bowl with warm soapy water
- buffer or bench grinder with unstitched cotton polishing wheel
- small dab of candle adhesive or floral clay

Getting Started

Many kinds of textured sheets, found objects, and tools, including mounted or unmounted rubber stamps, can be used to imprint the clay for this project. Shade Tex sheets with a hexagonal pattern were used to make this vase.

1 Make the base of the vase.

(Indented Ball) Roll a ball of black clay slightly larger than the diameter of the pin frog. Press a round-ended object such as a brayer handle about three-quarters of the way down into the ball, leaving the bottom of the base at least ¼" (5 mm) thick.

(Vase) Next, form the walls around the depression by stretching the clay upward. The walls should be about ¼" (5 mm) thick and slightly higher than the pin frog. Press the pin frog into the bottom of the base so the pin frog will fit securely once baked. Make sure the bottom of the base is at least ⅛" (3 mm) thick

and the hole's diameter is bigger than the 1 ¼" (3 cm) round cutter; if necessary, stretch it a bit. Remove the pin frog. Then place waxed paper on top of and underneath the base. Use a square Plexiglas sheet to flatten the clay and ensure that the vase will be level. Bake the base at 275° F (135° C) for 30 minutes, then allow it to cool and harden.

(Vase with clay log on top) Roll a ¼" (6 mm) thick log of soft, tacky black clay that's long enough to make a ring around the top edge of the base. Press the log gently into place and set the base aside.

TIP

Always use clean waxed paper for different stages of the project to prevents nicks, fingerprints, and other damage to the clay. This will reduce the amount of sanding time necessary to achieve the high-gloss finish.

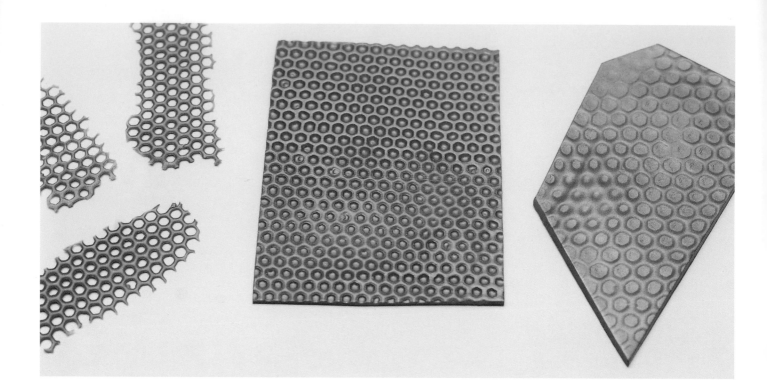

2 Make the top of the vase.

Fold the gold clay, then roll it through the pasta machine on the thickest setting 15 to 20 times, to align the reflective mica particles and bring them to the surface. Then divide the gold sheet of clay into 5 even parts.

To imprint the "ghost image" on the clay, roll 1 of the 5 parts through the pasta machine on the thickest setting. Trim the sheet so it's about 4" x 5" (10 cm x 13 cm), and lay it on a paper towel. Use a spray bottle to moisten the surface with water, which will keep the clay from sticking to your texture sheet. Place a texture sheet on the clay, and roll both through the pasta machine on the thickest setting. Next, gently remove the texture sheet, and place the imprinted clay on a piece of waxed paper. Blot the clay dry with paper towel, and trim any rough edges. Also dry the pasta machine. Allow the clay to stand for one hour, then remove it from the waxed paper, and press it gently on a plastic cutting board or a sheet of poster board, making sure it sticks to the board.

Using a flexible tissue blade, slice away long, paper-thin strips of the textured clay until all raised surfaces have been skimmed off. These pieces can be flipped over and recycled for use in another project.

Then roll another piece of gold clay through the pasta machine on a fairly thin setting. Place this sheet under the imprinted one, and roll gently over the surface with a brayer. Roll the combined sheets through the pasta machine on the thickest setting. Repeat this procedure with another piece of gold clay to completely flatten the imprinted surface.

Stack the remaining two pieces of clay, and roll them through the pasta machine on the thickest setting. Lay this sheet on waxed paper, then place the imprinted sheet on top of it. Roll firmly and evenly over the surface of the clay with a brayer. The multilayered clay sheet should be about ¼" (6 mm) thick. Trim the edges with a tissue blade to create a four-sided shape, although not necessarily a rectangle. Then cut a hole in the center using a 1 ¼" (3 cm) round biscuit or cookie cutter.

3 Assemble and finish the vase.

Lay the vase top face-down on a new piece of waxed paper. Turn the base upside down, and position it over the hole in the vase top. If the log on the top of the vase has stiffened, condition it again until tacky. Use the Plexiglas square to gently press the base to the vase top. Turn the vase over so that it's facing up, then set it on a piece of clean waxed paper. Remove the protective waxed paper from the vase top, and apply it again. Use the Plexiglas square again to gently press the top to the base. Smooth the corners of the vase top down through the waxed paper so they touch the work surface. This will ensure a steady, stable vase. Bake at 275° F (135° C) for 60 minutes.

To bring out the chatoyant, three-dimensional ghost image effect of the imprinted texture, sand the vase top in a bowl of warm, soapy water with successively finer grits of wet/dry sandpaper (400-, 600-, 800-, 1,500-, and then 2,000-grit). Wash the vase in clean, warm, soapy water, then dry it. Use a cotton-polishing wheel to buff the piece, then wash and dry it again. Finally, apply a small dab of candle adhesive or floral clay to bottom of pin frog to secure it in the bottom of the vase.

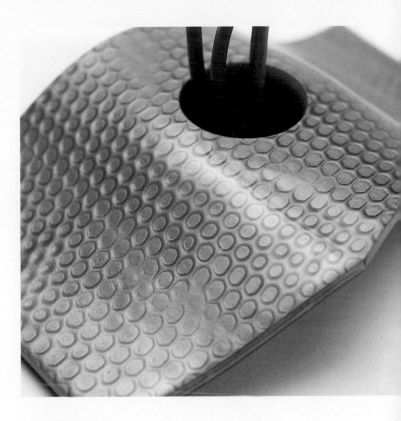

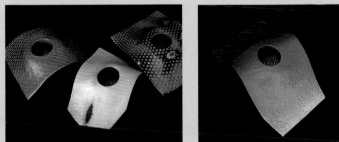

Variations

The graceful, simple form of these vases is the perfect canvas for experimenting with texture and color. Try simulating nature: wood, water, stones, foliage—these patterns will complement any flower. Specialty texturing tools are commercially available, but experimenting with found metal or plastic objects like screens or grids can lead to great discoveries. Also try creating a texture that can be felt as well as seen—use rubber stamps, carving gouges, or custom-made clay tools.

"Ghost image" clay can be used for many other projects, from bracelets to pins to picture frames.

Faux-Fabric Poof Box

Artist: Susan F

Shows and conferences often inspire clay lovers to create novel techniques. One theme at the second Ravensdale conference—held near Seattle roughly every three years—was "Reinventing the Box." Inspired by this theme, artist Susan Hyde created this poof box, which features a faux-fabric technique. She combined the streaky blend technique invented by Judith Skinner and Kathleen Amt and added her own special touch: the linguini effect. Use contrasting shreds of clay and embossing powder for further effect, make it into a cane or loaf, fold a sheet into a curvy box, and get sealed-in air to support the baking form.

Materials

- basic polymer clay equipment and supplies (see page 15)
- cardstock or large index card
- Transparent Liquid Sculpey (TLS)
- the equivalent of 2 to 3 blocks of Premo clay in metallic blue, cadmium red, ecru, turquoise, fuschia, and gold
- embossing powder or superfine glitter in a contrasting color
- handkerchief-size piece of fine cotton fabric
- pasta machine with linguini attachment
- ruler
- small straw, such as a coffee stirrer

Getting Started

For this project, the clay doesn't need to be conditioned in advance—it will be conditioned by the process of making the blend.

1 Make a six-color streaky blend.

Make a cardstock triangle template about 6" (15 cm) long and a bit less than 2" (5 cm) wide. Set your pasta machine on the thickest setting, and roll out a sheet of each color. Fold the sheets on the diagonal to make a double thickness of clay. With the craft knife, cut triangles from the double layers. Arrange the double-layer triangles head-to-foot to form a rectangle. Use half-triangles on the sides. Roll with the brayer, and press together with your fingers. Run this clay sheet through the pasta machine five times on the thickest setting, folding it in half across the "grain" each time and sending it through the machine fold first. Never fold it lengthwise before running it through the pasta machine or the blend will become muddy.

2 Add inclusions to the blend.

Sprinkle about a tablespoonful of embossing powder or superfine glitter on half of the clay sheet, fold it over, and pinch the sides to keep the slippery embossing powder from scattering; press down gently to join the halves. Run the clay through the pasta machine fold first; fold again, and repeat 10 times. You now have a streaky color blend. Trim it into a long rectangle.

3 Add contrasting linguini shreds to the blend.

Sprinkle a little baby powder on the surface of three 2" (5 cm) strips of unconditioned clay in bright colors that contrast, or even clash, with the streaky blended sheet. Spread the powder all over. Make "worms" from the bright clay by running through the linguini attachment of the pasta machine. If you don't have a linguini attachment, use a ruler and a sharp craft knife to produce plenty of linguini-size shreds. Place them on one end of the blended clay sheet; they'll become colorful speckles in the final piece. Fold the slab across the middle, run it through the pasta machine again, and repeat.

(1)

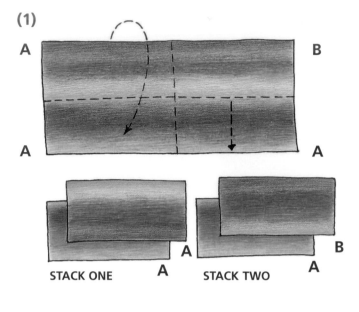

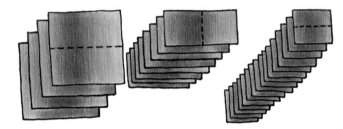

STACK ONE   A   STACK TWO   A

(2) FOR STRIPES:

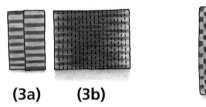

FOR PLAIDS:

(3a)   **(3b)**   **(3c)**

4 Make striped and plaid clay stacks.

Cut the clay sheet in half across the middle. Take one part, cut it in half in the direction of the streaks, and flip the halves together, fronts facing. This is stack one. Repeat with the other part, and place one half on top of the other without turning or flipping it so that the bottom of one side rests on the top of the other side. This is stack two. When you have finished, stack one will make a striped pattern and stack two a plaid pattern.

For stripes, slice stack one in half, across the streaks, and stack again. (See diagram 1.) Repeat twice so you have a little loaf with horizontal layers, like a club sandwich or layer cake. (See diagram 2.) Slice down the side to produce a striped piece.

For plaids, slice stack two in half, across the streaks, and stack again. Repeat twice, as you did for the striped stack. Then, tip the loaf over on its side so the layers are standing up and running straight toward you. Mark it in regular increments about ¼" (6 mm) apart, and slice it, cutting downward perpendicular to the layers. Separate the slices a little, and turn every other one around so the blends don't match. (See diagram 3a.) Pack and trim the stack into a neat loaf. The top will have a plaid pattern. (See diagram 3b).

When your "fabric" loaves are finished, cut several thin slices of each, giving you stripes and plaid. Roll out a thin sheet of any conditioned clay (it won't show once the project is complete). Patch the fabric slices together on this backing sheet in a pleasing pattern. Run each patchwork sheet through the pasta machine repeatedly, starting at the thickest setting and stepping down to setting #4 or #5. Before each rolling, rotate the sheet one turn so it doesn't stretch too far in one direction. The "cloth" will become quite thin and the pattern will expand. (See diagram 3c.)

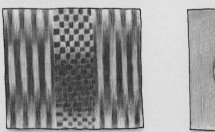

5 Make and laminate the poof box.

Roll scrap clay through the pasta machine on the thickest setting to make about a 6" (15 cm) square. Place a layer of your patchwork faux fabric over it. Cover it with waxed paper, and roll it down firmly with the brayer to fuse the layers. Cut out a circle of your faux fabric about 4" (10 cm) across. Turn the square over, place the circle in the center, and roll it down. This becomes the inside of the box and will be beautiful when you look inside.

Place the square between two pieces of cloth and roll hard again with your brayer to fuse the clay layers and give the box a nice cloth texture. Trim the square with a ruler and sharp craft knife to bevel the edges toward the inside of the box.

7 Make the poof box lid.

Remove the box from the oven, and let it cool just until you can handle it. Take your sharp craft knife and, holding it at an angle as if you were cutting the lid of a jack o'lantern, cut a square top from the box. You can follow the fabric patterns in the clay if you like. Cut on an angle that slopes in toward the center of the box. If you cut straight down, there won't be a ledge for the lid to sit on and it will fall straight down into the box. If you like, cover the bottom of the lid with a patch of faux fabric, because it's usually pretty messy from all the pinching and not symmetrical. Trim the patch even with the slope of the lid, and bake for 10 minutes, just to harden the clay. For the handle on top that will never come off, use a cane slice or any attractive piece of clay. Add it to a disk of unbaked clay (to make the surface smoother), dab on some TLS, press it onto the top, and bake for 20 minutes.

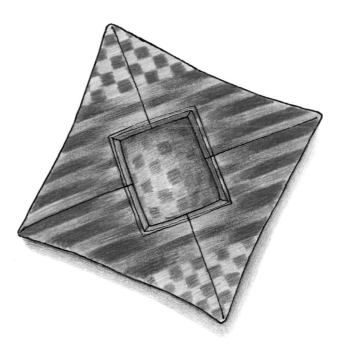

6 Inflate the poof box.

With the circle facing up, lift up two adjacent corners of the square, put the corners together, and gently squeeze the edges together. Bring up another corner and finally the fourth. It can be tricky to get the edges stuck together neatly. Alternatively, you can pinch them upward like a ruffled pie crust edge. When all the edges are stuck together, poke the straw into the little hole in the top where the points meet, and blow so the box inflates. Remove the straw, pinch the hole closed, and quickly get the box into the oven. The air inside will keep the box inflated. Bake 30 to 45 minutes at 275° F (135° C).

Variations

Faux fabric can be used anywhere patterned or decorated clay is wanted, from an ikebana vase top (see page 108) to a fitted box (see page 126).

Experiment with different kinds of shreds using a clay extruder with various attachments. Imagine making faux-fabric accents for clay figures, dolls, or other sculptures! Be sure to see page 122 for tips and inspiration.

Chapter 4
Creating the Structure

One of the most satisfying things you can make with polymer clay is a three-dimensional piece. As with all modeling media, sound structural techniques are integral to using polymer clay effectively, especially when making functional pieces—you don't want your creations to fall apart! In this chapter, you'll discover some of the many ways to create lovely, durable artwork.

One simple technique is to cover a form with thin veneers of clay. Glass, plain metal, and papier mâché are good candidates. If a rounded form is enclosed, no glue is needed. If the object has straight sides, you can coat it with white PVA glue and let that dry. Then add the clay, which will stick to the dry glue. This makes it possible to create vessels of nearly any shape. Use veneers with at least some translucent clay for candleholders that diffuse light beautifully. Also try encasing cardboard pieces, like the matchbox used for the Storyteller Doll on page 122.

You'll also discover the secret to making a perfect round box using an ordinary mailing tube. By layering sheets of clay around a cardboard cylinder, you'll be able to make a box with a top that fits so well, it will make a popping sound when you open it! Another technique you'll learn is how to make extraordinarily thin but strong polymer clay leaves that can be wired and used to build a lush centerpiece like the one on page 48. Made with a special clay mixture and reinforced with flexible varnish, the leaves can be handled and manipulated with ease.

Remember, the methods we explore in this chapter can be used to create new projects with just a little modification. Just follow the basic technique, and add your own special touch.

Leafy Mokumé Gané Vessel

Artist: Jody Bishel

Mokumé gané is a traditional Japanese metal-working technique used to create gorgeous, intricate patterns. Because the technique involves stacking thin layers, it can be easily adapted to polymer clay. Unlimited patterns of mokumé gané are possible, so experiment with different clay colors, tools, and materials, such as metal leaf or inclusions. A ripple blade is used in this project to create the dotted pattern. Use Premo-brand clay to reproduce the brilliant pearlescent sheen of this vessel. To make a lovely and functional candleholder, use tinted translucent clays or a mix of opaque and translucent clays.

Materials

- basic polymer clay equipment and supplies (see page 15)
- 1⅜ blocks of gold clay, Premo
- ⅛ block of copper clay, Premo
- ⅛ block of burnt umber clay, Premo
- ⅜ block of black clay, Premo
- ¼ block of silver clay, Premo
- squared-up lump of scrap clay
- 4" (10 cm) round glass vessel

- glossy polymer-clay-compatible varnish, such as Flecto Varathane Elite Diamond ISP
- Translucent Liquid Sculpey (TLS) or Sculpey Diluent
- copper-colored mica powder, such as Pearl Ex
- pasta machine
- ripple blade
- flat brush
- small round paintbrush

Getting Started

Ripple blades tend to catch more debris along the edge than straight blades, so clean as needed by wiping carefully with isopropyl alcohol on a paper towel. Painting the unsharpened edge of the ripple blade with bright nail polish will make it easier to avoid picking up the wrong side and cutting yourself.

1 Make the mokumé gané veneer.

Begin by rolling two separate sheets of marbled clay through a pasta machine on the thickest setting. For sheet A, marble together ⅜ block of gold clay, the copper clay, and the burnt umber clay. For sheet B, marble together the black and silver clay.

Cut both sheets into 1½" (4 cm) squares, and stack them to form a loaf. Alternate between sheets A and B. Then, roll gently over the surface to eliminate air bubbles and adhere the layers to each other. Press an edge of the loaf into the lump of scrap clay so the layers are vertical. Using the ripple blade, cut ⅛" (3 mm) thick slices. Try to make each slice of the same thickness. The scrap clay will hold the loaf steady while cutting. Then, roll the slices through the

pasta machine at the thickest setting, just enough to flatten them. Mix up the order of the sheets, then stack them again. The edges should be aligned so that two sides are wavy and the other two are straight. Again, roll gently over the surface. Next, press one of the straight edges of the loaf to the scrap clay. Using the ripple blade, cut ⅛" (3 mm) thick slices. The slices should reveal a dot pattern. If there are no dots, give the loaf a quarter turn, then cut again. Roll the slices through the pasta machine on the thickest setting, then roll the slices through again, one setting above the thickest. Continue rolling the slices through on successively thinner settings, stopping at setting #4. Give the slices a quarter turn between each rolling to keep the dots round and to avoid stretching out the pattern too much in one direction.

2 Cover the glass vessel.

Place the slices over the outside of the glass votive. Piece them together so that the edges meet; don't overlap them, which will create raised seams. Roll gently over the edges to smooth and fuse the seams. Bake the votive for 20 minutes at 275° F (135° C). Once the vessel has cooled, wet-sand the clay with 400-grit sandpaper, then 600-grit sandpaper to refine the surface and remove any imperfections. Use a flat brush to apply two coats of glossy polymer clay-compatible varnish, such as Flecto Varathane Elite Diamond ISP, then allow the vessel to dry completely.

3 Make and attach the leaves to the vessel.

Roll the remaining block of gold clay through the pasta machine on setting #4. Fold the sheet in half, and roll it though again. Keep repeating the process to brighten and intensify the metallic sheen. Be sure to make the sheet as wide as the pasta machine will allow. Then, cut five 2" (5 cm) wide strips from the sheet. Fold the strips lengthwise, and press gently, then open the strips. This will create a groove down the center of the strips. Next, cut out leaf shapes with the groove in the center. Flatten and smooth the edges of the leaves for a more realistic look. Use a clean scrap of paper over the clay to avoid leaving fingerprints. The edges of the leaves can be ruffled by gently stretching the area. Curl the point of the leaves gently, if desired.

To attach the leaves to the votive, first use a craft knife to scratch the areas on the vessel where the leaves will be attached—underneath the vessel and at the lip. Dab the scratched areas with TLS or Sculpey Diluent. Then, press the base of each leaf onto the moistened clay underneath the vessel, then attach the top to the corresponding area at the lip of the vessel. The leaves will look especially graceful if they arch away from the sides of the vessel, as shown on facing page. Bake the vessel again for 30 minutes at 275° F (135° C).

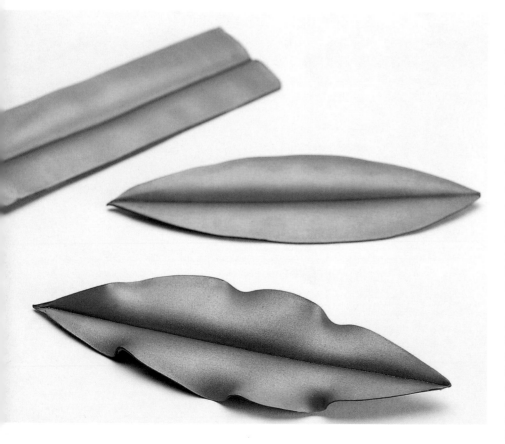

4 Finish the leafy vessel.

Wipe the leaves with an isopropyl alcohol-soaked paper towel to remove any oils. Then, mix the copper-colored mica powder into a small amount of varnish. Use a small round brush to paint an accent stripe down the groove in the center of each leaf. Let dry. Use a flat brush to apply one or two coats of varnish to the leaves.

Variations

Try varying the shapes of the leaves, using more of them, and arranging them less regularly. Also try using other glass forms, from vases to hurricane lantern chimneys.

Mokumé gané is an intriguing technique with infinite variations. To make a simple, versatile block, layer alternating sheets of clay and metal leaf. Try using heat-treated leaf, which has beautiful color variegations. And be sure to use at least some translucent clay, which will create visual depth and allow the metal leaf in the block to show through the layers. Then experiment with translucent slices over a base of contrasting color. Sand, then buff to a high shine for the most stunning effects.

Storyteller Doll

This storyteller contains a hidden compartment, which opens to reveal an accordion-folded book. An ordinary matchbox serves as the structure for the compartment, demonstrating how everyday materials can be readily integrated with polymer clay. The book pages can be decorated with any number of things—a favorite quote written in calligraphy, rubber stamping, drawings that tell a tale, or a collage of inspiring images. The simple structural techniques described here can be easily adapted to create a doll with personal or cultural significance.

Artist: Dayle Doroshow

Materials

- basic polymer clay equipment and supplies (see page 15)
- ½ block of clay for head
- acrylic paint
- 1 block of clay for body
- slices of millefiore cane slices, mokumé gané slices, or other surface embellishments
- small cardboard matchbox
- decorative paper
- elastic cord
- wire and beads for headdress
- 2" (5 cm) eye pin

Getting Started

The face of this doll was sculpted by hand. Push molds can also be used; they can be handmade or purchased and are available in various styles and expressions.

1 Make the doll's head and body.

The doll's head can be sculpted from an elongated ball of clay, using a thumbnail to create the eyes, a needle tool to create the mouth, and a small snake of clay to create the nose. Once the face is formed, coat 1" (3 cm) of a 2" (5 cm) eye pin with glue, starting at the looped end. Insert the eye pin, loop first, 1" (3 cm) into the head. Bake following the manufacturer's directions. Once cool, rub acrylic paint over the face, then wipe away the excess so the features are highlighted.

To form the body, roll a large ball of clay into a fat log. Taper the log into a cone shape, then flatten it with a brayer until it's about ½" (1 cm) thick. The body can be decorated with millefiore cane slices, mokumé gané slices, or any other surface embellishments. To add millefiore inlays, place thin cane slices on the log before tapering it, then roll the log to adhere the slices.

2 Make the book holder and pages.

Place the outside sleeve of a cardboard matchbox on the doll's body, aligning the top edges of each, and mark where the bottom edge of the matchbox meets the clay. Then, flatten this area of the clay until it's about ⅛" (3 mm) thick, first with your hand and then with a brayer. Make sure the clay extends past the sides of the body to create flaps. Next, press the matchbox sleeve into the flattened area of the body, and fold the side flaps of clay up the sides of the matchbox. Trim the excess clay.

To make the book, accordion-fold a piece of paper that has been cut to the height of the matchbox. Decorate the pages as desired. Then, cut the matchbox open on the right side, along the creased edge. Glue the first "page" of the folded paper to the back of the matchbox. Decorate the front of the matchbox with paper, or paint it. To make a closure for the book, poke a hole through the cover and right side of the box. Thread a looped elastic cord through the side hole, and knot it. Then, wire a bead through the cover hole. To close the book, slip the elastic loop over the bead.

3 Assemble the doll.

Coat the remaining 1" (3 cm) of the eye pin that extends from the baked head with glue. Then insert the head into ⅛" (3 mm) of clay behind the matchbox. Bake following the clay manufacturer's directions.

4 Add accents.

Use beads, wire, charms, and any other desired materials to embellish the storyteller. The coiled headdress here was made by wrapping delicate wire around a knitting needle.

Variations

The basic technique of enclosing a box within polymer clay has limitless applications. Try enclosing a wooden container, perhaps with a sliding top, to create a treasure keeper. Or build a figurine and give it a small glass bottle to hold; then, fill the bottle with scented oil or a fragrant herbal sprig.

Another option is to custom-make a box. Sketch out a template, using a real box as a guide if desired, then use cardstock or cardboard to construct it. (See the *Laminated Boxes* project on page 152 for more information on constructing oven-safe paper containers.)

Fitted Jewelry Box

Artist: Dan Cormier

Over the past several years, I've made various wearable vessels and small boxes with precisely fitted lids that often pop when you open them. I developed my own techniques for building these containers, and though I've made them in all sorts of shapes and sizes, they all rely on the same principle—using paper as a release to prevent two layers of clay from sticking. A form provides the initial shape, but each layer of clay becomes the form for the layer that follows. This jewelry box will teach you the basic steps, and when you're done, you'll have a place to keep some of your wearable polymer clay jewelry creations.

Materials

- basic polymer clay equipment and supplies (see page 15)
- several sheets of standard copy paper
- disappearing-color glue stick (colored when wet, dries clear)
- 2 pieces of 100% cotton rag paper or tracing paper, 4" x 12" (10 cm x 30 cm) and 2" x 12" (5 cm x 30 cm)
- cardboard postal tube, 2½" (6 cm) diameter, 6" (15 cm) length
- 4 blocks of clay, any brand and color, for the base of box
- cellophane tape
- 2 blocks of clay, any brand and color, for decorative veneer
- pasta machine
- flat-topped plastic bead vials in various heights
- Plexiglas rod

Getting Started

Before baking, some clays adhere to rag paper (and baked clay) better than others. If you have trouble, take some scrap clay and rub it over the surface you're trying to adhere to, just enough to create a "glue." This should help the next layer stick.

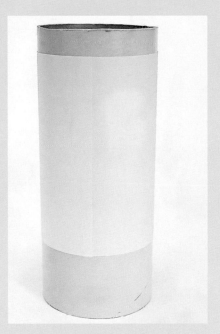

1 Wrap the tube with paper.

Lay a piece of copy paper on the work surface. Then, using the glue stick, apply glue along one of the shorter edges of the 4" x 12" (10 cm x 30 cm) piece of rag paper. The coat of glue should be ½" (1 cm) wide and should completely cover the area. Next, lay the cardboard tube over the unglued short edge of the paper, and begin rolling it around the tube until the paper attaches to itself. Be careful not to adhere the paper to the tube. Make sure the paper fits snugly around the tube, but still slides freely.

2 Make the base of the box.

Using your Plexiglas rod and pasta machine, prepare a sheet of clay about 3" x 10" (8 cm x 25 cm) (rough edges are okay at this point). Use the third-thickest setting. For example, if #1 is your thickest, use setting #3. Place your clay sheet on a sheet of office paper; working on paper will allow you to move and lift the clay easily. With your ruler and craft knife, cut a clean edge along one of the short ends of the clay sheet. Reposition your clay sheet so the cut edge is about ¼" (6 mm) away from and parallel to the edge of your paper; turn it so the cut edge is closest to you. Place the paper-covered tube on the clay sheet.

Use the work-surface paper to lift the clay sheet and gently press it against the tube. Apply only as much pressure as you need to release the clay from your work-surface paper and adhere it to the rag paper on the tube. Try not to distort or flatten the clean edge of the clay sheet. Start in the center and work out toward the ends until the clay sheet is attached to the rag paper. Continue rolling the sheet around the tube.

To preserve the clay's uniform thickness, don't let the ends overlap. Use the first cut edge as a guide to trim the clay sheet. When the clay sheet has almost wrapped the tube, gently roll the cut edge onto the sheet to mark it, making sure to extend the lines past the edges of the clay; this will be your trim line. Unroll the cut edge of the clay, then roll the rough edge over the marked area and trim. Set the excess trimmed clay aside. The clay sheet is now exactly the right size to fit the tube.

To seal the seam, gently support your clay-covered tube in one hand, and push one cut edge toward the other with your thumb so they stick together. Again, start in the center and work out to each end until the cut edges are sealed. By starting in the middle, you will get a clean seal and a snug wrap, and you will avoid trapping air between the clay and the rag paper. To smooth the outer surface of the clay and fully adhere it to the rag paper, wrap the clay-covered tube snugly in a sheet of copy paper, and roll it on your work surface. Tack the paper together with a little tape.

Now, trim the top and bottom of the clay. For this jewelry box, you'll need a cylinder 2½" (6 cm) long. Using a ruler and the end of your blade, mark the places where you want to make your cuts. Stand the tube up on the factory-cut end. Trimming the cylinder evenly is a bit tricky, so you'll use a plastic bead vial to create a platform supporting and steadying your blade. Stand a vial next to the tube, and lay your blade flat on the lid of the vial, with the cutting edge toward the tube. Slide the covering paper up or down the tube until one of your marks is in line with the blade. Hold the blade in place on the vial with one hand, and slide the tube over to the blade with the other. When the blade has cut into the clay sheet, rotate the tube to cut around the full circumference of the cylinder. To cut the other end of your box cylinder, remove the tape, reposition the clay and paper wrap along the tube, and repeat the rotating cut. Use a taller vial if necessary. Peel the excess clay off the tube, leaving a cleanly trimmed 2½" (6 cm) cylinder. Stand the tube on a baking tray, and bake according to the manufacturer's directions. Let the cylinder cool on the tube before continuing.

3 Make the lid of the box.

To make the lid, you will use the 2" x 12" (5 cm x 30 cm) piece of rag paper. Your clay sheet should be about 2" x 10" (5 cm x 25 cm). I used a different color. Repeat the first two steps, but over the baked clay now surrounding your tube. First, prepare the rag paper with glue and wrap it around the tube-and-clay form, making sure the rag paper is snug but moves freely over the baked layer. Then, wrap the rag paper with the new clay sheet, making sure the new clay layer is centered on the rag paper wrap and snug and the seam is sealed; the new clay shouldn't overlap or touch the baked clay beneath. Remember to smooth and adhere the clay fully by rolling it within a copy paper wrap. Trim the new clay cylinder to 1" (3 cm) long. Bake, and cool.

Now, release the clay cylinders by gently twisting and sliding them off the postal tube. The rag paper will enable them to separate easily. Remove the paper from both layers. The second, shorter layer will be larger in diameter than the other, and the first clay layer will nest snugly within it.

4 Make the top and bottom of the box.

Using the same setting on the pasta machine, prepare two small sheets of clay.

To make the top for the lid of the box, place one of the clay sheets on a piece of paper. Place the box lid on the clay sheet, and gently press it in place, without pushing it into the clay. With your blade, trim around the contour of the lid until all excess clay is removed. Carefully lift the lid from the work surface, and gently press the fresh clay with your fingers to secure it to the baked clay edge. This will ensure it adheres during baking. Repeat these steps to make the bottom for your base. Stand the lid and base, open ends facing up, on your baking tray. Bake and cool. You have completed a basic box.

5 Create a flush lid.

At this point, the box lid overlaps the base, like an ice cream carton. But in the finished jewelry box, the lid will be flush with the base. To create this we must add another layer of clay to most of the base.

First, prepare a sheet of clay about 3" x 10" (8 cm x 25 cm). You will use this clay sheet to wrap the base as in step 3, but because you want these clay layers to adhere, there's no rag paper buffer. Wrap the new clay around the base, and trim it top and bottom using the baked clay edges beneath to guide your blade. Now, using a vial to steady and support your blade, trim away about ½" (1 cm) of clay from the top (open) edge of the base. Stand the base on a tray, open end up, and bake. You now have a box with a lid that slips over the lining of the base and rests on the edge of the layer you have just added, creating a uniform outer layer.

6 Decorate the box.

The specific processes and techniques used to finish your boxes will depend on how you want to decorate them. You could use cane slices, mokumé gané, imitative materials such as faux ivory or stone, surface texturing, transfers, colored pencils, stencils, paint—whatever you like. The choice is yours. Clay veneers were used here.

For added strength and a clean finish, the box decoration is done in two baking stages: lid top and base body, then lid body and base bottom. First, make a sheet of veneer, and decorate it. Cover the top of the lid and the body of the base with the veneer, and bake, open ends up.

When the lid and base have cooled, finish your decoration by covering the body of the lid and the bottom of the base. Note that the wrap covering the lid body conceals the exposed edges of both the structural and decorative tops of the lid, and the base bottom covers the concentric wraps of the bottom's body.

Finally, stand the fully veneered lid and base on your baking tray with open ends up and bake. Once they've cooled, you can finish your decoration with any additional finishing techniques (see page 24).

Variations

Different diameter tubes, and even different shaped forms, can be used to create all sorts of containers with snug lids. For example, I have used smaller wood dowels and metal tubes to make wearable vessels—hollow pendants with space to hold a lucky charm, inspiring message, mad money, or aspirin.

Everlasting Leaves Centerpiece

Artist: Leigh S. Ross

This project uses polymer clay to preserve the natural beauty of Mother Nature's treasures—it's as easy as impressing fresh leaves and flower petals into the clay. The secret to creating flexible, paper-thin leaves and flowers is to mix Sculpey Super Flex with Premo. Sculpey Super Flex tends to be sticky, which can interfere with the impression process. Mixing it with Premo, and leaching if necessary, will reduce this tendency, making the clay easier to roll and handle. Rolling the clay paper-thin may take some practice. Try cooling it off between rollings by laying it in the refrigerator for five minutes, or holding it in front of an air conditioning vent.

Materials

- basic polymer clay equipment and supplies (see page 15)
- white clay (conditioned and leached), Sculpey Super Flex
- clay in leafy and floral colors, Premo
- freshly picked flowers and leaves
- Pearl Ex pigment powder
- 22-gauge craft wire
- spray varnish, such as Krylon Triple-Thick Crystal Clear Glaze Spray
- floral tape
- straw wreath
- E6000 glue
- Kemper Pro Needle Tool
- round tapered Clay Shaper
- pliers
- floral stem wire
- pasta machine
- wire cutters
- glass candle chimney and pillar candle

Getting Started

To prepare leaves, first clean them with dish detergent and water, then lay them on a paper towel to dry. Store them in a phone book to keep them flat until you're ready to use them. To prepare flowers, carefully separate the petals, then keep them in water until you're ready to use them. Lay them on a paper towel, and blot gently to dry them before decorating them with pigment powder.

1 Decorate and position leaves and flowers on the clay sheet.

To make leaves and flowers, mix equal parts of Sculpey Super Flex and the desired color of Premo clay. Roll out the mixture as thin as you can without it sticking, then leach it (See *Leaching* on page 18). Lay the clay sheet on a piece of waxed paper, parchment paper, or office paper.

Apply a layer of Pearl Ex to the underside of the leaves or petals. Spring green, pearl white, and brilliant gold were used here. Gently shake off the excess Pearl Ex and turn the leaves or petals over, placing the powdered sides down on the piece of clay. Press them down gently with your fingertips, but try not to move them around. Do this with as many leaves or petals as you can fit on the sheet of clay, or as many of that variety as you want. It takes 15 to 25 carnation petals to make one flower.

To make leafy accents to cover the base of the flowers, cut a small sheet of the leaf-colored clay, roll it as thin as you can, then apply a layer of green Pearl Ex. Set aside this sheet for baking.

TIP

To make a frilly carnation, the clay should be as thin as possible. Also, leach the clay sheet until it doesn't feel sticky anymore.

2 Impress and cut out the clay leaves and flower petals.

Lay piece of waxed paper over the leaves and petals, again being careful not to move them. Carefully holding the waxed paper in place, roll over the leaves with a brayer, using enough pressure to transfer the texture onto the clay. When this is done correctly, the clay picks up an incredible amount of detail from the leaves and flowers. Gently remove the waxed paper. Using an extra-fine needle tool or a fine needle in a pin vise (the thinner the needle, the easier it cuts the clay), trace around the outline of the leaf, cutting through the clay. Remove the excess clay.

Grab the stem, or the edge of the leaf, and pull it back from the clay. After removing all the real leaves, use the fine needle to clean up the edges of the clay leaves. Gently peel the clay leaves from the waxed paper, and turn them over on the paper, Pearl Ex side down.

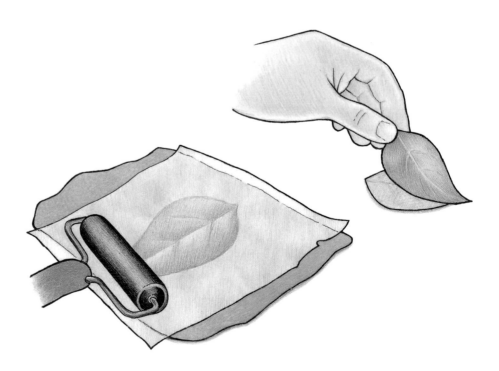

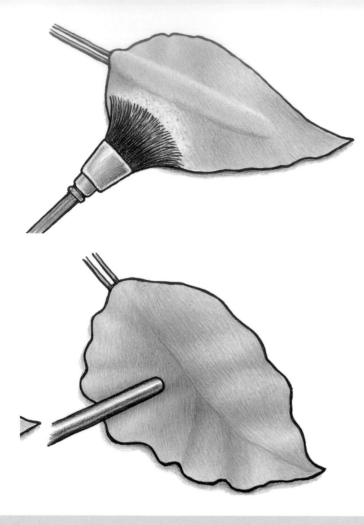

3 Shape and make stems for the clay leaves.

Cut 6" to 10" (15 cm to 25 cm) lengths of 22-gauge craft wire, and fold them tightly in half, with the ends meeting (the size will depend on how long the spine of the leaf is and how much of the leaf you want to have wired). These will be the stems of the leaves.

Lay a folded craft wire on the back of a clay leaf with the fold of the wire about three-quarters of the way up the leaf. Cover the wire with a strip of clay, and trim the excess off at the base of the leaf. Using the back end the Kemper Pro Needle Tool, a clay shaper, or some rounded tool, smooth the edges of the strip into the clay of the leaf. Don't press too hard or you'll smooth out the texture on the other side of the leaf. Then hold the leaf by the wire and cover the back with Pearl Ex.

Depending on the kind of leaf you're using, you'll want to give it a three-dimensional look before it's baked. You can use a rounded tool to carefully stretch the edges a little, which automatically gives you a curly effect on the leaves. You can also use a needle tool to deepen the leaf impressions. Fold the leaf gently along the vein lines that you want to show the most. When you have the look to the leaf that you want, place it down on a piece of paper on your baking pan. Bake at 265° F (129° C) for 40 minutes. Let cool, then seal with a spray varnish that is compatible with polymer clay, such as Krylon Triple-Thick Crystal Clear Glaze Spray.

4 Shape and make the clay flowers.

Shape petals as directed for the leaves, but use a smaller tool such as a round tapered clay shaper. Then, along with the green clay sheet that will be used to cover the base of the flowers, bake at 265° F (129° C) for 40 minutes. Let cool, then seal with spray varnish, such as Krylon Triple-Thick Crystal Clear Glaze Spray.

To make the wire stems, first cut 6" to 10" (15 cm to 25 cm) lengths of 22-gauge craft wire. Use pliers to bend down about 1" (3 cm) of the stem wire, making an elongated loop on one end of the wire; this helps to give you a better base on which to lay the petals while you're assembling the flower. Next, cut about a 2' (61 cm) length of floral tape. Wrap it around the loop of the wire, stretching the tape carefully, yet not too hard. Keep twisting the wire while you hold the tape taut, and run the tape down the wire about three-quarters of the way down.

Now attach the floral tape to the top of the wire again. Grab a couple of petals, preferably petals with tight curly edges. I like to put the tighter curls in the middle and the looser curls on the outside of the flower. Put the base of the petal up against the elongated loop at the top of the wire. Wrap the floral tape over the base of the petal, pulling the tape slightly. Slip in another petal, and wrap the floral tape around the wire a couple times. Add three or four more petals, then twist the tape halfway down the wire, and

break it off. Then start at the top again, attaching the tape to the wire, and add more petals. Keep adding petals evenly around the flower. When your flower is the size you want it, run the floral tape all the way down the wire, and break it off.

Cut a piece from the green clay with scissors. Cut one edge in a zigzag pattern for a decorative finish. Wrap the piece around the base of the flower, and trim off any excess. Using floral tape, secure it to the flower.

5 Assemble the wreath.

Plan the arrangement of the wreath. Position the focal flowers or leaves first. Then, remove them one at a time, coat the bottom of the stems with E6000 glue, and replace them in the same hole. Fill in the rest of the space by using a needle tool to make a hole in the wreath and then inserting a glue-coated wire into the hole. If you're using a straw wreath to assemble your centerpiece, the wires don't need to be any more than 1" (3 cm) long. Continue until all the leaves and flowers are glued in place. Trim the wires as necessary.

Set the pillar candle in the center, and voila! Enjoy your centerpiece. If you plan to burn the candle, place it in a glass sleeve or chimney so the wreath can't catch fire.

Variations

The technique described here is perfect for creating realistic whole flowers; simply wrap the entire stem and add a few wired leaves. Whole flowers, or individual leaves, can be used to make and decorate so many things—try using them to fill a vase, make a wall wreath, decorate a curtain swag, or create custom jewelry. Or build simple polymer clay circles, then attach smaller leaves and flowers to make napkin rings that coordinate with your centerpiece.

Chapter 5
Enhancing the Surface

You have luscious-colored clay to work with; you can make intriguing, useful, sturdy structures. So what goes on top? How can you frost this cake?

In about a million ways.

The range of possibilities for surface decoration is one of the most delightful attributes of polymer clay. It works with a host of other art, craft, and commercial materials. You can stamp it, mold it, paint it, emboss it, carve it, antique it, gild it, and transfer words and pictures onto it. It can be used to create anything from a cameolike pendant to an enameled wind chime to a Roman-style mosaic. This easy adaptability inspires artistic experimentation that's bound to lead to exciting discoveries.

Other arts become a banquet of inspiration for polymer clay crafters hungry to play with the clay's surface and create special effects. Paper arts such as rubber stamping, printmaking, and bookbinding contribute pigments, paints, inks, glues, colored pencils, iridescent powders and metallic leaf, photocopies, glitters, and embossing powder. Jewelry contributes carving, inlaying, enameling, texturing, mosaic making, molding, and antiquing. Even the kitchen can be raided for cookie cutters, candy molds, and sugarcraft tools for making fancy cake icing.

The interplay between texture, dimension, and surface decoration is another intriguing aspect of polymer clay crafting. Keep in mind how these elements will interact when planning a project. Because clay can be easily molded, manipulated by hand, or textured with various materials ranging from sandpaper to leaves, there are unlimited combinations to explore.

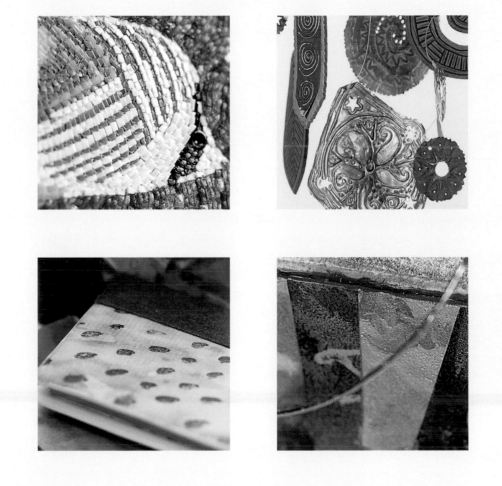

Molded Pine Pendant

Artist: Jacqueline Lee

Simple elements can be combined to produce elegant work. These pendants have the rich look of antique lacquerware from Japan. You'll make a simple but precise push mold and use it to cast a delicate pine sprig. By building this many-layered piece in stages and baking each one just enough to harden it, you'll keep the all-important surface layer perfect—no need to sand and polish it at the end.

Materials

- basic polymer clay equipment and supplies (see page 15)
- 1 yard (.9 m) of black pendant cord
- 2 ounces (57 grams) of Elasticlay
- 1 tiny pinecone
- 1 pine or yew frond
- cardstock
- 1 block of metallic copper clay, Premo
- gold bronzing powder or Pearl Ex powder
- Transparent Liquid Sculpey (TLS)
- 1 block of black clay, either Fimo or Premo

- 2 gold eye pins ½" (1 cm) long
- flat black acrylic paint
- 10" (25 cm) length of black crochet thread, cut in half
- 1 black hairpipe bead 1¼" (3 cm) long
- 1 round black accent bead
- 1 small black bead for necklace closure (hole should be just large enough accommodate a double thickness of the pendant cord)
- toothpick
- pasta machine
- dust mask

- tracing paper
- graph paper
- 2 small pairs of pliers
- small brush

Getting Started

Coat 1" (3 cm) of each end of the pendant cord with cyanoacrylate glue (unless you're using leather), and hang to dry.

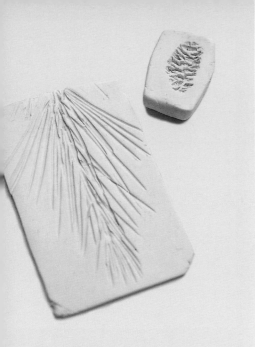

1 Make the molds.

Lightly condition the Elasticlay. Shape a small amount into a rectangle that's longer and thicker than your pinecone, and place it on a piece of cardstock. Coat the top of the rectangle with cornstarch, and press down on it lightly with the tile to flatten the surface. Center the pinecone on the clay rectangle, and press gently until it's half submerged. Carefully lift the pinecone straight up out of the clay, which will be your pinecone mold.

Roll some Elasticlay through the pasta machine on setting #1. Place the clay on a piece of cardstock. Gently press the pine frond into the surface of the clay to create an impression.

TIP

You may find it helpful to press the pine needles down with a small piece of clear glass borrowed from a frame. Carefully lift the frond away. Bake both molds according to manufacturer's instructions, and cool completely.

2 Mold and gild the pine parts.

Make a small ball from metallic copper clay. Fill the pinecone mold half full of water, and then press the ball of clay firmly into the mold. (The water will act as a release agent and keep the clay from sticking to the mold.) Expect some water to spill over the sides. Use the tissue blade to trim the clay until it's flush with the mold. It works best to trim from the center toward one end and then turn the mold and repeat. Press a small lump of excess clay gently against the edges of the clay in the mold, and pull back. The lump of clay will stick slightly to the clay in the mold and allow you to pull it out. You may have to repeat the press-and-pull maneuver around the whole outside edge. Repeat to make two molded clay pinecones.

Now you're ready to gild the pinecones. Wearing a dust mask, get a small amount of gold-colored bronzing or Pearl Ex powder on your finger by rubbing your finger around on the inside of the lid. Rub your finger gently over the mold-contoured surface (not the back) of the clay until the raised areas are nicely coated. Bake the pinecones at 275° F (135° C) for 10 minutes.

Roll a sheet of copper clay through the pasta machine on setting #3. Wet the pine frond sheet mold well, and lay the #3 layer of clay on top of it. Run them through the pasta machine together on setting #1. Lay the sheet with the molded copper pine frond on the ceramic tile. Use a sharp craft knife to trim away the excess clay. (Although this step isn't difficult, it does require patience.)

3 Make the pendant body and add the pine parts.

Roll a sheet of copper clay through the pasta machine on setting #1. Lay sandpaper on the clay, grit side down, and run it through the pasta machine on setting #1 again. Gently lift the sandpaper off the clay. The textured surface will be the top layer of your pendant. Lay the clay, textured side up, on a piece of tracing paper, and trim to about 3" (8 cm) square. Place the tracing paper with the textured clay over a piece of graph paper, and use the grid lines to cut out a rectangle of clay large enough to accommodate the pine frond. Round off the corners with your craft knife if desired.

Slowly and carefully lift the pine frond from the tile by running the tissue blade beneath it with (not against) the direction of the needle growth,

as if you're shaving the surface of the tile. Lift the freed end gently with your other hand so that it doesn't adhere back down. When the pine frond is free, lay it on the textured rectangle and gently smooth your finger over it to ensure that all the individual needles are in contact with the clay. Gild the pine frond following step 2.

After the baked pinecones have cooled, turn them over and make scratch marks in several directions on the backs to help them adhere to the next layer. Coat the backs lightly with white glue or TLS, staying away from the edges. Press the baked pinecones onto the pine piece. If this distorts the rectangle, simply place it back over the graph paper, and trim it back into shape. Bake at 275° F (135° C) for 10 minutes.

4 Finish the pendant.

Roll a sheet of black clay at the thickest setting, and place it on a piece of cardstock. This is the back layer. Trim one edge of the clay with a tissue blade; this will be the top edge. Holding an eye pin by the eye with a small pair of pliers, use a second pair of pliers to bend the pin section at a sharp angle. Repeat with the second eye pin. Press the eye pins into the trimmed side of the final layer with the eyes placed ½" to ¾" (1 cm to 2 cm) apart, protruding beyond the edge. Score the back of pine assemblage with a needle tool or craft knife, then press it firmly onto the back layer so that the eye pins are centered at the top and about ¹/₁₆" (1.5 mm) of the bottom layer is visible as a border. Trim the edge of the bottom layer all around to leave a ¹/₁₆" (1.5 mm) border. Bake at 275° F (135° C) for 20 minutes.

When the pendant has cooled, antique it by applying flat black acrylic paint with a small brush between the pine needles and in the crevices of the pinecone.

5 Assemble the necklace.

Fold a 5" (13 cm) length of black crochet thread in half, and—holding the ends together—thread them through one eye from the side, and draw the thread through until you're left with a dime-size loop of thread on the outside and two long ends in the middle. Lay the pendant face down, and separate the threads. Lay one thread up (perpendicular to the top edge of the pendant) and the other down (perpendicular to the bottom edge). Take care not to pull your loop through the eye.

Place one end of the hairpipe bead into the loop, and lay the bead, centered, across the top edge of the pendant. Grasp the ends of the thread (one in each hand), and pull the loop snugly against the bead. Then tie the thread into a knot against the back of the bead to hold it tightly in place. (You may want to make a double knot to be safe.) Put a tiny dot of cyanoacrylate glue on the knot to secure it. When it's dry, trim away the excess thread. Repeat this process for the other side.

Fold the necklace cord in half. Holding it at the loop end, thread it loop-first (going in at the front out at the back) between the eye pins, beneath the hairpipe bead, until you have a 1½" (4 cm) loop at the back. Fold the loop up, and thread both cord ends through it. Pull snug to form a lark's-head knot around the bead.

Clip the dry, stiffened ends of the pendant cord at an angle with clippers or sharp scissors. Thread both pieces of the pendant cord through an accent bead (it may be easier to do one at a time), and slide the bead into place just above the lark's-head knot.

Thread one end of the pendant cord through the closure bead, then thread the other end through the bead in the opposite direction. The cord should fit snugly in the bead so that when the ends of the cord are pulled to adjust the length it will be held securely in place.

Tie a knot in each cord end. Place a tiny dot of cyanoacrylate glue on the knot to secure it. When the glue is dry, trim the excess.

Variations

This necklace is constructed much like the main project, but instead of using a mold for the design, it's made using two Asian-themed rubber stamps. The main design is the Kanji character for Happiness.

For the top layer—layer one—roll a sheet of black clay through the pasta machine on setting #4. Place the sheet of clay on a piece of tracing paper. Rub gold-colored bronzing powder over just the top surface of the Kanji stamp with your finger, and then stamp an impression into the clay. Trim the clay neatly around the image and bake at 275° F (135° C) for 10 minutes.

For layer two, roll a sheet of black clay through the pasta machine on setting #5, then lay it on a piece of cardstock. Coat the surface of the ori-ental text stamp with gold powder as before, and press it onto the sheet of clay. When the baked Kanji piece has cooled, score the back, coat it lightly with white glue or TLS, and lay it over the middle layer. Lay a skewer gently against each side of the Kanji layer and use it as a guide to trim a narrow border from the unbaked layer. Bake at 275° F (135° C) for 10 minutes.

For layer three, roll out a small sheet of metallic copper clay on setting #3, then trim it to about a 2" (5 cm) square. Lay it on a corner of a sheet of gold leaf or composite leaf, and trim off excess leaf sheet with a sharp blade. Run the leafed clay through the pasta machine on setting #3 to ensure the leaf adheres well. Run it through again on setting #4. The gold leaf will show tiny cracks. Rotate the leafed clay a quarter turn, and run it through again on setting #5.

When the baked Kanji layers (layers one and two) have cooled, turn the baked piece over, repeat the scoring and gluing process as before, and press the piece firmly onto the leafed layer. Trim the left and right sides of layer three flush with layer two. For the top and bottom borders, lay the bamboo skewer gently against layer two as a guide, but trim the leafed layer about 1/16" (1.5 mm) wider than the skewer. Bake at 275° F (135° C) for 10 minutes.

Make the fourth and final layer following step 4 from the Molded Pine Pendant (you won't need to do any antiquing), and assemble the necklace following step 5.

TIP: MAKE A FAUX HAIRPIPE BEAD

Roll a clay snake about the diameter of a pencil, and use a tissue blade to cut a segment about ¾" (2 cm) long. Pierce it lengthwise with a toothpick that has been dusted with cornstarch. Lay the pierced segment on a flat surface. Use two fingers to roll the bead and gradually spread your fingers apart. Roll until the bead lengthens to ¼" (6 mm) from each toothpick end. To bake, suspend the bead above the surface by resting each end of the toothpick on a small piece of excess clay. Bake at 275° F (135° C) for 20 minutes. Trim the bead to size while it's still warm. When it's cool enough to handle, hold the bead in one hand, and use pliers to pull out the toothpick; it may help to twist the toothpick first and then pull. Use the tissue blade to trim off the rough ends of the bead so that it's about the same width as the pendant.

Mosaic Plaque

Artist: Margaret

Creating a polymer clay mosaic can be thrilling, because there's no limit to the colors that can be used, as there is with other mosaic materials. The "water" in this mosaic was created by blending blue and translucent clay with embossing powder in various amounts to create an array of shades. The final result is a beautiful water scene with shimmery depth and sophistication. This ungrouted mosaic was created by placing uncured "tiles" on an uncured background, eliminating the need for adhesive. The resulting classic look is reminiscent of the intricate, expressive works created by the ancient Romans.

Materials

- basic polymer clay equipment and supplies (see page 15)
- picture for reference and tracing
- 1 block of white clay, Fimo or Premo
- 1 block of translucent clay, Fimo or Premo
- dark blue embossing powder
- 1 block of blue clay, Fimo or Premo
- 1 block of black clay, Fimo or Premo
- 1 block of yellow clay, Fimo or Premo
- imitation gold leaf
- tracing paper
- matte varnish, Fimo or Sculpey
- pasta machine
- tapestry needle
- penny or penny-size circular cutter
- paint brush

Getting Started

Be sure to include the most important details when tracing an image for a mosaic, such as the eye, fins, and gills of this fish.

1 Transfer the mosaic pattern to the clay.

First, trace the selected image in pencil. Next, use a pasta machine to roll out a piece of clay about 3½" x 2¾" (9 cm x 7 cm) on setting #1. Make the rectangle as even as possible, but don't trim the edges. Place the clay on a bakeable work surface.

Then lay the tracing face up on the rectangle of clay, and smooth it out. Run a tapestry needle over the lines of the pattern to create slight but visible indentations in the clay. Remove the paper after tracing all the lines.

2 Fill in the traced pattern with tiles.

Roll out the clay to be used for the tiles on setting #5, and place the slabs on baking parchment or waxed paper. From these slabs, cut several short strips ⅛" to ³⁄₁₆" (3 mm to 4 mm) wide. Using a craft knife with a curved or angled blade, cut small squares from the strips, and begin placing the tiles along the image outline.

To create the shades of blue for the water, first roll out a sheet of translucent clay using a pasta machine on setting #1 (the thickest setting). Then, cut out a 1½" x 1½" (4 cm x 4 cm) from this sheet. Mix in about ¼ to ½ teaspoon of embossing powder, a little bit at a time, until the clay is denim blue. Cut the clay into four equal pieces. Set one aside to be used as is. Then cut out six penny-size pieces of clay from the remainder of the translucent sheet, using a craft knife and a penny or a circle cutter as a guide. Mix one piece of translucent clay with one denim blue piece; two pieces of translucent clay with another denim blue piece; and the remaining three translucent pieces with the last denim blue piece. Finally, create a blue-gray color by mixing 2 parts white, ½ part blue, ½ part black clay. For the gold accent tiles, roll translucent clay through the pasta machine on setting #6 (very thin). Then, carefully lay the metal leaf on top and smooth it out.

TIP

To make an eye like the one seen here, press a small ball of clay into place with a ball stylus tool or ball-headed pin.

TIP

To enable you to hang the plaque, adhere a looped string to the back using permanent glue, or drill two holes at the top for a knotted cord. A smaller piece would make a striking brooch or pendant.

3 Fill in the remaining parts of the image.

For guidance and inspiration, refer to the image used to create the traced pattern. Fill in the major features, such as the fish's stripes and spots, then continue with the background. Place the tiles in rows to keep the mosaic neat. Pay attention to the flow of the lines that the rows create. The tiles in the body of the fish here have been laid in diagonal rows, but the tail is made up of horizontal rows; this helps to define the image

and creates movement in the piece. To create the illusion of water, alternate between shades of blue, and lay the tiles in wavy lines as seen here.

Once the mosaic is complete, put a piece of blank tracing paper over the tiles and use a smooth roller, such as a brayer or jar, to gently embed them into the slab of clay. Then remove the tracing paper, and bake according to the manufacturer's directions. Once the piece is cool, finish with two coats of matte varnish.

Variations

Like all surface techniques, this one could be used to ornament many different objects. Glue your plaque to a plain journal cover, clock case, or vase. Want to wear it as a brooch? Add a pinback (first clean the metal with alcohol, roughen it with a nail file, then glue it to the plaque with cyanoacrylate glue). Make a mosaic disk to fit commercial bezels for a pendant, earrings, ring, or brooch.

I work wet-on-wet, but that isn't the only way to make polymer clay mosaics. Some artists place prebaked "tiles" ranging from tiny threads to substantial pieces on top of unbaked clay. And some artists make canes that look like mosaics.

Wind Play Wind Chime

Artist: Linda Goff

*Make this unique wind chime using polymer clay and color-plated aluminum tooling foil. The basic form is easily made using an ordinary jar as a support. Transparent Liquid Sculpey mixed with powdered pigments was used to glaze and reinforce the delicate embossed foil elements. The clay elements were carved using a **V**-shaped linoleum cutting tool; try using wood-carving tools of various shapes as well. Be sure to hang the finished wind chime where it will receive some protection from the sun and weather, such as a window or a porch.*

Materials

- basic polymer clay equipment and supplies (see page 15)
- 4 conditioned blocks of gold polymer clay
- chime tubes
- 2 conditioned blocks of polymer clay in assorted colors
- cotton swabs
- tracing paper
- tooling foil
- Transparent Liquid Sculpey (TLS)
- Sculpey Diluent
- metallic pigment powders
- acrylic and oil paints
- E-6000 glue or other two-part adhesive
- water-based satin varnish, such as Flecto Varathane Diamond Elite (black and silver can)
- nylon or heavy cotton thread
- 20-gauge wire
- metal ring for hanging the chime
- pasta machine
- cylindrical glass jar about 13" (33 cm) in circumference
- rubber stamp
- linoleum cutter with **V**-shaped blade
- bone folder
- stylus tools for embossing the foil
- stack of newspapers at least ¼" (6 mm) thick
- scissors
- paint palette
- round-nosed jewelry pliers

Getting Started

Design shapes for the foil accents that will be applied to the body of the wind chime by sketching ideas on tracing paper. Then cut them out to make flexible templates that can be easily used on a curved surface.

1 Make the body of the wind chime.

Roll the gold clay through the pasta machine on the thickest setting. Trim that clay so the sheet is 3" x 14" (8 cm x 36 cm). Cut away the top edge to create a decorative pattern and the bottom edge to create a wave pattern. Wrap the clay sheet around a cylindrical glass jar so the short ends overlap, and make sure they're aligned. Press a rubber stamp into the overlapped clay so it stays on the jar. Bake following the manufacturer's directions. Don't remove the clay from the jar.

2 Carve the body of the wind chime.

With a pencil, trace the templates of the foil accents on the body of the wind chime. Then carve decorative lines around the shapes and other areas of the body using a linoleum cutter. Fill the carved lines with conditioned clay in a contrasting color. Remove any excess clay using a bone folder, cotton swabs, and isopropyl alcohol. Bake following the manufacturer's directions. Once the clay has cooled, carve more decorative lines between the filled lines. Leave the new lines unfilled.

3 Make foil shapes.

Using a pencil, trace the same templates used on the body of the wind chime on the front of the tooling foil. The traced outlines should be slightly larger than the templates. Next, place the foil on a stack of newspapers at least ¼" (6 mm) thick, then emboss and/or pierce the foil with a stylus tool, paper punch, or needle tool. Embossing the front (here, the green side) of the foil will create a recessed pattern; embossing the back (here, the silver side), a raised pattern. After embossing, neatly trim the foil to the edges using scissors.

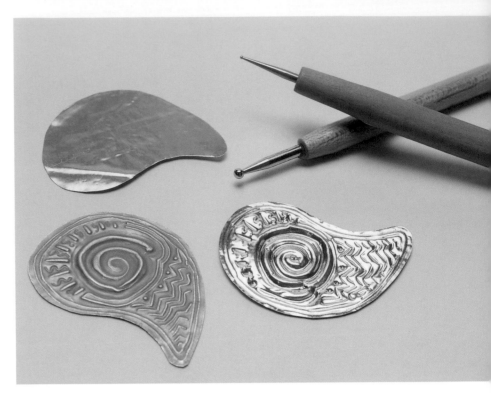

4 Decorate the body of the wind chime.

Fill three sections of a paint palette halfway with TLS. Thin with TLS diluent according to manufacturer's directions. Tint the TLS by mixing a small amount of metallic pigment powder into it. (More powder will yield a more opaque color and less powder a lighter, more translucent color.) Brush a layer of colored TLS onto the embossed foil shapes, and let it settle into the recessed areas. The brush can be cleaned with turpentine, paint thinner, or isopropyl alcohol. Bake the foil, TLS side facing up, for 20 minutes following the manufacturer's directions. Once they've cooled, decorate them with acrylic paint. Then use E-6000 glue or similar two-part adhesive to attach the foil accents to the body of the wind chime—but make sure you follow the glue manufacturer's directions exactly. Apply a fairly thick layer of glue on both the foil piece and the body, wait about 10 minutes, then press them firmly together. Remove the body of the wind chime from the jar.

TIP

Once the foil is coated with TLS, the colored surface can be easily wiped away, before curing, to reveal the silver metal underneath. Try wiping only the raised areas of the accents to make them stand out. Use a dry paper towel wrapped around a finger to remove the color.

5 Make and attach dangles to the body of the wind chime.

Roll some clay through the pasta machine on the third thickest setting. Cut shapes from the sheet of clay, and bake them on a flat or curved surface, such as a jar, for 30 minutes. Once the dangles have cooled, decorate both sides using the same techniques described in steps 2, 3, and 4 for decorating the body of the wind chime. Also make some dangles entirely of foil. Apply water-based satin varnish, such as Flecto Varathane Diamond Elite, to all areas of baked TLS to prevent scratches. Then drill a hole about ¼" (6 mm) from the top edge of each dangle. Also drill a hole for each dangle or row of dangles on the bottom edge of the body of the wind chime. Next, attach the dangles at various lengths using nylon or heavy cotton thread.

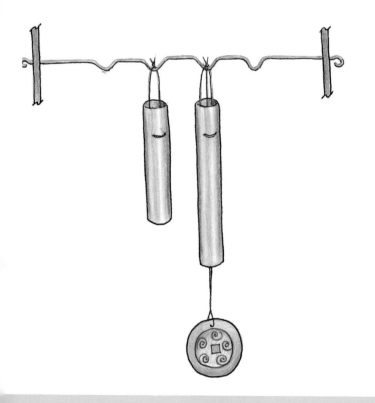

6 Attach the chime tubes.

Measure the diameter of the wind chime body, and cut a length of 20-gauge wire twice as long. Using round-nosed jewelry pliers, bend V shapes in the wire to hold each chime tube in place. The tubes should be positioned far enough apart to hang separately when still, but close enough together so they chime when moved gently. Drill two holes in the top of the body directly opposite from each other. Thread the ends of the wire through the holes and bend the ends to secure. Clip off any excess wire. Next, hang the chime tubes from the wire using nylon or heavy cotton thread. Make a wind catcher by hanging one of your large foil dangles through the inside of a chime tube so it is about 2" (5 cm) below the bottom of the tube. To hang the wind chime, first drill four equally spaced holes in the body of the wind chime, about ¼" (6 mm) from the top edge. Then, thread a piece of nylon through two of the holes, directly opposite each other, and tie securely. Repeat the procedure with the other two holes to create an **X**. Finally, cut another piece of nylon, and tie one end to a large metal ring; tie the other end around the center of the **X**.

Variations

Try using the construction technique described here to build a mobile, such as a suncatcher. Use translucent clay for the dangles, then carve and back-fill to create an opaque pattern. When sunlight hits the clay, the interplay between dark and light will be charming. Experiment with dangles of varying thickness, different shapes and sizes of carving tools, and clay inclusions such as glitter. Be sure to sand and buff the baked clay for the most translucent effect.

Book Covers with Freehand Transfers

Artist: Meredith Arnold

This freehand design, drawn with artist's felt-tipped pens on a scrap of synthetic fabric, was transferred to raw polymer clay using ordinary isopropyl alcohol. The result is a controlled yet flowing design, reminiscent of watercolors. For durable book covers, use a strong polymer clay that has some flexibility after it's baked, such as Fimo or Premo. Sculpey III isn't suitable. It's also a good idea to experiment with this technique first before finalizing the design of the book covers. Try combining different colors, simple and detailed designs, and various amounts of alcohol.

Materials

- basic polymer clay equipment and supplies (see page 15)
- 2 pieces of cardstock, 2" x 5 ½" (5 cm x 14 cm), folded lengthwise
- 2 paper clamps, 1" (3 cm) size
- precut stack of paper, 2" x 2 ¾" x ½" (5 cm x 7 cm x 1 cm) deep or less
- tight-weave cheesecloth or machine-made lace, 2" x 2" (5 cm x 5 cm)
- 1 piece of kraft paper or lightweight brown paper bag, 2" x 2" (5 cm x 5 cm)
- 1 block of white or light-colored clay
- Berol Prismacolor felt-tipped pens
- polyvinyl acetate (PVA) glue, such as Crafter's Pick Ultimate Glue
- masking tape
- thin synthetic fabric, such as coat lining material, 6" x 7" (15 cm x 18 cm)
- unlined index cards
- cotton swabs
- leather or Ultrasuede for binding
- bone folder or spoon
- small paint brush
- scissors
- pasta machine (optional)

Getting Started

Many copy centers offer paper-cutting services and charge by the number of cuts, regardless of paper quantity. This project uses a stack of 8 ½" x 11" (22 cm x 28 cm) paper cut into four equally sized smaller stacks.

1 Make the book block.

Crease the folds of the cardstock sharply, using a bone folder or the back of a spoon. Place the folded cardstock pieces on either side of the stack of paper, in the same orientation. (The folded edges should align with what will be the spine of the book.) Next, make sure the pages and cardstock are squared up, then attach paper clamps to both bottom corners of the paper block as shown. This will allow the block to stand freely on the work surface.

Fan the pages of the paper block in one direction, then apply a light coat of white PVA glue to the spine with a small paintbrush. Fan the pages in the opposite direction and apply another light coat of PVA glue. Squeeze the pages of the block together tightly, then lay the cheesecloth over the spine. Pull on the longer edges of the cheesecloth to hold the pages together tightly until the glue squishes through the weave. Hold in position for about 1 minute to allow the glue to set.

Once the pages remain together tightly without being held, apply another light coat of glue on top of the cheesecloth, and place the kraft paper over it. Burnish along the spine, and wipe off any excess glue. You now have a book block. Place the block between two sheets of waxed paper, and weigh it down for about 10 minutes. Once the glue has set, remove the waxed paper. Trim the kraft paper and cheesecloth to no less than ¼" (6 mm) from the spine, on all sides.

Make a template for the book cover by tracing the book block on a piece of cardstock. Make the rectangle ½" (1 cm) longer and wider then cut it out.

2 Make and decorate the book cover.

Roll out a 5" x 6" (13 cm x 15 cm) sheet of polymer clay using a pasta machine on a medium setting, such as #4. Place the sheet on a piece of paper, and set aside.

Tape a piece of waxed paper to the work surface. Tape the edges of the synthetic fabric to the waxed paper, making sure the fabric is taut. Using Berol Prismacolor felt-tipped pens, decorate the fabric. The ink will bleed, so choose colors that will blend well, and leave some open space in the design to compensate.

Next, place the decorated fabric on the polymer clay sheet, ink side down. Put an index card over the fabric, and burnish with a bone folder or the back of a spoon. Make sure the fabric completely adheres to the clay surface. Then, dampen a cotton swab with isopropyl alcohol; squeeze out the excess. Gently dab the fabric with the cotton swab, making sure the fabric stays adhered to the clay. Some of the pigment will appear on the cotton swab; this indicates that the transfer process is working. If the fabric becomes so saturated that it buckles, stop applying the isopropyl alcohol and just burnish it back in place; the end result will be different from the intended design, but still attractive. More moisture intensifies the watercolor effect, but if too much is used, it will ruin the transfer. Place an index card over the fabric and burnish to blot up excess liquid and pigment. Allow the fabric to dry for 3 minutes, then remove the index card.

Using the book cover template, carefully cut out two pieces of the decorated clay. Place the clay on an index card on a baking sheet. Bake at 265° F (129° C) for 25 minutes. If the clay pieces warp during baking, immediately place index cards over them, and weigh them down while they cool.

Using the rough side of an emery board or extra-fine sanding block, lightly sand the undecorated sides of the clay under running water; this will allow the glue to adhere better. Then, sand the edges of the covers while holding them together to ensure that they end up the same size and shape.

TIP

If a pasta machine isn't available, roll the clay to the thickness of a computer diskette. Place diskettes to the left and right of the clay, and tape in place. Roll over the clay and diskettes with a rolling pin or brayer.

3 Assemble the book.

To avoid accidentally gluing the book shut, place a piece of waxed paper between the glued cover and first page of the book block. Apply glue to the front of the book block, on the cardstock. Carefully position the book block over the undecorated side of one clay book cover. Make sure the spine edges are aligned and the other three sides of the cardstock are centered on the clay book cover. Press down firmly, then wipe off any excess glue with a dampened paper towel. Repeat the procedure to adhere the back cover of the book. Place a weight on the book, and let it dry.

4 Cover the spine.

Cut a rectangular strip of leather slightly larger than 2" x 1¼" (5 cm x 3 cm). Center the leather over the spine to check the fit. It should overlap the book covers; trim if necessary. Spread PVA glue carefully and evenly on the underside of the leather. Then, center it on the spine and press into place, making sure the corners are secure. Wipe off any excess glue, stroking away from the leather. Be careful; it can be difficult to remove glue from leather. Let dry before using.

Variations

Use rubber stamps to make impressions on the unbaked clay covers. After baking, apply acrylic paint with a dampened paper towel. Not all brands of acrylic paint work well on polymer clay; a few that do include Plaid Folk Art, Delta Ceramcoat, and Liquitex paints, available at most U.S. craft-supply outlets. For a slate effect, apply white paint to black clay. Wipe away excess, leaving some paint in the recessed rubber stamp impressions for a patina effect.

Decorate the cover with other types of transfers.

Basic transfers are created from carbon-based toner images. Either photocopied or laser-printed images will work if the toner contains carbon. If the transfer isn't successful when you use the following process, the image doesn't contain the necessary carbon to transfer. Roll out a sheet of clay with a nice flat surface. Burnish image onto the sheet of clay. Apply isopropyl alcohol to the back of the image with a cotton swab. The paper should become translucent-like. Blot any excess rubbing alcohol using an index card or other piece of paper. Let dry for half a minute or so and gently remove. The image should be very dark and crisp.

Laminated Boxes

Artist: Ellen Marshall

This project highlights the compatibility of polymer clay, rubber stamping, and paper arts supplies. The Chinese "take-out" box seen here was made using a simple one-piece paper foundation that was laminated with decorated clay. First the sheets of clay are textured with sandpaper, then they're painted with artist's inks to create vibrantly colored patterns. After the paint is dry, the unbaked clay can be cut apart and arranged in various ways, such as the delightful striped pattern on this "take-out" box. These miniature treasures make cherished party favors. A bigger box could hold a gift of candy or cookies, but make sure the treats are well sealed in plastic wrap.

Materials

- basic polymer clay equipment and supplies (see page 15)
- durable, heavyweight paper such as cardstock
- acrylic paints in assorted colors
- Transparent Liquid Sculpey (TLS)
- ¼ block of clay in a color to match the box, for a 2" (5 cm) box (larger boxes require more clay)
- 2 blocks of clay in a light color
- heat-resistant double-sided mounting tape in ¼" (6 mm) and ¾" (2 cm) rolls (such as Terrifically Tacky Tape)
- decorative paper cord for box handle
- artist's inks in assorted colors
- photocopier
- sponges and rubber stamps
- pigments and ink pads
- pasta machine
- small paintbrushes
- chambered watercolor palette
- soft makeup brush

Getting Started

We built the boxes for this project from scratch, using a commercially available box template. But it isn't necessary to build a box; any paper or cardboard box can be decorated using this technique.

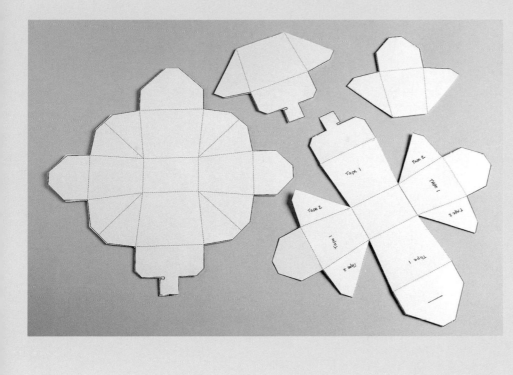

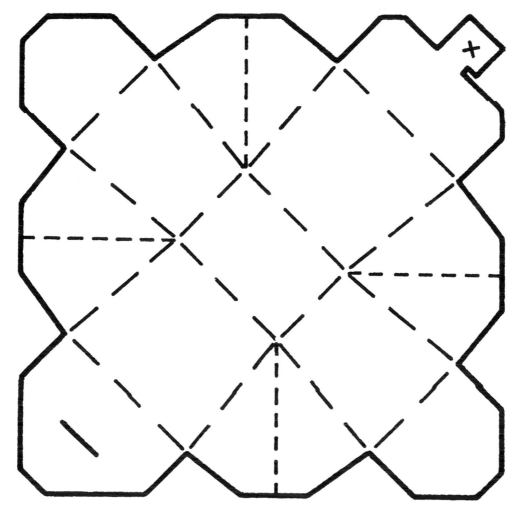

1 Prepare the templates.

Photocopy the template for the paper foundation box (see below) onto a piece of durable, heavyweight paper such as card-stock. Cut along the solid lines of the template with a craft knife. Then, cut along the edges of the two wider sides of the box, and remove the resulting triangles of paper. The narrower sides of the box will now have flaps for folding and securing the box. Lightly score the remaining dotted lines, then fold them in the same direction. Also, cut a slit in the middle of the box top, opposite the closing tab. If desired, make smaller templates of the box sides for use in planning the surface design.

After folding, cut slot in this cover piece for tab **X**

2 Decorate the foundation box and the clay.

Sponge or rubber stamp pigment ink on the entire inside of the box and the fronts of the box's top flaps. Paint the bottom and the folded edges on the outside of the box with acrylic paint; once dry, paint over these areas again with TLS, which will strengthen the paper. Bake following the manufacturer's directions.

Roll out sheets of clay using a pasta machine on a fairly thin setting. Make two 7" x 8" (18 cm x 20 cm) sheets of clay, piecing smaller sheets together to achieve the size, if necessary. (Boxes larger than the one shown here require more clay.) Dust the backs lightly with baby powder, and lay the sheets on pieces of cardboard.

Cover the clay sheets with plastic wrap and then with a piece of sandpaper, and use a roller to press the sandpaper into the clay, to create texture. Then, use a palette knife to loosen the clay sheet from the cardboard. Remove the sandpaper and plastic wrap. Now the clay is ready to decorate. Use brushes, stamps, or sponges to apply inks, let dry, then apply additional ink or painted accents. Use ink sparingly; if applied too heavily, it will collect in the recessed areas of the clay surface. Pearlescent and metallic colors were used on these boxes.

TIP

Inks can be dried more quickly with a hair dryer. Just be sure to use a cool setting.

3 Laminate and construct the box.

To plan the laminated design, cut strips of clay using a sharp craft knife and a metal ruler, and arrange them on the smaller templates.

Apply double-sided mounting tape to the template. Use two strips of tape for each panel of the box that will face outward when it's folded together, as seen here. Remove the protective cover strip to reveal the adhesive. Brush TLS over the box panels, making sure that the exposed tape is covered. Then, cut strips of clay and arrange them on each panel. Bake following the clay manufacturer's directions. When the box has cooled, carefully paint the edges of the clay panels with acrylic paint. Let dry.

Next, apply one piece of double-sided mounting tape to each of the four box flaps, close to, but not on, the areas that will be folded. Trim any excess tape. To construct the box, remove the protective cover strip from one flap. Fold the flap and the whole panel toward the inside of the box. Then fold the adjacent panel toward the inside of the box, bringing the edges of both panels together. Make sure they're aligned, then press them firmly together. Repeat with the remaining flaps.

Brush a little TLS into each corner edge of the box. Using the colored clay, roll thin snakes and fill the corner edges, smoothing the clay out so

it's flush with the box. Bake following the manufacturer's directions for the clay, and let cool.

To make the handle, drill holes on opposite sides of the box. Thread the ends of a pretty paper cord from the outside into the holes, then knot the ends of the cord on the inside of the box.

Stand by Celie Fago

Variations

A cohesive mosaic design can be created using unbaked sheets of clay in various colors, all decorated with a single design in coordinating colors. Start with sheets of unbaked clay. Apply the design by stamping, stenciling, or silk screening it, and let the clay dry. Build the mosaic by cutting strips or blocks from the decorated sheets and fitting them together on a thin, unbaked foundation sheet. When you're satisfied with the arrangement, cover the clay with tissue paper, and roll gently over the tissue with a roller to adhere the mosaic pieces to the foundation sheet. Cut the clay as desired to shape it. You can use the sheet flat, draped like fabric, or wrapped around a bead or box; bake following the manufacturer's directions.

Exploring Precious Metal Clay

by Celie Fago

Almost Alchemy:
The Story of Precious Metal Clay

When I first heard about Precious Metal Clay (PMC) I thought I had misunderstood. I'd been working with polymer clay, making jewelry for about seven years, and apprenticing to a metalsmith, studying metalworking for seven years. A clay that turned to precious metal when fired? Impossible. A few months later in 1998 a colleague showed me a bead made with this same new material. The bead had a look to it, a deeper texture than you could get with any metals technique I knew, and a resonance with its companion polymer beads that I couldn't quite identify. I was transfixed. The rest, as they say, is history. Like most people I didn't believe it possible—at first. Now, although its story has become as familiar in the telling as my own, I still marvel at the magic of a metal whose history is as a clay; I still marvel at the magic of PMC.

It was only after working with PMC for those first six months in 1998 that I discarded the idea that it was simply a shortcut to metalwork. Like polymer clay, PMC is a pioneer material and a clay. Understanding the nature of a material that's clay then metal has caused me to move away from attempts to replicate silversmithing and toward an understanding that an essential quality of great metal clay jewelry is the vestigial "clayness" found in the best PMC work. An undefinable quality, a range of textural effects that defy its recent history as clay but distinguish it forever from cast or fabricated silver. Whereas PMC is in its infancy, having been invented a mere 7 years ago, polymer clay is in its adolescence. The skills honed in working with polymer clay lend themselves splendidly to PMC. They are excellent companions. The pure silver adds aesthetic richness and, since it's precious metal, actual value to the polymer. Polymer clay, for its part, offers PMC the glory of color.

Chapter 6
Precious Metal Clay
Basic Techniques

This revolutionary new material was invented by Mitsubishi Materials Corporation of Sanda, Japan. It consists of three ingredients: tiny particles of pure silver (or pure gold), water, and an organic binder. When it's wet, or fresh, it's claylike and malleable and can be sculpted, textured, rolled, pushed into a press mold, or draped around a kernel of cereal to create a hollow form bead. When it's s air dried or leather-hard, it can be carved, cut, filed, drilled, and joined to make complex forms. When PMC is fired in a small electric kiln, the water evaporates, and the binder burns away.

The material shrinks as the metal particles fuse together, sharpening the surface detail, leaving an object made of pure silver. PMC comes in lump form (silver and gold), paste (or slip), and sheet. It also comes prepackaged in a syringe and can be extruded to ornament a surface. Several related products are in development.

This chapter covers the basic techniques for working with PMC. I have also included many tips and techniques that I have discovered and developed while using this unique material. The projects that follow range from simpler beads and earrings to more elaborate frames and pendants. I hope that they provide inspiration and a useful base of techniques on which to build your own designs.

Composition

Precious Metal Clay (PMC) is composed of three ingredients—fine pure silver particles so small they could be described as a flour, a proprietary binder, and water. The binder is organic, naturally occurring and nontoxic. Water accounts for 10 to 20 percent of the material. The silver powder and the binder are stable, but the water content begins to evaporate as soon as the package is opened, or over time, with improper storage.

PMC comes in four different forms: lump (silver and gold), sheet, paste, and packaged in a syringe.

- **Lump**—Silver lump PMC comes in two types: standard PMC and PMC Plus. The former was invented about 7 years ago by Mitsubishi Materials Corporation of Sanda, Japan; it shrinks 28 percent when fired. A few years later, that same company developed a new clay called PMC Plus. Because of a key difference in the silver particles that make up PMC Plus, it's stronger after firing than standard PMC, and it shrinks by only 12 percent.

- **PMC Plus sheet**—The 2" x 2" (60 mm x 60 mm) square sheet is a paper thin, specially formulated material that's had its moisture content stabilized and therefore isn't subject to evaporation. It resembles ultra suede, is flexible like fabric, and doesn't dry out.

- **PMC Plus paste**—This form is prepackaged slip.

- **PMC Plus prepackaged in a syringe**— This is specially formulated slip that doesn't slump when you extrude it onto a surface. It can be used for decoration or for repairs.

Sheet, paste, and syringe style PMC are all formulated from PMC Plus and should be fired accordingly. You can unwrap a package of PMC and use the entire ounce in making a small vessel, or you can stretch an ounce, economically, and make many smaller pieces. The textured leaf shapes shown on page 102, were two of seventy-two such shapes made from 1 ounce of standard PMC.

Keeping PMC Moist

Two discoveries I made early on made working with PMC immeasurably easier. The first has to do with extending the working time of fresh PMC by rolling through plastic wrap to minimize evaporation. The second has to do with working leather-hard. Borrowed from ceramics, the term *leather-hard* simply means "dry" when used to describe PMC. It may mean air dried, or force dried under a light or in an oven set at 225° to 285° F. For all intents and purposes, when the material is dry or leather-hard it's stable indefinitely.

Standard versus Plus

Because of their slightly different balance of ingredients, PMC and PMC Plus have different attributes in all three stages—fresh, leather-hard, and as metal after firing. Fresh standard PMC takes detail beautifully. It rarely requires oil to prevent sticking, and it's both flexible and strong while leather-hard. PMC Plus rebounds slightly from texture, so the impression isn't always as crisp as that of standard. It's slightly more difficult to join to itself, and when fresh, it always requires oil to prevent sticking. PMC Plus has less binder holding the metal particles together so when it's leather-hard it's not as durable as standard. It's fragile and care must be taken not to bump or drop a piece. Besides taking details of impressions a bit better to begin with, standard PMC sharpens detail because it shrinks more, whereas the 12 percent shrinkage of Plus doesn't have much effect on detail. After firing however, it's denser and stronger than fired standard PMC, so PMC Plus is more appropriate for rings and thinner designs. Because it has more binder, standard PMC is remarkably strong in its leather-hard stage, and as a result, it carves more easily than PMC Plus. Leather-hard standard PMC can be successfully cut with a protected tissue blade, but this same method may shatter leather-hard PMC Plus. Instead, use a jeweler's saw with a 3/0 blade for PMC Plus. Both materials can be drilled with a hand drill, a Dremel, or a flex shaft.

Storage

Store PMC tightly wrapped in plastic, in its original package, and in airtight plastic bags with folded-up wet paper towels inside. Refresh the paper towels on a regular basis, especially if you

live in a dry climate. If you discover that a package of clay seems dry when you push your finger into it, take a bit of sponge or paper towel, dampen it, and put it in the package under the tightly wrapped PMC.

Rehydrating

To rehydrate rock hard PMC, stab holes in it with a needle tool, then run it under the tap (or use distilled water) for 30 to 60 seconds. Rewrap it tightly in plastic along with a tablespoon or two of water. In several hours it will reabsorb the water and give slightly to the pressure of your finger. Repeat the above process, but instead of running it under water, stab holes in it, then wrap it tightly with some water in with the clay. You may be able to knead the clay at this point, or you may need to repeat the first steps one or two more times. Once you have some experience with PMC, you'll be able to recognize a good working consistency, and remember that you can always turn clay into slip by adding extra water.

Forming

Rolling out PMC: As a general rule, if you flip your PMC over every three or four rolls, it is much less likely to stick to your work surface.

Water versus oil: What to do about cracking PMC?

When closing a joint in fresh PMC, or joining one fresh piece to another—like an embellishment to a bead—you'll need to add a bit of water. After you've made the joint, it's helpful to smooth it over with an oiled finger or oiled brush handle. Experiment, and you'll soon know when you need to switch from water to oil. Too much water will make mud. If this happens, wait a few seconds, then smooth over the wet spot with an oiled finger. Balancing the moisture level simply takes some getting used to. Keep your water and your oil within reach.

Tenting

If your PMC is cracking, roll it out through plastic or try "tenting"—that is, tearing off a large sheet of plastic and working under it. Put a barrier up to protect your work area from any breeze. Or, try rehearsing a particular design in scrap polymer clay until you can work a bit faster.

Top left: PMC Plus; top right: Standard PMC; below: PMC Sheet.

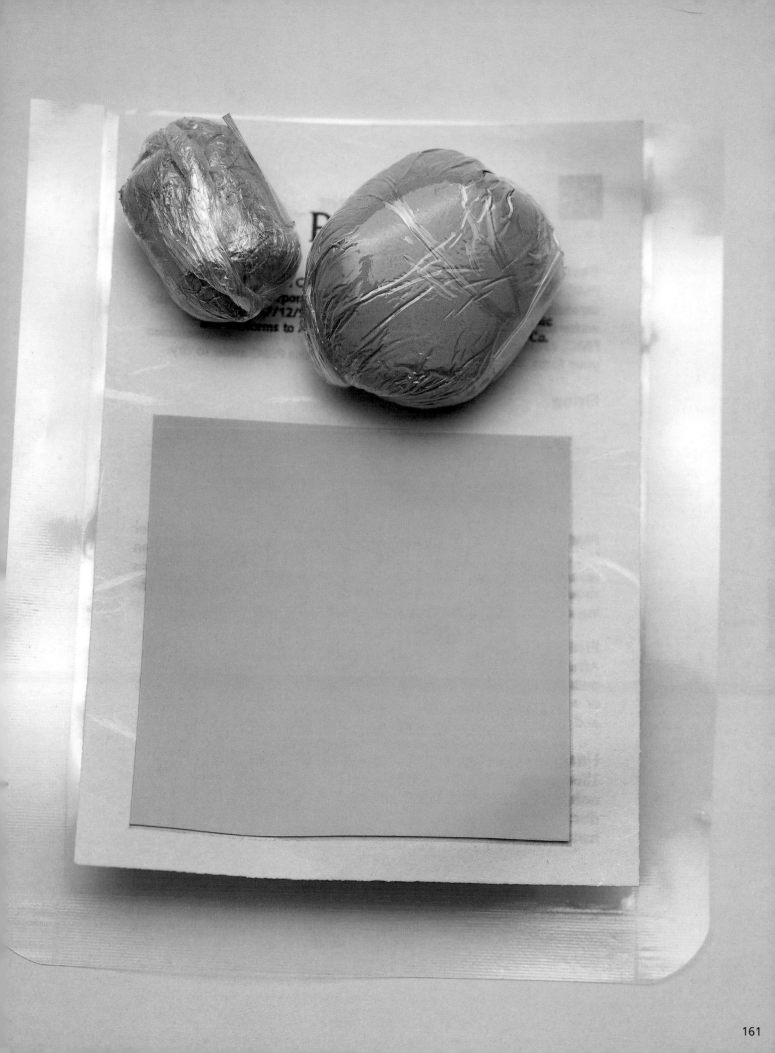

Setup and Tools

Although your PMC will ultimately be transformed into metal, you'll do most of your work in PMC while it's clay. Both philosophically and in the matter of tools, this is an important consideration. Here are a few essential tools. Generally the tools you use for polymer clay will work with PMC.

- For rolling polymer clay, I use a 1½" (4 cm) diameter PVC pipe, available at a hardware store. For PMC, I use a ½" (about 1 cm) diameter PVC pipe **(A)**, 6" to 7" (about 15 cm) long (both cut with a tube cutter).

- For cutting fresh PMC, use a tissue blade, a Nu-Blade, or a craft knife **(B)**. On leather-hard standard PMC, use a protected tissue blade. (Glue two Popsicle sticks with 5-minute Epoxy onto either side of the dull edge.) A hard blade may shatter leather-hard PMC Plus. Instead, use a jeweler's saw with a 3/0 blade.

- A small airtight container **(C)** is another essential for storing slip. A plastic film canister will do, but small round pill containers with attached tops are even better. They are typically sold in twos, giving you one for PMC Plus and one for standard PMC. PMC Plus is grayish white, whereas standard PMC is more of a buff or tan color. Remember to label your containers.

- I use and recommend two brushes **(D)**: a small, pointed watercolor brush for applying slip or water and a square-tipped one, kept clean, to remove excess slip.

- Use foam rubber scraps (¼" to ½" [5 mm to 1 cm] thick) from a fabric store **(E)**, accordion folded, and stuffed into a cup for drying delicate assemblies. Laid flat on your work surface, foam pieces give you a place to dry rounded PMC objects so they won't develop a flat side.

- Teflon sheet **(F)** is sold as nonstick baking sheets in kitchen stores and as Teflon Pressing Sheets in fabric stores. They can be cut up into convenient palette sizes, or you can roll directly on them. If you don't have access to Teflon, plastic report covers, sold in stationary stores, are another possibility, but I strongly recommend Teflon.

Work surfaces

Many materials can be used as a work surface—for example, glass, marble, Plexiglas, acrylic, a laminated place mat, or a plastic report cover. Any smooth, nonporous surface will do. I use and recommend only glass—not window glass, which is dangerously thin, but a 10" x 15" (25 cm x 38 cm) sheet of ¼" (6.5 mm) plate glass **(G)**, with smoothed edges. It's inexpensive, and it's available from auto glass stores. It makes an excellent surface because PMC doesn't readily stick to it, and it isn't scratched by cutting blades. What's more, a lump of PMC set on the glass and covered with plastic will remain viable for 24 to 48 hours. If you won't be working for more than a day, invert a dish over the plastic on top of the PMC to seal it on the work surface. For a shorter duration, dip your finger in water and run it around the PMC on the work surface, and press the plastic wrap to seal it.

Other tools

- A small container **(H)** with a section of kitchen sponge pushed into it, full of water. You can use a paper cup trimmed to 1" (3 cm) height. Keep the water level high enough so that you can easily get some water on the end of your brush.

- Another small container **(I)**, with a piece of foam rubber in it, filled with olive oil. Olive oil is specifically recommended because it's less likely to get sticky and rancid.

- A pin tool **(J)**
- A small spray bottle full of water **(K)**
- Plastic wrap **(L).** I recommend Saran because it's heavy, and it doesn't stretch or cling; avoid waxed paper of any sort.
- Rolling rectangle **(M)**—that is, a 2 ½" x 7" (6 cm x 18 cm) piece of plate glass or rigid plastic to use for rolling ropes of clay or "wire"
- Scrap polymer clay, for rehearsing ideas and for securing a texture to a work surface
- Palette knife **(N)** in plastic or metal for making slip
- Good pair of fine tweezers **(O)**
- Brass tube sections **(P)** are useful for cutting out circles of PMC.
- Use drinking straws **(Q)** for cutting out circles of clay.
- Stacks of playing cards **(R)** help you roll consistent thicknesses of PMC.
- Foam rubber **(S)**, accordion-folded and pushed into a cup, affords a good place for drying delicate PMC assemblies.
- A brass sliding millimeter gauge **(T)**
- Fine sandpaper (320, 400, 600, and 1,000 grit)
- Micron-graded polishing paper (1,200 grit, from a jewelry supplier)
- Salon boards—double sided, medium fine (from a pharmacy)
- Round needle file (from a jewelry supplier)

Note: *Although you may use tools that contain aluminum (such as circle cutters), avoid prolonged contact between the aluminum tool and fresh PMC because the aluminum will cause contamination.*

Universal measuring system

Decks of cards have become the universal tool for rolling even slabs of PMC to specific thicknesses. Tape together the following sets of cards: 2 sets of 2 each, 2 sets of 3 each, 2 sets of 4 each, 2 sets of 5 each, and 2 sets of 6 each. For a deep relief, a two-sided texture, or a piece you intend to carve, you can combine the card stacks: 4 and 3 to get 7 or 5 and 3 to get 8. The main drawback of using cards is that they're plastic coated and therefore slippery. Other ideas for rolling PMC to a consistent height include using strips of cardboard, using rubber gaskets, in a range of sizes, slipped on the ends

of your rolling tool, or wrapping masking tape around the ends of your rolling tools to correspond to the card system.

Making Slip

Think of slip as glue. It's what you'll use to assemble leather hard parts and fill small cracks. You can also apply it as a surface texture. Slip needs to be thick. To test it, use the slip to attach one leather-hard piece to another, count to 10, and turn the piece upside down. Slip that's a good working consistency will hold the pieces together.

Pinch a piece of fresh PMC clay off, and put it on your work surface. Spritz it or pour a few drops of water on it, and smear it with your palette knife against the glass repeatedly. The material resists for a while, but then the two mix. The consistency you're aiming for is much thicker than paint and could be likened to frosting—that is, it holds peaks. Using distilled water will help eliminate mold in the PMC. If mold forms, just scrape it off. Save small scraps and shards to add to a slip jar.

Joining

Joining fresh PMC to fresh PMC requires a few drops of water and then a bit of smoothing over the joint until you can no longer see it. If the clay is too wet, it's beginning to crack, or you aren't making progress, put it aside to dry. When it's completely dry and easier to handle, you can add clay, fill cracks, and smooth rough areas.

Repairing Leather-Hard PMC

When making repairs, use the thickest version of PMC you can handle in the situation. If you can, use PMC right out of the package (after brushing water on the spot). If the repair is in too tight a spot, or if something else makes the thickness of PMC out of the package difficult to use, then repair it with thick slip.

Adding Texture and Embellishments

Most people's first foray into PMC involves texturing. The simple process and beautiful results make it a good place to begin.

For a rigid texture

Oil the texture. Roll out PMC to a height of 3 cards (or 4 cards for a deep relief), through plastic wrap. Lift the PMC with the plastic in place onto the oiled texture and secure it to your work surface with a small lump of polymer clay at each corner or with tape. Roll across the PMC a few times, then lift up a corner to see if it has taken a good impression. Transfer the clay to a teflon palette, texture side up, cover with plastic, and proceed with your design.

For a flexible texture

If you're using something like the plastic netting that onions come in, roll out the PMC to a height of 3 cards, transfer it to Teflon, lay the oiled netting onto the PMC, cover with plastic wrap and roll over it.

Top left: carved polymer clay plates and bottom left: clay paper, and polymer clay plate from Tear-Away technique (by Celie Fago). Right: assorted found textures. Center: drywall sanding screen.

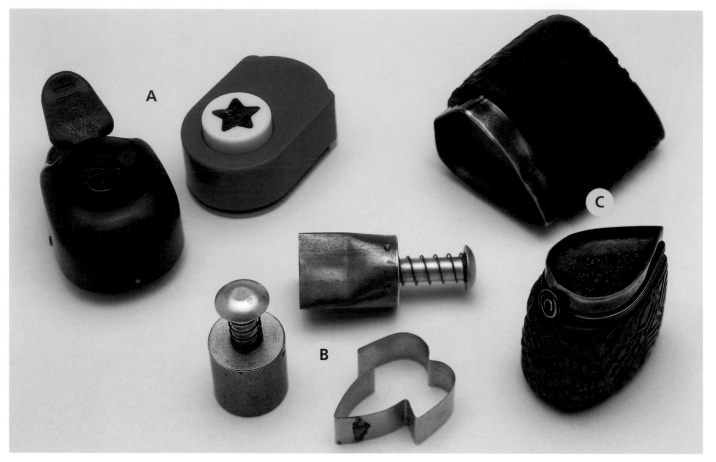

Shown above: paper punches (A), shaped cutters for polymer clay (B), custom cutters made from carved polymer clay and brass (by Celie Fago) (C).

For a double-sided texture

This takes a bit of practice, but it's worth it. Because you'll be impressing both sides, start by rolling the clay out to a height of 4 cards, and if it seems too thin, go higher. It's also a good idea to choose textures with low relief. Secure the first texture to your work surface with a small lump of polymer clay (or tape) at each corner, and oil the texture well. Transfer the clay, with the plastic wrap in place, onto the first texture, and roll once or twice firmly across it. Place the second, well-oiled texture carefully on top of the clay, and roll once or twice across it. Check the impression. Two-sided texturing is much easier if the top texture is flexible. Then, it's an easy matter to check the progress of the impression by lifting up an edge.

If you don't like the way a texture looks or you change your mind and want to start over, ball up the clay you've used and spritz it lightly with water. Knead it for a few seconds through plastic, then add it back to the original ounce. Take a fresh piece from another part of the ounce to start again. Kneading the clay like this, or "wedging," is a good general strategy for getting bits of clay with different moisture levels homogenized.

Embellishments

Make the following embellishments in fresh clay, let them dry to leather-hard. Store the twisted "wires" in drinking straws and the spheres and bails sorted into plastic pill minders for later use.

Twisted "wire"

To make small twisted wires, roll out ¼ ounce of PMC, under plastic wrap, to the height of 4 cards. It should form a rectangle at least 2¼" (5.5 cm) long. Transfer the PMC to a Teflon palette. Using a well-oiled tissue blade, cut a strip as wide as the PMC is thick so that it's square. Then, take an end in each hand, and gently twist the strip. To prevent it from untwisting, firmly push both ends onto an oil-free glass surface, or another surface to which the PMC will stick, like marble or stone. Continue making twisted wires until you have enough for the project you're working on, plus a few extras in case some break. Don't worry about sizing. Just add in a little extra length, and plan on trimming the wires with a protected tissue blade once they're leather-hard. When dry, they'll detach from the glass on their own. You can usually straighten pieces that develop a curve. Weight the leather-hard pieces under a book or store them in cocktail straws to help keep them straight. To make larger sizes of twisted wires, simply roll out a thicker slab and cut bigger square lengths of clay.

Spheres

Although there are several ways to make spheres, this one is the most efficient. Roll PMC out to a height of four cards, and with the plastic wrap in place, transfer it to a Teflon palette. Lightly oil a tube section (or a drinking straw), and press out several circles of clay. Pick one up—being careful to re-cover the others with the plastic wrap—and place it on your palm. Now roll vigorously with a finger, against your palm until you have a perfect, round sphere. Trial and error will tell you whether to add a bit of water or oil as you roll. Experiment, and try both until you can successfully roll spheres without cracks. Dry the spheres on a scrap of foam so they don't develop flat areas.

Spherical bails

After you've become proficient at rolling spheres, try the following technique for making a spherical bail. The word bail refers to that part of a piece of jewelry that connects a pendant to a chain. For the following technique to be successful, you must use copious amounts of oil. Have ready the following: a needle tool, a large wooden knitting needle (or a sharpened pencil or other large tapered tool), olive oil container, and a scrap of foam. Follow the preceding instructions for making a sphere, but start with more clay and make a larger ball. Cut a circle of clay, and roll it swiftly into a smooth ball. Place it in your palm while you oil your needle tool. Make a hole through the center of the ball using a turning and pushing motion, while spinning it against your palm. The instant you encounter resistance, re-oil the needle. Just as you reach the other side, take it out and re-oil it, and start back through from the other side, re-oiling as necessary. Now, pick up your pencil or bigger tapered tool; slather the tip with oil, and start through the hole using a turning and pushing motion, re-oiling at the first sign of resistance. Once you get the basic tool through, you can start expanding the hole diameter by rolling the ball back and forth against your palm. The key is oil. When you're satisfied with the bail, set it aside on foam to dry. Attach it with slip when it's leather-hard.

Though it's possible to do this with PMC Plus, it's more difficult. For PMC Plus, I recommend forming the sphere, letting it dry, and drilling it with a hand drill, Dremel, or flex shaft. For either material, clean up the hole in the sphere when it's leather-hard with a round needle file.

Ring Sizing

In the Ring Project, a simple technique is described for sizing a ring for a particular finger. Ring sizing is an inexact science. Ring sizes refer to several competing systems, and your finger size fluctuates over time. The following numbers assume a ring of average thickness—$1/16$" for small sizes and $1/8$" for larger (1.5 mm for small sizes and 2 mm for larger) and a width of about $1/4$" (5 mm). If your ring will be very wide, add a half a size to your calculations.

There are two ways to use the ring chart. If you have a ring sizer, find the size you want, match it to the ring sizes in the left hand column and follow it across to the type of clay you're using. If you don't have a sizer, wrap a piece of paper around the middle knuckle of the finger for which you're making a ring. That millimeter measurement is the size your ring should be after firing. Match that number to the numbers in the second from the left column (metal). Now follow across to the number in the column for PMC or PMC Plus, and cut a strip that length in fresh clay. Generally, PMC Plus is the better choice for rings.

Mandrels

A ring mandrel is a long, tapered steel tool. If your PMC ring has become misshapen during firing or it's tight on your finger, slip it onto the mandrel and tap it with a rawhide mallet.

Warpage

Once PMC is in the kiln, gravity will flatten most warps. Any additional flattening can be done after firing by placing the piece on a bench block or other flat surface and using the heel of your hand or, failing that, tapping with a rawhide or plastic mallet.

Firing

When the PMC is dry, place it on a shelf in an electric kiln. During the firing, any remaining water evaporates, the binder ignites and burns up, then the metal particles fuse together in a process called sintering. My electric kiln—designed for use with (silver) PMC—takes about 40 minutes to ramp up to the set temperature. This can vary depending on individual electrical supply. Set the temperature according to the chart shown at left.

RING CHART

Ring Size	Metal (mm)	PMC Plus (mm)	PMC (mm)
2	44.6	50.7	61.9
2 1/2	45.8	52.0	63.6
3	47.1	53.5	65.4
3 1/2	48.4	55.0	67.2
4	49.6	56.4	68.8
4 1/2	50.9	57.8	70.7
5	52.1	59.2	72.4
5 1/2	53.4	60.7	74.2
6	54.6	62.0	75.8
6 1/2	55.9	63.5	77.6
7	57.1	64.8	79.3
7 1/2	58.4	66.4	81.1
8	59.7	67.8	82.9
8 1/2	60.9	69.2	84.6
9	62.2	70.7	86.4
9 1/2	63.4	72.0	88.0
10	64.7	73.5	89.9
10 1/2	65.9	74.8	91.5
11	67.2	76.4	93.3
11 1/2	68.5	77.8	95.1
12	69.7	79.2	96.8
12 1/2	71.0	80.7	98.6
13	72.2	82.0	100.3

FIRING CHART

	temperature		time
Standard PMC – silver	1650° F	900° C	two hours
Standard PMC – gold	1830° F	1000° C	two hours
PMC Plus – silver	1650° F	900° C	10 minutes
or	1560° F	860° C	20 minutes
or	1470° F	800° C	30 minutes

Pieces ready for the kiln on a kiln shelf: top left, spherical PMC bead in a bed of vermiculite; top right, flat pieces directly on the kiln shelf; bottom right, ring on a layer of alumina hydrate; bottom left, flat piece directly on kiln shelf.

The lower temperature offers exciting possibilities that have yet to be fully explored; glass and enamel powders that will discolor at the higher temperatures will be more stable at 1470° F (799° C) and can be combined with PMC Plus.

Although the two clays can be mixed, standard PMC needs to be fired for the full 2 hours to attain maximum strength. If you mistakenly use standard slip to close a joint in a PMC Plus object, and fire it for 10 minutes; the joint will be weak. To rectify this, re-fire for a full 2 hours at 1650° F (899° C).

Any kiln that will reliably maintain the set temperature for the above duration can be used, but the ideal choice is a small kiln with a programmable thermostat and a temperature controller designed for use with PMC. Kilns designed for enameling and glass will also work.

Firing Materials

Kiln shelves

Shelves make it easier to load and empty the kiln. They also protect the floor of the kiln from meltdown accidents. Suggested materials include:

- soldering pads (depicted)—Available from jewelry supply companies, these pads are fragile but when handled carefully will last a long time.

- soft firebrick—Available from ceramic supply companies, this brick can be cut with a hack saw or jeweler's saw into 1" (3 cm) slabs (thinner will break). This brick is also good for making noncombustible support forms.

- Cordierite—This ceramic tile, available from ceramic suppliers, is a good choice for firing PMC; however, its weight limits its use to the bottom shelf.

If you're firing several pieces, you may want to stack your shelves. Stacking is safe up to 1" (3 cm) from the ceiling of the kiln. Cut up soldering pads or firebrick to make 1" (3 cm) pieces to put at each corner for stacking the shelves. Pre-made kiln posts are available from ceramic suppliers.

Leave about 1" (3 cm) of space between the edge of the shelf and the walls of the kiln, and make sure the pyrometer (heat sensor) isn't pressed against one of the shelves.

Other Kiln Furniture

Firing volumetric pieces require a little extra effort to prevent slumping. A terra-cotta dish, the kind you'd put under a potted plant, will work. Fortunately they aren't expensive because they survive only a few firings. An alternative is carving a depression in soft firebrick or molding a dish from paper clay and letting it air dry. Paper clay is a premixed paper product containing paper pulp, binder, and volcanic ash. The latter keeps it from burning up in the kiln, so paper clay shrinks very little (unlike papier mâché), making it a good choice for a noncombustible support form or for a saggar dish in which to fire volumetric forms. Fill the saggar dish with any of the following materials and nestle your beads or volumetric pieces so that about two-thirds of the bead or piece is buried (see picture).

Bedding materials

- Alumina hydrate—a fine gray-white powder used in ceramic studios (It discolors slightly with use.)

- Vermiculite—a soil additive that is a form of mica

- Plaster of Paris—plaster that can be used straight from the bag (Don't add water. If it sticks together during firing, just break it apart.)

- Investment—a material similar to plaster that is used in jewelry casting

- Loose wool—ceramic fiber material available by the pound from ceramic suppliers

- Safety note: Wear a mask when using these products, and clean up spills with a dampened paper towel, not a vacuum cleaner.

These bedding materials can be piled directly onto your kiln shelves, but they tend to spill off. When firing rings, sprinkle alumina directly onto the kiln shelf and place the ring on the layer of alumina. Contain beads and other volumetric forms in a terra-cotta dish or carved out firebrick.

Once the binder has burned away (in the first ½ hour), but before the metal particles have fused together, the PMC pieces are susceptible to gravity. Place your pieces in the dish with the heaviest part at the bottom. For example, the point of a cone should be buried in the bedding material; the open end should be up.

A little while into the kiln cycle the binder will burn up, briefly producing an odor similar to that of a spill in a hot oven. It generally last 3 to 4 minutes and is no cause for alarm. There are products, such as wax or snack food armatures

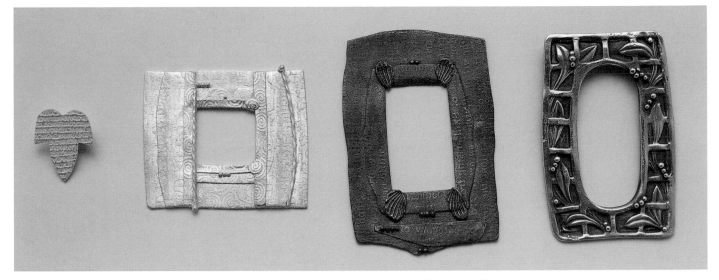

Steps in finishing PMC: from left to right, fresh from the kiln; brass brushed; blackened; highlighted by polishing.

with a high-fat content that will cause smoking during the first part of the cycle. They'll burn off harmlessly within a few minutes, but it's important to leave the kiln door closed. (Check with the PMC Guild for information on firing services.)

Cooling versus Quenching

When the kiln cycle is finished, unplug the kiln, and choose one of the following options: (1) Let the kiln sit with the door closed for several hours, or overnight. When completely cool, open the door and unload. (2) Wait 5 minutes; wearing fireproof gloves, carefully crack the door open 1" to 2" (3 cm to 5 cm). When the red glow has subsided, in 10 minutes, unload the kiln. Wear fireproof gloves and use barbecue tongs or extra-long tweezers, and either drop pieces carefully into a metal container full of water (that is, "quench" them) or transfer the pieces to a heat-proof surface and allow them to cool completely. Either technique is fine for PMC, but if your silver pieces contain synthetic gems or enamels or other materials that may be subject to thermal shock, let them air cool.

Finishing

Fresh from the kiln, all PMC pieces appear to be a matte white color. This color isn't a coating or residue, it's simply the color of the unpolished metal. The highly reflective shine usually associated with silver is the result of polishing; the color of silver is the reflection of light.

Polishing

Polishing choices occur along a continuum, with matte (right out of the kiln) at one end and shiny (or highly polished) at the other. If you looked at matte white silver under a magnifier, you'd see the top surface is made of countless peaks and valleys that trap light, creating what we know as a matte surface. Polishing smoothes out these peaks and valleys, causing light to bounce back—what we know as shine. The degree of shine and the type of finish are personal choices, but it's recommended that freshly fired pieces be polished or burnished until they no longer appear white. Fine or pure silver doesn't tarnish, but if it's left it its white state, it will trap dirt and dust and appear dingy over time.

Other polishing tools

Pieces fresh from the kiln may be scrubbed with brass or soft stainless steel bristle brush (available from jewelry suppliers). When scratch brushing, work at a sink, with the piece cradled in one hand and the brush in the other. Put dish detergent on your brush, scrub vigorously, rinsing the piece periodically so you can check progress. Continue until no trace of white is left. A scratch brush is efficient at getting into the deep relief of a design. You can use a steel burnishing tool on surfaces with no texture, but it isn't a good tool for getting into the relief of a design.

Use steel wool (0000), synthetic steel wool (000 or 0000), or a fine satin finish wheel on a bench grinder or polishing lathe (available from jewelry suppliers). Like burnishing tools, these tools may not reach into all recessed areas; however, they do produce a satin finish. A rock tumbler with stainless steel shot and specially formulated detergent is another option.

Antiquing

Antiquing involves two steps: blackening and highlighting. Use the following products with adequate ventilation, and wear rubber gloves. Liver of Sulfur, a traditional jeweler's patinating agent, is sold as a dry, yellow gravel and also as a premixed liquid. To use the gravel, mix a small piece with very hot water. Make a hook with brass or silver wire to immerse the piece for a few seconds. Rinse the piece in cold water, and repeat until you've achieved the desired color then wash piece in soapy water. The gravel must be stored in an airtight container, in the dark.

Silver Black and Black Max are acid-based proprietary solutions sold ready mixed by jewelry suppliers and, occasionally, bead stores. Dip the piece according to the directions above, or apply the solution with a brush. After rinsing, wash pieces well in soapy water and dry.

Shown here on a pine pillow: a leather-hard PMC piece partially carved, and a fired and finished carved PMC piece. Below, a leather thimble, linoleum carving tool with custom polymer clay handle (by Celie Fago), and two wood carving tools.

Highlighting

The objective of this step is to remove the black from the raised areas while leaving the black in the recessed areas to achieve a contrast in the final, polished piece. Soft or bushy tools, like a polishing cloth or steel wool, won't achieve this effectively.

A 1,200-grit micron graded (blue) polishing paper, wrapped tightly around a stick or salon board, will travel across the surface of the object but won't get into the recessed areas. The polish achieved by using this "blue" paper is shinier than steel wool, but it's still within the definition of a satin finish. For more shine, wrap a rouge or other polishing cloth tightly around a rigid stick or salon board and, after you've finished using the polishing paper, use the same technique with a rouge cloth. Wash and dry.

Carving PMC and Polymer Clay

Polymer clay must be entirely cured to carve well. To test for doneness, try carving a spiral. If the spiral breaks as you're carving, the polymer clay may need more time or a higher temperature in the oven.

The polymer clay texture plates pictured on page 81 are made from conditioned Premo polymer clay. (I prefer the metallics and pearlescents for carving.) Roll the clay out to the thickest setting on the pasta machine. Put the clay between two pieces of wax paper, and put it on a small piece of plate glass. Put another piece of plate glass on top, and put it in a preheated oven at about 275° F (135° C). After 25 minutes, increase the temperature to 285°F (141° C) for 10 minutes. The glass keeps it perfectly flat, and the wax paper keeps it from developing shiny spots against the glass.

The best tools for carving polymer clay and PMC are wood gouges. Both **V**- and **U**-gouges work well (1.5 and 2 mm). Gouges are made for linoleum and wood carving and are sold through art stores, wood-carving and printmaking supply catalogs, and some polymer clay suppliers. Place the piece to be carved on to a small pine pillow or folded face towel to prevent it from sliding around.

Carving PMC

Pushing a tool through polymer clay doesn't require much effort. But because PMC has metal in it, it offers resistance to the carving tool and requires a bit more force. To protect your holding hand from the force of the carving tool, use a leather thimble (from a quilter's supply) like a catcher's mitt on one of the fingers of the hand holding the piece. Drive the tool across the surface of the PMC into the finger that's wearing the thimble.

Standard PMC, because it has more binder in it, carves cleanly, without chipping. PMC Plus, because of its higher silver content, is a bit more challenging to carve.

Combining PMC and Polymer Clay

There are many ways to combine the two materials featured in this book. Scrap polymer clay can be used as a rehearsal material. Practice making a form in polymer clay and when you like it, re-create it in PMC. When you're pleased with a particular form in polymer clay, bake it, then put it on a copier or scanner bed, and reduce it 28% or 12% (depending on whether you're using standard PMC or PMC Plus) to get an idea of the after firing size. These 3-dimensional sketches are a great design tool that will help you visualize the end result. You can use a lump of scrap polymer clay pressed onto a corner of your work surface to anchor a wooden stake for drying a PMC bead on the other end. Aesthetically, the two materials make a unique and lovely combination. Fired and finished, PMC offers an aesthetic counterpoint to the resonant color of polymer clay.

Using Tear-Away Clay Papers to Texture PMC

1. Roll out PMC to a height of 3 cards, and place it on a Teflon palette. Lay well-oiled clay papers onto PMC, and roll it into the PMC through plastic wrap.

2. Gently peel off the paper. Don't be surprised if some of the polymer clay remains on the surface of the PMC. Tear-away clay paper is fragile and will yield only a few impressions, but while it lasts, it creates a lovely surface texture.

Using a Tear-Away Etched Polymer Clay Plate to Texture PMC

The polymer clay portion of the Tear-Away is a bit more durable. You'll get many good impressions from one plate.

1. Secure the polymer clay plate to your work surface using masking tape or balls of scrap polymer clay, and oil the plate well.

2. Roll PMC out to a height of 3 cards, and lay it onto the polymer clay. Gently and firmly roll once across the surface. If you aren't happy with the impression, ball up the clay and try again.

There are numerous ways to combine PMC and polymer clay. You can work thinly and economically in the metal clay with the intention of adding a decorative backing in polymer clay. Silver bezels or frames around polymer clay are a lovely and traditional way to complement both materials, as are polymer clay buttons that contain PMC as a decorative or structural addition. Mastering rings in PMC teaches you to make cylindrical forms. Working in polymer clay offers many opportunities to use silver cylindrical forms. You can use them as ornaments on bracelets (see gallery), as a starting point for necklace terminations such as cord ends, and as a base for polymer clay inlay. You'll discover your own possibilities for invention in this material once you master a few basics.

Although it's possible to duplicate many conventional metal-fabrication techniques using PMC, the vestigial clay character in finished PMC works accounts for a great deal of its charm.

TEAR-AWAY TECHNIQUE FOR POLYMER CLAY

Polymer Clay

Originally developed for polymer clay by Gwen Gibson and adapted here by Celie Fago,* the tear-away technique offers a unique way to texture PMC or polymer clay by creating etched plates and clay papers from photocopies of your collages, designs, or copyright-free artwork. The process consists of burnishing a photocopy onto polymer clay, resting it, and then tearing it away. Because the photocopy toner bonds with the clay, the paper brings a layer of clay with it when it's torn away. Once baked, this "clay paper" becomes a lovely, delicate texturing tool. The clay the paper has been torn from is impressed with a delicate relief of the image from the photocopy. When it's baked, it becomes a durable texturing "plate."

STEPS

1. Roll out conditioned polymer clay to a number 1 or 2 on your pasta machine (use thickest or next-to-the-thickest setting). Cut a piece a bit larger than your intended image, and place it on a portable surface that can go into the oven—for example, plate glass, an oven tray, or wax paper.

2. Place the photocopy face down on the clay, and fold a corner up to use as a tab. Burnish the copy onto the clay using a circular motion, first with your fist and then with the bone folder, for about a minute.

3. Position the piece 6" to 8" (15 cm to 20 cm) under a lamp, and let it rest for about 7 minutes. Burnish it for 1 minute, and then let it rest again under the lamp for another 7 minutes.

Tip: Experiment with the variables: heat, time, friction, different clay brands (I've had good luck with Sculpey III) and photocopies. Too little heat, or friction, and nothing happens; too much heat, and the photocopy image transfers to the clay.

4. Holding the surface steady with one hand, grasp the paper tab, and tear the paper off the clay. For best results, tear low and quickly, in one smooth motion. Bake the etched clay plate and the paper portion, which will be rolled up, according to manufacturer's instructions. Wait until after baking to unroll the clay paper.

The 'clay paper' can be unrolled and flattened out and used as a collage element or as a picture in itself, or it can be used as a texturing tool for PMC or polymer clay. The etched clay plate can be used for texturing as well. You can also rub acrylic or oil paint into the etched surface for a scrimshaw-like effect, buff it up when the paint is dry, and use it as a picture or a pin.

* For further study, see Gwen's video *Ancient Images*. See the resources section for more information.

Chapter 7
Creating with Precious Metal Clay

The following projects are designed to demonstrate the range of possibilities of Precious Metal Clay (PMC), an array of different techniques, and how to successfully combine polymer clay and PMC. Each project also provides general skills and specific tips with the idea that you'll ultimately transform this information to suit your own working style.

The maple leaf earrings (on page 184) not only illustrate the use of texture but the concept of using shrinkage as part of composition. The ring project (on page 176) provides an easy method of sizing rings and closing joints and introduces simple, elegant ways to use PMC Sheet. Beauty and function combine in the toggle clasp project (on page 172), which can add a personal touch to an old necklace or complement and complete one of your own creations. The frame project (on page 188) is a wonderful example of the marriage between polymer clay and Precious Metal Clay; it uses polymer as a texture, as an image to frame, and as a decorative support for the frame itself. The celestial spheres project (on page 180) shows you how to create a hollow form bead using a combustible core and then applique small embellishments onto the bead. The box pendant (on page 192) is a more challenging project. It teaches precision, the use of noncombustible support forms, and the challenges of working with leather-hard PMC.

These projects are meant as a starting point: Experiment as you work, and don't be discouraged by mistakes, because you'll make discoveries, as well. Remember, PMC is a new material—and the possibilities are truly limitless.

Carved Circle and Bar Toggle

Artist: Celie Fago

PMC allows you the freedom to design a unique toggle any scale or size to fit a particular design—from a delicate bracelet toggle to a bold design for a large bead necklace. The toggle seen here is a carved bar and circle made from PMC Plus. In a complex design, just as in a simple one, you'll need to consider how a toggle functions: The bar piece needs to be long enough to be securely captured by the circle piece. You can study the proportions of commercial toggle clasps in a jewelry catalog or you can make a working model from polymer clay to better understand how a particular design will work in a specific setting. A beautiful toggle can also be the centerpiece for a necklace.

Materials

- basic Precious Metal Clay equipment and supplies (see page 162)
- 1 sheet copy paper
- 1 package of PMC Plus
- 2 large jump rings
- photocopier
- foam rubber scraps
- chain nose pliers
- carving tool (2 mm **V**-gouge Micro Carving Tool or your choice)
- hand towel or small pine sachet pillow
- hand drill with a ¹/₁₆" (1.5 mm) drill bit (or a Dremel or flex shaft)
- round needle file

Getting Started

When drying rounded shapes, place them on foam rubber and turn them over every 10 to 15 minutes so that they don't develop a flat side.

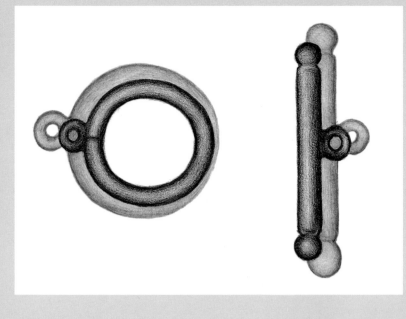

1 Determine the size you want your toggle to be.

Make a simple rendition of a circle and a bar that size, on paper. If three-dimensional "sketching" works better for you, make and bake a bar and circle in polymer clay the size you want your toggle to be. Copy the paper or the polymer clay "sketch" at 115 percent. This is the size you need to make the toggle using fresh PMC Plus to compensate for 12 percent shrinkage that occurs during firing.

2 Form the toggle.

To make the featured toggle, first roll ½ package of PMC Plus into a rope about ¼" (6 mm) in diameter with a rolling rectangle. Don't use oil, but if the clay begins to dry out, tent it with plastic wrap as you roll. (See *Tools* and *Rolling Techniques* on pages 160–162.)

Next, cut a section about 2¾" (70 mm) long, and cut a bevel on each end. Brush water on each end, and form it into a circle so the beveled ends match up, smoothing the joint well with an oiled finger or a brush. Remember that you can add clay to the joint once it's leather-hard or sand any excess clay away, so concentrate on getting the beveled ends attached so the circle so it will hold its shape while drying. Lay the circle on a piece of foam rubber to dry.

To make the bar, cut another section of the rope about 1¼" (30 mm) long and set it on foam rubber to dry.

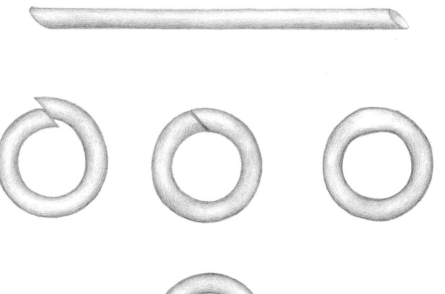

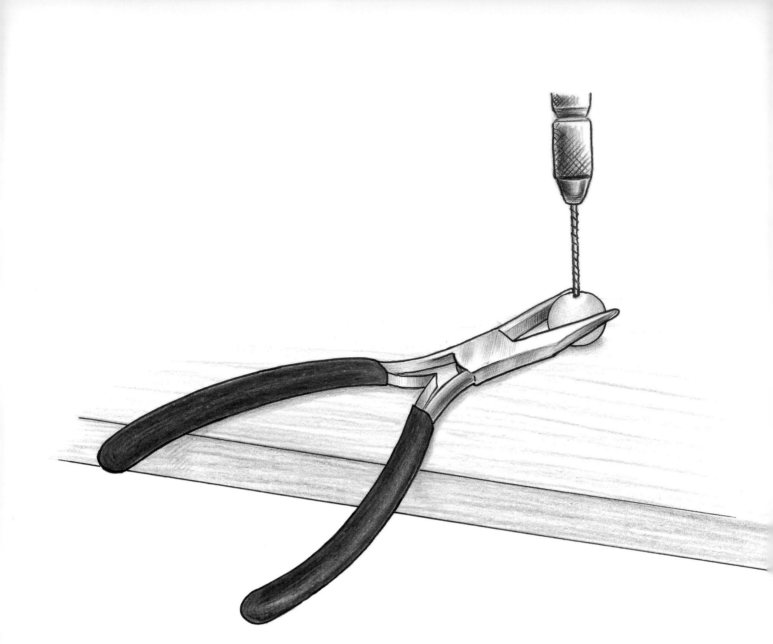

3 Make the decorative spheres for the toggle.

Cut four more segments from the PMC Plus rope, each about 4 mm long, and roll them into balls. (For other methods, see *Embellishments* on page 164.) Set the balls on foam rubber, and allow them to completely dry. Then, holding the balls flat on a table and firmly in the jaws of chain nose pliers, drill holes through two of the balls with a 1/16" (1.5 mm) drill bit, a Dremel or a flex shaft, to accommodate the jump rings that will be used to attach the toggle to a chain. (Image shown features a larger bead; actual sphere for this project is smaller.) Clean up the holes with a round needle file. Refine the circle and bar with nail boards and/or sandpaper (320, 400, then 600 grit), and fill any cracks with slip. If there are large cracks, brush them with water, and then push PMC Plus right out of the package into the cracks.

4 Carve the toggle pieces.

The featured toggle was carved using a **V**-gouge Micro-Carving tool, which was designed for carving wood. It's helpful to nestle the piece to be carved onto a folded hand towel or a small pine or sachet pillow. This will keep it from sliding around and also cushion it to prevent breakage. (See *Carving* on page 168.)

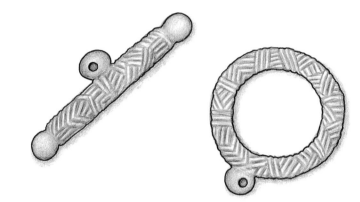

5 Attach the leather-hard pieces.

See *Making Slip* on page 163. Affix the two undrilled balls to the ends of the carved bar. Attach one of the balls with a hole to the middle of the bar as seen here, and set it aside to dry. Then, attach the other drilled ball to the outer edge of the carved circle, as seen here, and set it aside to dry. These attachments need to be well secured with thick slip, checked for gaps when dry, and refilled where necessary to ensure a structurally sound toggle. Fire flat on a bed of alumina hydrate or vermiculite. (See *Firing* on page 165.) Scrub with a brass brush, and finish as desired. Finally, attach the toggle to a necklace or bracelet using jump rings.

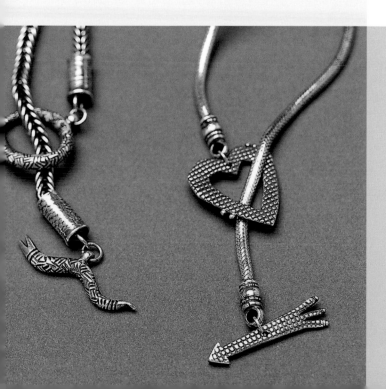

Variations

The toggle on the left was carved using the method described above. The wiggling snake functions as the bar in this variation. The snake with its tail in its mouth, an age-old symbol of infinity, serves the function of the circle. The heart and arrow toggle is made from clay that has been textured on both sides and cut out with a heart-shaped cookie cutter. The arrow shape was cut by hand with an oiled tissue blade.

PMC Appliqué Ring

Artist: Celie Fago

PMC Sheet opens up a whole new realm of design possibilities. Paper-cutting tools, such as punches and edgers, create stylish designs simply and easily. There is a vast array of patterns and motifs available in these craft cutters. You can make your design unique by cutting freehand details such as triangles or arrows to add to your ring, using a craft knife, a protected tissue blade, or a wavy blade. Try a design by cutting shapes from copy paper first. When you're satisfied, proceed to the PMC Sheet.

Materials

- basic Precious Metal Clay equipment and supplies (see page 162)
- copy paper
- clear tape
- 1 package PMC Plus
- 1 PMC Sheet
- paper scissors
- paper punches in assorted shapes, such as a star, moon, or spiral
- ripple or wavy blade
- ring mandrel
- rawhide or plastic mallet
- brass brush

Getting Started

If you have trouble with the PMC Plus sticking to your work surface, try rolling directly on a piece of Teflon taped to your work surface. Remember to flip the clay over every three or four rolls, which will help minimize sticking.

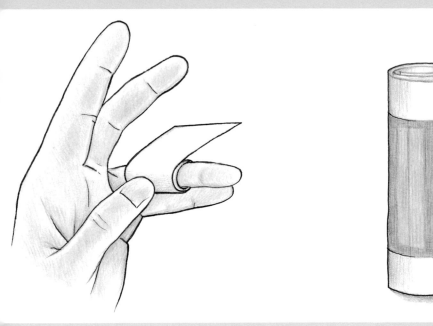

1 Make the ring form.

Cut a piece of copy paper into a rectangle about 3 ½" x 1 ¾" (9 cm x 5 cm). Wrap the paper around the middle knuckle of the finger for which you want to make a ring, then use clear tape to close it. This is the size you want your ring to be after firing. Since PMC Plus shrinks 12 percent during firing, it's necessary to add a millimeter of thickness to the ring form. To do this, cut two or three strips of paper and wrap them around the ring form while it's on your finger. It will take seven revolutions of copy paper to add the needed thickness. Next, wrap the whole thing with a piece of Teflon paper, then use clear tape to close it. If you're have trouble getting the paper strips tight, try wrapping the paper form with masking tape instead of paper. (See *Ring Sizing* on page 165 for alternative methods.)

2 Form the ring.

Wrap a small scrap of paper around your ring form to measure the circumference, then lay the paper flat on your work surface to use as a length guide. Lightly oil the work surface, and roll out ½ a package of PMC Plus, through plastic wrap, to a height of three cards. Using a well-oiled tissue blade, cut the PMC Plus into a strip slightly wider than you want your finished ring to be and approximately ¼" (6 mm) longer than the paper guide. The featured ring was rolled out to a height of three cards, and cut to a width of ⅝" (16 mm). Next, cut one end of the PMC strip at a blunt right angle.

Next, wrap the PMC strip around the Teflon-covered paper form, and overlap the ends. Try not to stretch the clay. Using an oiled tissue blade, cut through the two layers of PMC at an angle in one smooth motion so that both ends are beveled. Gently lift the top layer of PMC, and remove the excess clay from the bottom layer. Abut the two beveled ends, and seal the joint with a few drops of water. Smooth the joint to seal it well using an oiled finger, a brush, or similar tool.

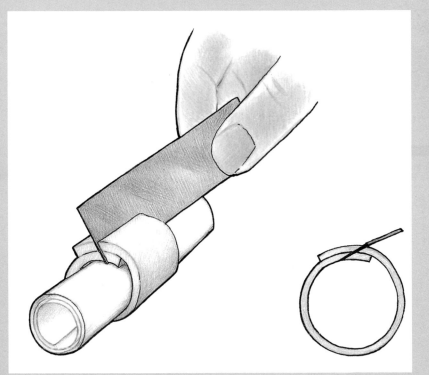

3 Dry the ring.

As the clay dries to leather-hard, it will lose moisture and shrink slightly. Sometimes this is just enough shrinkage to force open a weak joint. Monitor the drying, and after 15 minutes or so, carefully slide the ring off the form and place it upright, in a safe spot to dry. The easiest way to do this is to slide the teflon off with the ring in place. Then use tweezers to grasp the Teflon strip inside the ring and, with a half turn inward, pull the Teflon out. Now, place the upright ring in a safe place to dry. If the joint opens or your ring develops other cracks, fill them with thick slip. Make sure all parts of the ring are completely dry before repairing anything.

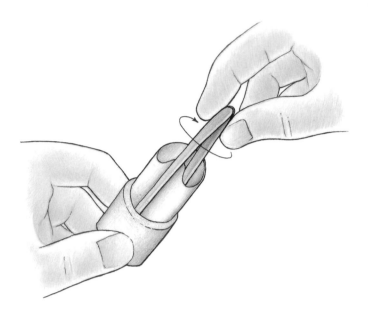

4 Sand and level the ring.

When the ring is dry, sand and true up as necessary. To true up your ring, slide it back onto the paper form after removing one or two layers of paper so there is still a snug fit. Position the ring so that it is protruding slightly off the end of the paper form. Sand it on a piece of medium-fine sandpaper (400- or 320-grit) laid flat on a piece of glass or other flat surface. Sand both edges in this way, then smooth any flaws in the rest of the ring. Smooth the inside by rolling a piece of 400-grit sandpaper to a size that moves freely in the ring. Proceed to 600-grit and then to 1000-grit if desired. Set aside.

5 Decorate the ring.

Using hand punches, cut out spirals, hearts, or other shapes from the PMC Sheet. Shapes can also be cut freehand using a craft knife or a protected tissue blade to make your ring design unique. Cut strips from the PMC Sheet with a wavy blade to complement your design. To attach the cut pieces to the ring, lay the shape in the desired place, then run a bead of water around it using a paintbrush. Press gently to attach. Another way to attach the cut pieces is to dampen a spot on the ring and press the piece onto the wet area. If the piece becomes too moist, or if you try to move it once it has been attached with water, it will tear.

6 Fire the ring.

Fire the ring upright on a kiln shelf that has been sprinkled with alumina hydrate. The alumina will reduce friction as the ring shrinks and ensure that it doesn't end up bigger on the bottom than the top. If it does become misshapen in the kiln, you can tap it back in to shape by slipping it onto a ring mandrel and tapping it with a rawhide or plastic mallet. (See *Firing* on page 165.) Scrub with a brass brush, and finish as desired.

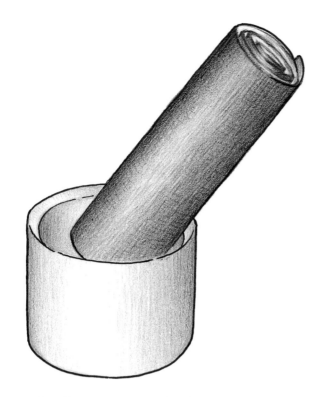

TIP: BEVEL THE INSIDE EDGES OF THE RING.

After sanding and leveling, beveling the inside edges of the ring will allow it to slide smoothly on and off your finger and will make it look more finished and more professional. To do this, roll up a piece of 400-grit sandpaper so it can move freely in and out of the inside of the ring at an acute angle. Then, sand using a gentle back and forth motion while turning the ring. Be sure to bevel both sides of the ring.

Variations

Freehand Designs and Texturing.

Cut a strip of PMC Sheet, long enough to encircle your leather-hard ring. Using a craft knife with a new blade, cut out a pattern of interior shapes. The featured ring on the top shows a pattern of leaf shapes that were cut using this method. You can practice your design on a sheet of paper. If your ring's circumference is greater than the length of the PMC Sheet, use two or more sections to encircle the ring, making the seams a part of the design or abutting the ends, letting it dry and carefully filling in the seams with slip until they are invisible.

Follow the directions for making the ring described in the main project. Then, to adhere the strip to the leather-hard ring, first quickly paint the ring with medium-thin, lump-free slip. Let the ring dry and reinforce any gaps as necessary with slip or water. Fire, scrub with a brass brush, and finish.

The cut-out shapes on this ring (bottom) were attached to a leather-hard textured ring. Once fired, the cut-outs fuse to and take on the shape of the ring's surface, adding an additional element of texture and dimension.

TIP

To make thicker paper, which creates a more dramatic relief for your ring design, spray one PMC Sheet with a fine mist of water. Wait 5 seconds then place a second PMC Sheet on top, and press gently. Allow to dry, then use it as you would any PMC Sheet.

Celestial Sphere Beads

In this project you'll use found core materials to make round, hollow form beads. The smaller bead pictured was made by using a round piece of cereal as a core. The cereal is painted with white glue and covered with a layer of PMC. When it's dried, the bead is embellished with designs in fresh PMC. Round cereal, puffed corn, or round snack foods make good core materials for spherical beads. This project uses a cereal core of an average diameter of 10 cm. Adjust the numbers for other combustible cores. Fresh or freeze-dried cranberries also work but with any food that contains water it's important to apply a quick coat of acrylic gel medium as a moisture barrier and let it dry before you begin.

Artist: Celie Fago

Materials
- basic Precious Metal Clay equipment and supplies (see page 162)
- small combustible cores, such as round cereal
- scrap polymer clay
- 1 package of PMC Plus
- small brass tube or small straw
- square-ended tool (small ruler)
- wire cutters

Getting Started

To sand a round shape without developing any flattened areas, fold the sandpaper to form a curved trough. Then, sand using a back-and-forth motion, and rotate the object frequently in the trough.

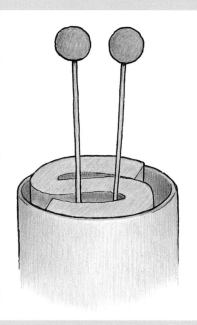

1 Prepare the bead cores.

Choose two relatively round balls for the bead cores. Make handles for them by poking a wooden skewer into each one. Apply a light coat of white craft glue to the cores, which will help adhere the PMC. Insert each skewer into a ball of scrap polymer clay pressed onto the edge of your work surface, within easy reach. Or, set the skewers into a glass with a piece of ½" (1 cm) foam rubber accordion-folded and stuffed inside. Roll out approximately ⅓ ounce of PMC Plus, through plastic wrap, to the height of three cards. Transfer the clay, with the plastic wrap in place, to a Teflon palette.

2 Covering the cores.

Lift the plastic sheet and cut a circle for each core, about 32 mm in diameter. (You may want to use an oiled plastic circle template laid on the clay. If so, cut around the circle with an oiled pin tool.) Use a tissue blade or a knife to cut a star shape out of each circle, visualizing the size of the ball you want to encase as you work. You may want to practice this technique once or twice with polymer clay. Using an oiled tissue blade or palette knife, carefully transfer one of the star shapes onto a glue-coated core. Be sure to cover the second circle with plastic wrap. Twist and remove the wood skewer from the core. Press the clay onto the core, starting from the top and working your way around. Press out air bubbles as you go. Smooth the seams together first with a little bit of water from the end of your watercolor brush, then with a lightly oiled finger. Close all the "darts" and smooth the resulting seams. Don't worry about covering the hole; it can be reopened later. You may stretch the PMC slightly, trim any excess with the tissue blade, or add more clay as needed. When all the seams are closed and the core is entirely covered, roll it vigorously between your palms to transform it from a lumpy mass into a lovely sphere. Insert the wooden skewer again, gently poking a new hole if the first one is covered. Roll the bead again between your palms until smooth. Set it aside, into the ball of polymer clay, and let dry.

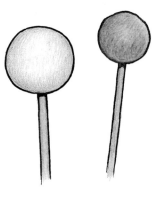

Repeat the process to make a second sphere, and let dry. Once dry, fill any cracks with thick slip. If the cracks are large, dab with water and use clay right from the package to smear into the cracks. When the repaired areas are dry, refine the shape of the beads with 400- to 600-grit sandpaper that has been folded into a curved trough. Then, with the bead resting on your work surface, position a hand drill with a ¹⁄₁₆" (1.5 mm) drill bit into the existing hole, and drill straight down through the bead to the opposite side.

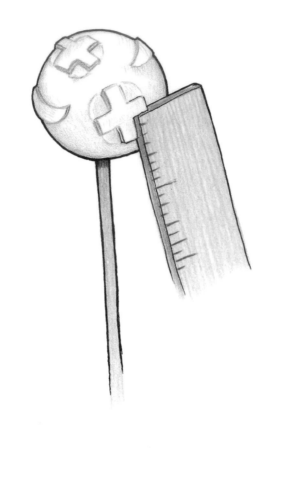

3 Decorate the spheres.

Roll out an almond-size bit of PMC, through plastic wrap, to a height of two cards. Transfer it to a Teflon palette leaving the plastic in place. Using the end of a lightly oiled small brass tube or small straw, cut out several circles of clay. Pick a spot on the sphere, and moisten it with a little water from the end of your pointed brush, then transfer a circle to the wet spot. Press to attach. Now convert the circle, and subsequent circles, into other shapes—such as a star, plus sign, or cross—by pressing a square-ended tool repeatedly around the circle. Io make a star, press the tool five times around the circle, evenly spaced. To make a plus sign, press the tool four times around the circle, evenly spaced. To make a crescent moon, press the tube or straw into the PMC again, off-setting it slightly. To make a dough-nut, transfer a circle to a dry spot on the sphere, and immediately press a smaller circle into the middle of the first circle. The center should come out readily with a slight twist of the tube. Now run a bead of water around the outside edge of the doughnut and use gentle pressure to attach it. Continue adding shapes until you're satisfied with your sphere beads, then let dry.

4 Fire and finish.

Once the beads are dry, remove the skewers. If the skewers don't come out readily, cut off the ends with wire cutters so the ends are flush with the surface of the beads. The remaining wood left inside will burn out harmlessly during firing. Then, nestle the spheres into a bed of vermiculite or alumina hydrate in an unglazed ceramic dish. Leave the top third or so of the spheres protruding above the surface of the vermiculite or alumina hy-drate. Put the dish onto a shelf in the kiln, and fire at any of the three firing choices for PMC Plus. (See *Firing* on page 165.) Scrub with a brass brush, and finish as desired. (See more on finishing on page 167.)

Variations

Embellishing with shards and slip.

Try using shards left over from other projects, such as the carved toggle on page 172, to decorate beads. Follow the directions for making beads described above, let them dry, then refine them. Gather leftover shards onto a piece of plastic wrap. Paint the bead with thick slip, then gently roll it in the pile of shards, guiding it along with the skewer handle. It's easy to fill in any bare spots later, when the bead is leather-hard—just paint the bare areas with thick slip, and fill with more shards. Dry and fire as directed in the main project. You can also combine shards and appliqué pieces in one design. To learn about other types of appliqué, see the ring project on page 176.

To make slip-covered beads, follow the directions for making beads described above, let them dry, then refine them. Then, paint thick, lumpy, slip over the beads until you are satisfied with the surface design. The best effects are achieved with very thick slip.

Maple Leaf Earrings

Artist: Celie Fago

This project demonstrates the concept of relative shrinkage. Using the same-sized cutter or template to cut out both the PMC and the polymer part of this project illustrates the 28% shrinkage of standard PMC. As it happens, the relative proportions (the polymer at full size and the PMC shrunk by 28%) work very well together in finished jewelry. If you are using PMC Plus, the shrinkage is only 12%, so the PMC will be larger relative to the polymer piece, but still proportionately balanced. Both the PMC and the polymer shapes in this project were cut with a commercially available leaf-shaped cutter.

Materials

- basic Precious Metal Clay equipment and supplies (see page 162)
- basic polymer clay equipment and supplies (see page 15)
- standard PMC
- texturing materials
- conditioned polymer clay in 3 or 4 colors
- scrap polymer clay
- pair of large loop earwires
- chain-nose pliers
- cutter or template of your choice, oiled
- ring mandrel or other hard, round form
- rawhide mallet
- drinking glass or ceramic coffee mug
- soft cloth or polishing lathe for polymer clay

Getting Started

If you are using a rigid texture, put the PMC onto the oiled texture. With netting or other flexible texture, it is easier to put the texture on top of the PMC. First, roll the clay out and transfer it to a piece of Teflon. Then, lay the oiled flexible texture on the clay, and go over it with a roller.

1 Texture the PMC.

Roll out PMC, through a sheet of plastic wrap, to a height of three cards. With the plastic in place, lift the PMC, gently position it on the oiled texture. Roll over the clay firmly once or twice, through the plastic, with your roller. Lift a corner, and if the PMC has taken a good impression, transfer it to teflon paper, with the textured side up. See *Texturing* on page 163.

2 Cut out the earring shapes.

Cut your chosen earring shape out with an oiled cutter. To cut a freehand design, use an oiled tissue blade. To use a plastic template, make sure it's well oiled, then lay it on the clay and trace around the shape with a pin tool. Repeat to make a second shape. Set the shapes aside to dry.

3 Refine the shape of the earrings.

Once the PMC is leather-hard, hold the two earrings together and run a nail board or sandpaper, held perpendicular to the outside edge to refine, and to match, the two shapes. Using a hand drill with a ¹⁄₁₆" (1.5 mm) drill bit, make a hole in both shapes near the tops. Make sure you leave enough distance between the hole and the edge of the earrings so that after firing and shrinking it will not be weak. For the featured maple leaf shape, the hole should be ⅛" (3 mm) from the top edge of the earring. Dry the shapes.

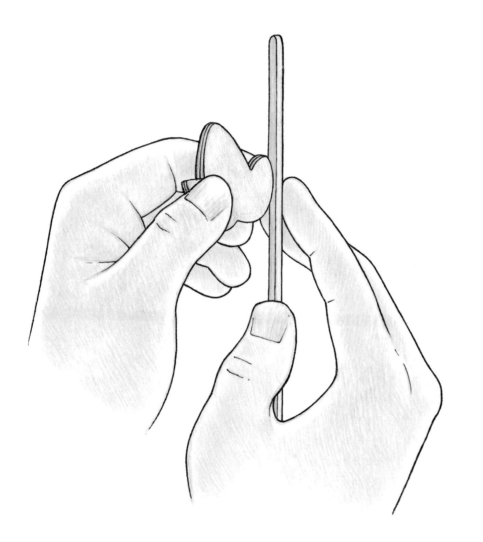

4 Fire the earrings.

See *Firing* on page 165. Fire flat on the kiln shelf. Unload the kiln following the usual procedure, and scrub with a brass brush (see *Polishing* on page 167). Then, lay the earrings over a curved surface such as a ring mandrel (available from jewelry supply companies). If you don't have a ring mandrel, use a dowel or your PVC roller. Gently push the pieces into a curve against the mandrel, or tap with a rawhide mallet. Repeat with second shape. Finish as desired.

5 Make the polymer clay elements.

To make textured polymer clay elements, first use a pasta machine to roll out half a block of conditioned polymer clay on setting #3 (medium thick). If you aren't texturing, roll out the clay on setting #4. Sprinkle baby powder or cornstarch on both sides of the clay sheets to prevent it from sticking to your texture or to your rolling tool. Then, lay the polymer onto the texture, and roll over it once firmly. Lift a corner; if the texture looks good, transfer the polymer clay to your work surface or waxed paper, and cut out two earring shapes with the same cutter used to cut the PMC pieces. The featured earrings were made by conditioning pearl blue, gold, copper, and a little bit of black Premo polymer clay separately, then rolling them out together. This multi-colored sheet was then textured with a carved polymer clay texture plate (see page 163).

You may bake the shapes flat or, if a curve is desired, put a drinking glass or coffee cup on its side on a baking try. Balls of scrap clay strategically positioned on either side of the glass will keep it from sliding around on the tray. Gently press the earring shapes on to the glass. If the amount of powder residue on the earring backs prevents them from sticking, put a smidgen of hand lotion on the tip of your finger and wipe the powder off the back of the earrings and try again. Bake according to manufacturer's directions. The low heat needed to bake the polymer clay won't affect the glass. Once the pieces have cooled, sand them with 600-grit and then 1,000-grit sandpaper, if desired. Buff with a cloth or on a polishing lathe set up for polymer clay. Drill a hole with a 1/16" (1.5 mm) drill bit near the top of the pieces. Finally, assemble the earrings by threading the earwires through a PMC and a polymer clay piece.

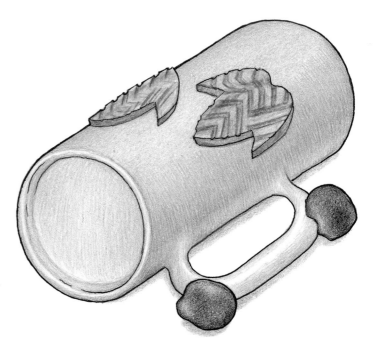

TIP

Put an extra piece of clay, the same brand and thickness as your earrings, in the oven for the duration of the baking cycle. When it's cool, try to break the extra piece. If it breaks, you know your earrings need to bake longer or at a higher temperature. Experiment with these two variables to make durable earrings.

Variations

These earrings were cut out with a custom-made tool. The tool was made by bending 24-gauge brass sheet into a leaf shape and then baking it in a polymer clay handle. The handle was then sanded and carved. Try pressing a small metal cookie cutter into a ball of polymer clay. Bake it according to manufacturer's directions, sand, and then carve it. The leaf earrings pictured were made with Premo clay and carved with a 1.5 mm **V**-gouge, micro-carving tool.

Textured Silver Frame with Inset

Artist: Celie Fago; Photo: Robert Diamante

This delicate silver frame can be used to house a small photo, or a beautiful polymer clay image, as seen here. There are many ways to texture and embellish a frame like this, and it can easily be transformed into a pendant or a brooch. Be sure to read Embellishments on page 164 for ideas and inspiration when designing your own frame. Also, try experimenting with different frame shapes, finishes, and polymer clay transferring techniques— the possibilities are endless. The spiral image on the featured frame was made using a collage transfer and the Tear-Away technique.

Materials

- basic Precious Metal Clay equipment and supplies (see page 162)
- basic polymer clay equipment and supplies (see page 15)
- 1 ounce of standard PMC
- Tear-Away etched plate, clay paper, or other texture, oiled
- 1 block of black polymer clay (featured piece was backed with Premo)
- image for transfer
- texture, such as sanding screen, for back of frame
- Translucent Liquid Sculpey (TLS)
- 3" (8 cm) length of 14- or 16-gauge brass, steel, or sterling wire
- five-minute epoxy
- cotton batting
- bench block or other metal surface
- hammer
- use frame templates on page 298

Getting Started

Virtually any black-and-white line drawing can be easily transferred to polymer clay. Repeating the motifs from the picture in the frame creates a resonance that unifies these two materials. You can do this with transfer techniques and Tear-Away, by making embellishments for the frame that match the image, or by carving patterns from the image onto the frame when it's leather-hard. For carving PMC you'll need to make it extra thick because you'll be cutting into it with the carving tool.

1 Make the PMC frame.

Roll out standard PMC, through plastic wrap, to a height of three cards, nudging it into a rectangle as you go. If you're making a piece larger than 2" x 2" (5 cm x 5 cm) roll the PMC to a height of four cards. Transfer the rectangle to a Teflon palette keeping the plastic wrap in place.

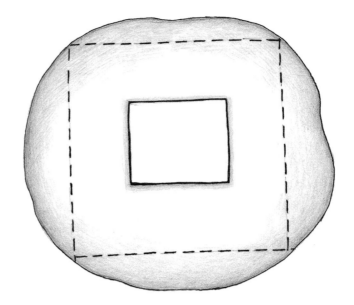

2 Texture the PMC.

First, see *Using Tear-Away Plates and Clay Papers to Texture PMC* on page 169. Then, make an etched polymer plate using the Tear-Away technique. Secure the etched plate to your work surface with some scrap polymer clay at each corner. Oil the etched plate, and lay the PMC over the top, leaving the plastic wrap in place. Roll once firmly across the surface to impress, then lift the PMC to check the impression. Roll over the PMC again if necessary. Then, remove the plastic, and turn the PMC over onto to the Teflon palette, texture side up.

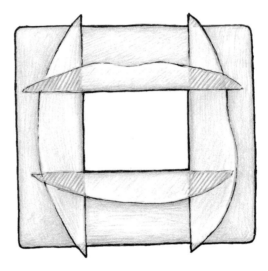

3 Cut out the frame opening.

Using an oiled craft knife, cut an opening in the center of the frame. Trim the outside edges of the frame and position those pieces around the opening, or trim and position only two of the outside edges, leaving the other two as is. Attach the trimmed pieces to the frame with a few drops of water. Let the frame dry.

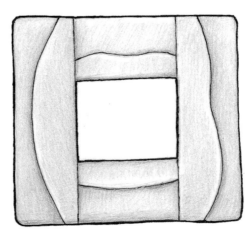

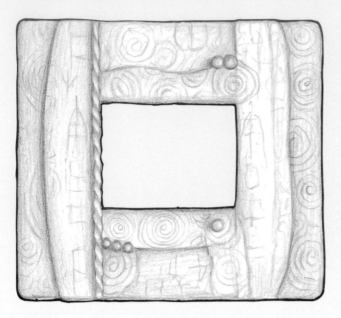

4 Decorate the surface.

Once the frame is leather-hard, check for gaps in your attachments, and reaffix with thick slip. Decorate the surface with small balls of clay and lengths of twisted PMC strips. Attach the embellishments with thick slip. (See *Embellishments* on page 164 and Step 2 in the following project.) Once the slip has dried, refine the form with a nail board or fine-grit sandpaper. Fill any cracks, gaps or weak joints with thick slip. Let dry.

5 Fire the frame.

Fire the piece flat on the kiln shelf (see *Firing* on page 165). Brass brush, antique and polish the surface as desired. Scrub the back of the frame well with steel wool, sandpaper, or a brass brush until glistening clean in preparation for gluing. (See *Finishing Techniques* on page 167.)

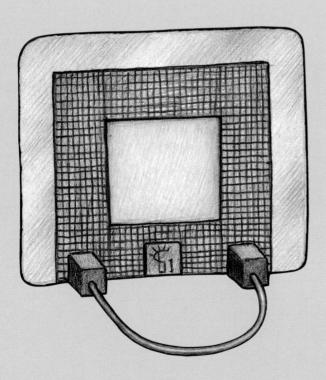

6 Make the polymer clay inset.

Transfer an image that will fit in your frame's window to a piece of rolled out polymer clay. Lay the polymer clay on a baking surface with the transfer facing up. Lower the PMC frame onto the polymer clay so the opening frames the transferred image. Press down gently to secure. Turn the piece over, and use a craft knife or tissue blade to trim the polymer clay so it s ⅛" to ¼" (3 mm to 6 mm) larger than the frame opening.

To create a finished look on the back side of the frame, first roll out some polymer clay to about the height of the transfer inset. Texture the surface as desired. Drywall sanding screen was used here. Using a tissue blade, cut thin strips from the clay sheet, long enough to enclose the back of the transfer inset. Apply TLS to the edges of the transfer inset, and abut the textured strips to make a frame. To make a spot to sign or carve your name, cut out a ½" (1 cm) long square from the middle of the bottom strip. Flip it over so the smooth side is facing up. Dab the edges with TLS and reposition it in the same spot. Make sure the bottom strip extends to the bottom edge of the PMC frame.

Next, make two ⅜" (10 mm) square cubes of polymer clay. Use a 3" (8 cm) wire to poke a hole about halfway into one side of each cube. Position the hole one-third of the way up from the bottom of the cube. Then, position the cube along the bottom edge of the polymer clay strip, and affix with TLS. Bake the entire frame assemblage on cotton batting, face down, according to the polymer clay manufacturer's directions. Let cool. Sand polymer if desired.

To assemble the frame, first use a craft knife or needle tool to roughen all surfaces to be glued—the part of the frame back and the part of the polymer piece that will be glued to each other. Then clean all surfaces by swabbing with alcohol. Prepare five-minute epoxy according to manufacturer's instructions. Glue polymer clay assemblage to the back of the PMC frame. To make the frame stand, bend the 3" (8 cm) wire into a **U**-shape loop, and poke the ends into the holes in each cube. If the wire ends don't fit snugly, remove and place them on a bench block or other metal surface, and tap them with a hammer to flatten. Keep tapping and testing, until you get a snug fit.

Variations

Turning a Frame into a Pendant.

It's easy to turn a delicate frame like this one into a pendant. The quickest way is to add holes for jump rings (see above, right). Before the PMC has dried, use a small straw or metal tubing to poke two holes into the top edge of the frame. If the clay is leather-hard, use a hand drill with a 1/16" (1.5 mm) bit or a Dremel tool. For both methods, reinforce the holes with doughnuts of fresh clay attached with slip.

To make the doughnuts, first roll out PMC, through plastic wrap, to a height of two cards. Use the same small straw or metal tubing you used on the frame to cut out circles of PMC. Then, use a smaller straw or tube to cut and remove the centers of the circles. Paint some slip around the holes on the frame, and position the doughnuts over the holes. Press into place, and clean up any excess slip with a clean brush. In this pendant, the holes were reinforced with

doughnuts on the front and back. If they don't complement your design, put them only on the back.

To make an alternative frame support (see above, left): When the frame is completely finished do the following: Roll a plump log of conditioned black clay approximately 1/2" (2.5 cm) in diameter. Trim a sectin that is about as wide as your frame. Powder the bottom edge of the frame and gently push it down in to the log of clay, stopping to repowder if it sticks. Stop about two-thirds of the way through the snake. It should stand up fairly well on its own. Make a **U**-shaped loop of wire and poke the ends in to the log to give it greater stability. Remove the frame and bake the stand according to manufacturer's directions. When it's cool you can remove the **U**-loop and adjust the fit by tapping it with a hammer as per above directions.

Bird Box Pendant

Artist: Celie Fago

Combustible support forms were used in the bead project on page 180; in this project, you will learn how to make a noncombustible support form, which is used to keep PMC from slumping during firing. The parts for this box pendant are textured and cut out of fresh clay, dried to leather-hard, then assembled with slip. Since force drying results in warpage, air dry the box parts to facilitate assembly.

Materials

- basic Precious Metal Clay equipment and supplies (see page 162)
- basic polymer clay equipment and supplies (see page 15)
- 1 ounce of standard PMC
- texture sheets
- graph paper
- foam rubber scraps
- cereal box
- small piece of paper clay or fire brick
- copy paper
- flat piece of polymer clay with transferred image, unbaked
- five-minute epoxy
- metal or plastic right angle or triangle
- round needle file
- photocopier
- jeweler's saw
- tweezers
- scrap polymer clay

Getting Started

Use a piece of plastic wrap laid over graph paper to help measure rolled-out PMC more accurately when cutting it.

1 Roll out and cut the box pieces.

Roll out about ⅛ ounce of standard PMC, through plastic wrap, to a height of four cards. Texture the clay then transfer it to a Teflon palette. Cut out a rectangle measuring 1¼" x 1⅛" (32 mm x 28.5 mm), and set it aside to dry. Repeat to make an identical rectangle, and using a craft knife, cut an opening in the rectangle. Make sure there's a ¼" (6.5 mm) border of clay on all four sides. Set aside to dry. These pieces will be the front and back of the box pendant. (See page 299 for a template diagram.)

Next, roll out ¼ ounce of clay, through plastic wrap, to a height of four cards, nudging it into a long rectangle as you roll. Texture it, then cut four ¼" (6.5 mm) wide strips that are just a little longer than the sides of the rectangles. The strips will be used for the top, the bottom, and both sides of the box; because they're slightly longer than needed, you can sand them to create a perfect fit when they're leather-hard. Set the strips aside to dry.

To make the border for the frame opening, roll out about ¼ ounce of PMC, through plastic wrap, to a height of four cards. Texture it as desired, then transfer it to a Teflon palette. Cut a rectangle from the piece that's about ⅛" (3 mm) wider all around than the frame opening. Then, cut out the center of the rectangle, leaving an ⅛" (3 mm) border.

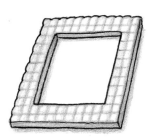

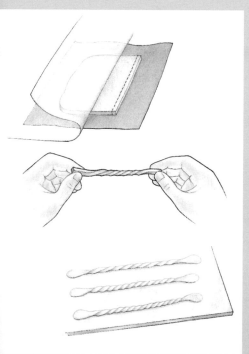

2 Make the decorative details for the box pendant.

To make twisted wires, roll out ¼ ounce of PMC, under plastic wrap, to a height of four cards. It should form a rectangle at least 2¼" (5 cm) long. Transfer the PMC to a Teflon palette. Using a well-oiled tissue blade, cut a strip as wide as the PMC sheet is thick so it's square. Then, gently twist the strip into a square wire. To prevent it from untwisting, firmly push both ends onto a glass surface, or other surface to which the PMC will stick, like marble or stone; be sure to remove all traces of oil. Continue making twisted wires until you have one for each side, plus a few extra in case some break. Don't worry about sizing them exactly to your box sides. Just make them a bit longer than the sides, and plan on trimming them with a protected tissue blade, once they are leather-hard. When they dry, they will detach from the glass surface on their own. Sometimes the pieces will develop a curve, but standard PMC is flexible and can be

gently straightened. You may want to put the pieces under a book or other weight so they remain straight until it comes time to use them. They can also be stored, straightened, in cocktail straws. With the box seen here, the leather-hard wires were placed on the sides, bottom, and top of the box.

To make tiny spheres: Cut an extra strip from the rolled out PMC, divide it into squares, and roll four tiny spheres to decorate the corners of the box. Set them on a scrap of foam rubber to dry.

To make a bail: Pinch off a piece of PMC the size of an almond, and cut a cube measuring ¼" (6.5 mm) square. Put a hole in it using a large, well-oiled knitting needle, and set it aside to dry. As an alternative you may form the cube, let it dry, then drill a hole in it. Remember that it will shrink, so use a large needle, or at least a ¹⁄₁₆" (1.5 mm) drill bit.

3 Refine and true-up the pieces of the box pendant.

Hold the front and back pieces together, face to face, and rub the edges on 320-grit sandpaper that has been laid onto a perfectly flat surface, such as glass. Sand until the two pieces are exactly the same size. Check the corners against a right angle, and continue sanding until they're trued up and smooth. Sand the ¼" (5 mm) wide side pieces until they're true and sized to fit the rectangles. If you need to trim them first, use a protected tissue blade, which will cut through standard PMC without breaking it.

To sand the pendant opening and the border for the opening, make a small sanding tool by cutting a strip of cereal box (or equivalent) and folding 320-grit sand paper around it. This tool should be a bit narrower than the smallest dimension you're sanding. Trim and true up the twisted "wire" lengths so they're each slightly longer than the side and the bottom pieces of the box. Reserve the twisted length that will go on the top until later. Refine the cube bail by sanding it and enlarging the hole with a round needle file as necessary

4 Make a noncombustible support form.

The form, which will prevent the box from slumping as it heats up in the kiln, should be made from a nontoxic, noncombustible material. Good choices are paper clay, which is available from craft supply stores, and fire brick, a common and inexpensive material available from ceramic suppliers. Paper clay is superior to regular papier-mâché because it shrinks very little, and it can be sanded once dry, like fire brick. Because it contains volcanic ash, it won't burn up in the kiln.

The only part of the box vulnerable to slumping is the front, where the frame window is cut out. To support this area, make a form from paper clay or firebrick that is slightly larger than the window opening and 4 mm high. The easiest way to measure for your piece is to lay the box front (before assembly) on to graph paper and poke a hole at each corner. Draw a line to connect the four pin holes and make your combustible core 1 to 2 mm larger than that, all the way around, and 4 mm high.

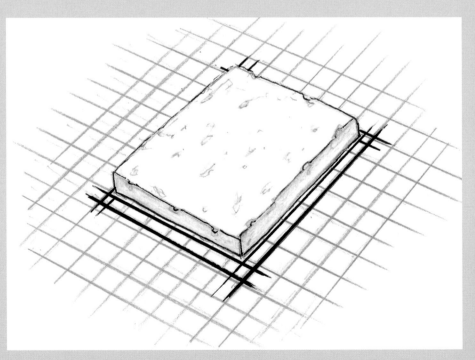

If using paper clay, sculpt it into a rectangular shape slightly larger than the size you want, and let it dry. If using fire brick, cut it slightly larger than the size you want, using a craft knife or a jeweler's saw. Then, sand the form to the size you want using 320-grit and then 400-grit sandpaper.

5 Assemble the box pendant.

Check the fit of the pieces and sand as necessary. Then, paint a line of thick, smooth slip on the back piece, along one side and along the top. Paint slip on the ends of one side piece and the top piece, then position them on the back piece, with tweezers or your fingers. If your slip is the correct consistency, these two pieces will stand up without support. Hold the pieces steady while you remove excess slip from the outside edges with a clean brush. Allow the assembly to dry completely. Attach the other ¼" (6.5 mm) side piece and let dry. Reinforce the seams as necessary from the inside, and let dry. Attach the border for the frame opening to the front piece, and let it dry. Then, attach the front piece to the three-sided assembly, and let it dry.

The bottom ¼" (6.5 mm) piece, which will be fired separately, needs to be sized now. Try the fit, and sand as necessary so that it is a little larger than the space for it. You can easily file it down after its fired, but it is a lot harder to add material if the box bottom is too small.

TIP

The bail hole can be oriented parallel to the pendant, as seen here, or perpendicular to the pendant.

7 Insert the polymer clay image, and bake.

Slide the image into place, adding rolled-out strips of polymer clay behind the insert to fill up the area and so there's more surface area for gluing the ¼" (6.5 mm) bottom piece on after baking. Bake the whole assembly according to manufacturer's directions. Remove the polymer to sand and buff if desired, then glue it in, and the bottom piece on, using five-minute epoxy.

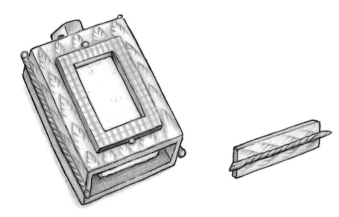

6 Attach the decorative elements and fire.

Make a pencil mark at the center of the top of the box. Attach the bail to this spot with enough thick slip so it squeezes out into a flange around the bottom of the bail. Let it dry.

Next, miter the ends of the twisted wire pieces so they meet neatly at each corner, trimming the top section as necessary to account for the bail. To miter an end, hold one twisted wire length close to the end, at an angle, and rub it gently back and forth against 320-grit sandpaper. Attach the three twisted wire sections to the box using slip, and let dry. Attach the last wire to the bottom ¼" (6.5 mm) piece using slip, and let dry. Reinforce as necessary. Attach a ball to each corner with slip.

Center the support form inside the box and place it, along with the ¼" (6.5 mm) bottom piece, in a bed of alumina hydrate or vermiculite, and fire. (See *Firing* on page 165.) Once cool, remove the support form, and finish as desired.

Chapter 8
Creating Fantasy Figures

This grinning bird, looking up, settled over his gigantic bird feet, teeth gleaming through his smile, is a perfect starting project, particularly if you are completely new to working with clay. Making the bird, fun in itself, is also useful practice in the essential skills that you will need for the rest of the projects in this book such as: making basic shapes and learning how to work on a specific area of a critter without ruining the rest of it.

The color scheme should follow this one guideline: use two well-contrasting colors—one for the fluffy parts (the body, the wigs, and the tail) and one for the bony parts (the beak and legs).

The size of the bird doesn't matter, as long as its proportions make sense. The bird shown here is less than 1" (2.5 cm) tall. (But don't underestimate him!)

¼ block yellow clay
(we used Sculpey Premo)
½ block green clay
⅛ block white or glow-in-the-dark clay
⅛ block orange clay
⅛ block black clay

Safety pin
Taped-point clay shaper

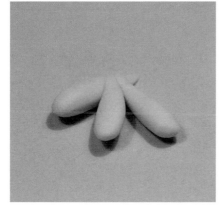

1 A bird is built the way a house is built, from bottom to top, so we will start with the feet. The foot of an average bird consists of three toes. To make a toe, roll a small ball of clay between your index finger and thumb until it becomes oblong. Make the back end slightly sharper by exerting a little bit more pressure while rolling. The pointed end will go under the bird, and the round end will be the tip of the toe. That way, the bird will have nice, chubby toes instead of scary claws.

2 Continue with the other two toes, and stick the pointy ends firmly on top of one another. Make sure to sufficiently overlap the toes, so that they will provide a firm, solid base once the bird is cooked. The outside toes should form a 90-degree (right) angle so that the bird can stand firmly on his feet.

3 Repeat the procedure to make a second foot. Make sure to include the same number of toes in each foot—it is considered to be good taste.

4 Next, create an egg shape, which will become the body of the bird. Roll a ball of clay between the palms of your hands, gently squeezing your palms toward the end, while still rolling, to achieve an egglike shape. Stick the body firmly to the feet. Remember that the body keeps the feet together, so if you want to have a solid bird, you'll need to apply a little pressure. Be careful not to disfigure the oval shape of the egg while pressing.

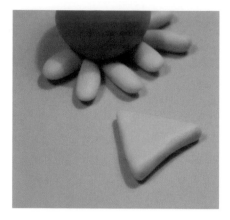

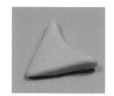

5 The bird's mouth is made from a triangular piece of clay. Make a small, flat triangle with equal-length sides. Flatten one point of the triangle to make it slightly thinner. This end will be the tip of the beak.

6 Pull the other two points in opposite directions, and curve the side between them. This side of the beak will be fastened to the body, so it should roughly follow the curves of the bird's body.

8 This step, where you first use the safety pin, involves separating the upper jaw from the lower one. Stick the pin into the beak where the curved part starts, and carefully pull toward the cheeks. Be careful not to pull too hard—you want to leave the jaws joined.

7 From this point on, working on the beak will be easier if you attach it to the body of the bird. Stick the beak to the body horizontally. Whether you will make a highbrow or a lowbrow bird depends on how high on the body you place the beak. Putting it in the upper part leads to a lowbrow bird with a belly. Gently push the top of the beak down. (This feature of the bird is probably the only one that bears resemblance to an eagle.)

9 Use the safety pin again to widen the distance between the jaws. Try to make a hole in a sideways, teardrop shape. You will put the teeth in this space.

A BIRD WITH TEETH

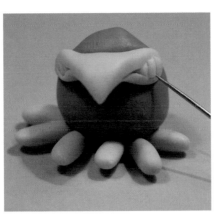

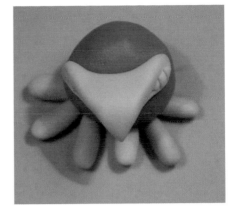

10 Fill the holes with white polymer clay. If you want your feathered songster to have bad teeth you can, of course, use yellowish clay. You can also put a cigar in the bird's mouth instead or even make him stick out his tongue. But teeth...teeth are classic.

11 Use the safety pin to divide the white polymer clay into individual teeth. Be careful not to touch the beak. Repeatedly rock the tip of the pin back and forth rather than just drawing it straight from one jaw to the other to avoid creating a "wake" of clay around the pin and ultimately ruining the shapes you previously created.

12 Here is a bird's eye view of the bird.

13 Roll out two small balls of white polymer clay for the eyeballs. For the eyelids, roll out two colored balls approximately the same size and a color darker than the beak. Squash the colored balls flat. Don't make perfect spheres, though. You want a slightly elliptical shape, so start with an elongated ball. Wrap the ellipses around the eyeballs, so that they cover half of the circumference and the rim sticks out, sort of like a baseball cap. You can see the making of the eyes in the photo above.

▲ ▶ **14** Add the eyes to the body of the bird. Stick them to the egg and to the beak at the same time. The beak and the eyes form the face of the bird, so make sure to set them close together.

▲ **15** Next, you need to make wings for your bird. Make them by squeezing two small balls into disks.

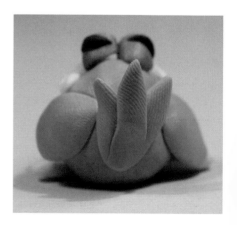

▲ **16** Stick one rounded end of the wing to the body at the height of the beak. Slightly spread the lower, loose end of a wing away from the body. Repeat this procedure to attach the other wing.

▲ **17** Make the tail just like you made the feet, but use the same color clay that you used to make the body. Then, flatten the oblong rolls to resemble feathers. The number of feathers, just like the number of toes, can vary indefinitely.

▲ **18** Attach the tail to the bottom of the bird.

19 Turn the bird around. Now you need to give it eyes that see, a nose to breathe with, and a belly button. (Have you been wondering what an ordinary bird is doing in a book of fantasy characters? Well, it is the belly button that merits his inclusion.)

Using the safety pin, poke two deep holes into the eyes, one in the belly, and two on top of the beak. For the nostrils, pull a little bit to the side—the holes don't need to be perfectly round. Also, roll out two tiny strips of black clay, and put them on top of the eyelids to be the eyebrows.

Where to put the hole on the eyeball is a very important decision. Here are a few of the possible options:

MAKING EYES

The fact that we made a hole to create eyes and didn't just add a tiny black speck of clay is important. A small black spot is perceived the same way from any angle that you look at it. Because of this, the eye looks artificial. A hole, on the contrary, has depth and direction. In addition, only a limited number of angles provide the impression that your eyes and those of the bird lock, which gives the creature more character.

Dizzy ▶

◀ Looking left

Normal ▶

◀ Stunned

20 Here, the bird is looking up. Because it is a tiny creature, looking up is the easiest way for it to make eye contact with whoever is looking at it. That way the bird becomes more interactive and doesn't just sit there.

22 Use the tapered-point clay shaper to blend the cheeks with the rest of the beak.

Then, bake the bird following the clay manufacturer's instructions and let it cool. For more tips see the baking section in the beginning of this book.

21 The bird looks finished, but one final step remains—you can make it look cheekier. How? Just add cheeks. Use the same shape you made for the toes, only shorter and sharp at both ends. Then bend it as shown, and add it to the finished beak.

Congratulations—you have completed the project. By changing the color and the shape of the different parts, you can create any bird, from a penguin to a pelican. The small bits that you change make the personality of the creature. See the following page for more variations you can try.

TIP

White or Glow-in-the-Dark?

When you make the eyes and teeth, use glow-in-the dark clay instead of plain white polymer clay. The typical white is too white, and eyes and teeth usually have some translucency to them. Glow-in-the-dark clay not only lacks that undesirable opaqueness, but it also gives your creatures life after dark. For the best night results, after you have baked your bird, use a safety pin to fill the eyeholes with raw black polymer clay. Then turn the lights off, and observe.

Variation Ideas

Bird with an Extravagant Tail
The fellow is also sticking out his tongue.

Penguin

Make the penguin following the basic principles of the bird project. The only innovation is the white belly, made in the same way we made the wings and the feet.

A tip on how to make the penguin feet: After using the clay shaper, squeeze the toes with your fingers to flatten them.

Scared bird

THE EASTER BUNNY

The goal of this project is to teach you how to make a basic rabbit. Once you master that skill, the transition to an Easter Bunny will be quite easy—you only have to put an Easter egg in the rabbit's hands.

The Easter Bunny will be made in a somewhat different order that the bird. We start with the body and add the arms and legs later.

1 block light blue clay
¼ block yellow clay
¼ block orange clay
⅛ block purple clay
⅛ block glow-in-the-dark clay
⅛ block pink clay
¼ block red clay

Needle or safety pin
Tapered-point clay shaper
Cup-round clay shaper

▶ **1** Using a piece of blue polymer clay and the palms of your hands, roll a ball approximately 1½" (3.8 cm) in diameter. Don't worry about making a perfect sphere —first, it would take too much time, and second, we don't need that level of precision. To make a character with a lot of character, we are counting on a combination of shapes that are often imperfect.

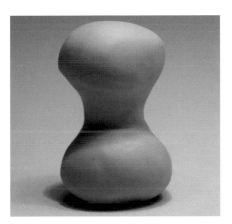

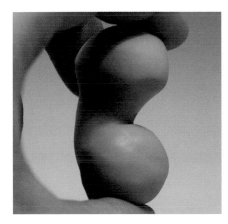

▲ **2** In this step hold the ball by the "equator" between your thumb and middle finger, and, by rolling back and forth, make it look like an apple core. Then gently smooth all edges until the shape starts looking more like an hourglass or an "8."

▲ **3** If you paid attention to the imperfection argument from the first step, by now one of the two ends should be slightly bigger than the other. This bigger end will be the torso of the rabbit, whereas the smaller end will be his head. Slightly bend the torso of the future Easter Bunny forward—the direction in which the belly is rounder and where the face of the critter will be.

Note: Stick the rabbit's bottom to the work surface until it flattens, and leave it there, as shown in step two. The figure should be able to stand without any props. Do not be alarmed if it is unstable, because we will add legs and a tail later, which will serve as additional support. This step is necessary because the upright position will be natural for the rabbit, which means that the "8" won't be flattened and distorted as it might be if just leave it lying, like an ∞.

4 Make a canoe shape out of the same color clay you used for the body. A canoe shape is flat on the surface, round on the bottom, and tapers off toward the ends. The canoe will be one of the ears. It should be about as long as the head/torso is tall.

Long ears are probably the most characteristic element of a rabbit, along with the small tail and the teeth. Even if you choose to ignore most of these instructions, as long as you give any critter long ears, two prominent teeth, and a tiny round tail, chances are you will end up with a rabbit. Once you practice here, you can go back and test this hypothesis on the bird for some interesting results.

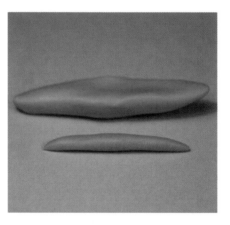

5 It's time to make the soft part of the rabbit's fur. I have used a 50-50 mix of orange and yellow clay to create the rabbit color. (To mix colors, mush two pieces of different-colored clay together until they are completely blended into a new color.) Much in the same way you made the bird's toes, roll out a long worm of clay, with two sharp ends this time.

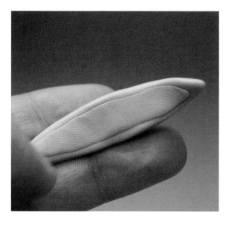

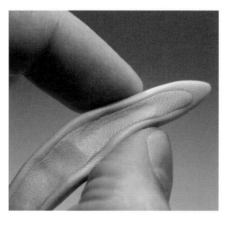

6 Flatten the clay worm into a tapeworm. Then put it on top of the flat surface of the canoe shape. Press firmly so that the yellow clay sinks in the blue one. The whole ear might flatten a little bit, but that is nothing to worry about.

7 Gently bend the ear until the blue rim comes slightly forward, as shown. Do the same to the other end of the ear but not to the central part. The ear is done for now. Don't forget you need to make another one of these.

8 Put your thumb on the rabbit's future face, and flatten it a bit. Then, with the help of a stick of any sort, poke two holes into the upper part of the future head, at one o'clock and eleven o'clock. This is where the ears will go. Make sure the holes are deep enough to accommodate about a quarter of an ear.

▲ **9** Put the ears in the holes, as shown, and gently squeeze the surrounding head to keep them firmly in place. You can also use a clay shaper to smooth the seam from the back of the ear. Bear in mind that because we are not using any armature at this point, it is quite natural for the ears to flap in the wind while you work on the rest of the rabbit. Just be careful not to rock their foundation (where they are fastened to the head).

▲ **10** Fold one of the ears in two and a little to the side, without covering the lower, inner yellow part. (Rabbit ears are quite revealing—this position implies a wink.)

▲ **11** Use a pin to draw the rabbit's face. Lightly trace the basic features where a more sophisticated face will soon smile.

▲ **12** Put the tip of the tapered-point clay shaper into the holes for eyes, and, with a rotating motion, widen the craters to make eye sockets.

▲ **13** Using the cup-round clay shaper, open the rabbit's mouth, as shown here.

▲ **14** Using purple polymer clay for the eyelids and glow-in-the-dark clay for the eyeballs, make the rabbit's eyes. Then put them into the eye sockets. The eyes are made exactly like those in the bird lesson. (See page 199 to review detailed eye making instructions.)

◀ **15** Make a small blue dome, or a hemisphere, to put in the center of the critter's face. This new protrusion will serve as a pedestal for the rabbit's nose.

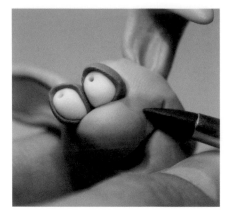

 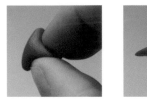

18 Further lengthen the two upper ends of the triangle. Make them thinner as well because you will need to bend them.

16 Put the blue dome in the center of the rabbit's face, right under his eyes. Then, using the tapered-point clay shaper, blend it into the whole.

17 After all this preparation, we're ready for the nose. Using pink polymer clay, make a triangle with three equal sides. You can use any other shade of polymer clay, but the goal is to achieve the effect that is a specialty of another imaginary character—Rudolf the Red-Nosed Reindeer. Squeeze the triangle as shown.

19 Bend the two ends down toward the bulk of the nose to make the nostrils.

20 While it is still warm, stick the nose to the rabbit's face.

 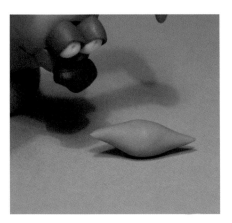

21 Next, we make the rabbit's cheeks. The technique is largely the same as that used previously for the bird. Here, however, we'll give more volume to the shape in the center. Make the two ends pointy.

TIP

Stickiness of Clay

When you work on a piece of clay, it warms up and becomes stickier, from all the kneading and the temperature of your hands. The stickiness makes the bonds between the clay pieces stronger. Use that property to make a critter that breaks less. Don't wait too long before you attach add-on parts to the bulk of a critter, especially when you do not intend to blend the add-on shape with its surroundings using a clay shaper, like you did with the little dome a couple of steps ago.

▲ **22** Curve the shape into a croissant, and attach it to the face. Place one of the sharp ends near the lower outer corner of the eye and the other no further than where the neck starts—unless, of course, you want the rabbit to have sagging cheeks.

▲ **23** Pinch the rabbit's cheeks between your index finger and thumb. (Just like one of these uncles who always say, "Look how much you've grown!")

▲ **24** Using that same index-finger-and-thumb hold, but in a perpendicular direction, pinch the cheeks some more, using the tip of your nail to create a sharper shape.

▲ **25** Repeat the same action again, further down the cheek.

▲ **26** Drawing in the clay with a needle or a pin makes the critter's features stand out. It also helps to highlight shapes. Stick the tip of the pin almost between the eyes, and draw a curved line toward the lower outer corner of the eye.

▲ **27** Draw the eyebrows. Make sure they are slanted like this— / \ —to give the critter a good-natured look.

◀ **28** Use the pin to make the hair. You need to be more energetic with the pin—stick it deeper and break the clay while drawing it out to create the effect of hair. It is more important to create the impression of small tufts than to focus on individual hairs.

30 Use the pin to separate the two teeth. Start from the lower end of the teeth, and press toward the upper lip. By using the upper lip for resistance, you not only create a better shape but also fasten the teeth more firmly.

31 Make a ball out of the yellow clay, and squash it into a disk. Stick the disk to the belly of the rabbit, and give the creature a belly button by using a pin. Ideally, the belly button should not be in the center of the circle but a little toward the lower part.

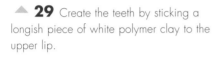

29 Create the teeth by sticking a longish piece of white polymer clay to the upper lip.

32 Now its time to create the feet. Round off all the sharp edges from a piece of blue clay, and, referring to the photo, hold the two ends and exert some pressure toward the middle.

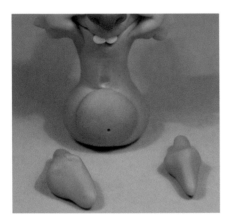

33 This is how big the feet are in proportion to the body. In addition to having long ears, rabbits are supposed to have big feet, because they run fast. So there is no real danger of overdoing the feet—make them as large as you want. The proportion shown in the picture is only a recommendation.

34 Attach the feet to the bottom of the critter. Make sure they are perpendicular to the body so that the rabbit will be well balanced.

35 The two feet overlap, because this is a very modest rabbit. They are less likely to break off, as well, once you have baked the critter. You shouldn't always let the fragility of materials dictate the posture of your creations (for example, we ignored it while making the ears), but if functional limitation can be reconciled with artistic goals, as it can be in this case, why not?

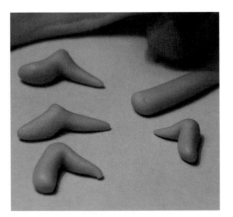

36 The hands are made using a basic technique you are already familiar wi from making the bird's toes. Make the finge from the same little shapes that have one pointy end and one round end. Then make the arm the same way, the only difference being that it is longer. The majority of the critters in this book will have four fingers, which is a popular convention when it com to cartoon characters. Typically, the index finger here should be slightly bigger than th middle finger and the pinkie, and the thumb should be slightly chubbier.

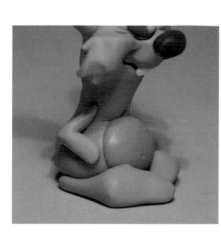

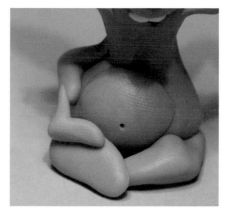

37 Bend a bunny finger between your index finger and thumb to create a joint, as shown. Repeat for all the fingers and the arm itself, too.

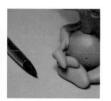

38 The arm and hands are added bit by bit to the body of the critter. First, attach the arm on the side, where the neck ends and the torso starts.

39 Attach the pinkie firmly, so that the pointy end is attached to the bottom of the arm and the thick end is on the hand.

40 In the same way, proceed with the next finger, making sure that it is firmly attached and that it doesn't entirely cover the previous one.

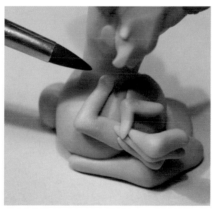

41 The base of the thumb makes a right angle with the other fingers and also covers the spots where they are attached to the arm. Use a clay shaper to smooth the surface and make all the joints firmer. Add the opposite arm.

42 Adding an Easter egg is the easiest way to transform an ordinary rabbit into an Easter Bunny. Roll out a small egg of red polymer clay. Stick it firmly to the body where the arm that is supposed to hold it ends. We will put the egg first and then add the fingers around it.

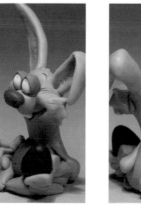

44 To make the tail, stick a ball of blue clay to the bottom of the Easter Bunny. This appendage should also counter any backward motion it might be inclined to make.

43 Using the same steps as for the other hand, add the fingers one by one. The only difference this time is that they have to be firmly wrapped around the egg without covering too much of it.

45 The Easter Bunny is nearly finished. To add a last touch of charm, use the safety pin to draw stitches (long lines crossed with shorter ones) along all the central axis of the critter. That way the Easter Bunny will look like a toy. This is also a good time to draw the individual toes on the bunny's foot. Finally, draw a crack on the egg—an egg that is about to hatch is much more exciting.

Bake the rabbit following the clay manufacturer's instructions, and let it cool. For more tips on baking, see page 27.

TIP

Fingerprints—or Why You Should NOT Try to Get Rid of Them

According to some people, fingerprints should be removed. However, fingerprints offer many positive things. First, most creatures have a certain sort of texture to their surfaces—unless, of course, we are talking about an alien, a frog, or a porcelain vase. The fingerprints that you leave fulfill that function of creating a texture, which produces a more natural look. A fantasy character does not need to look real, but it does need to look natural to a certain degree to be believable.

Second, you have to come very close to a creature to see the fingerprints. (But is this not the case with most things—the closer you come, the more you see the imperfections? It's a natural phenomenon.)

Last, but not least, your fingerprint is your signature that can never be forged. By leaving your fingerprints, you give the creatures identity in both the figurative and the literal sense.

Variation Ideas
Easter Bunny with a Basket, Easter Bunny with a Frying Pan

Easter Bunnies are, by definition, cute and must have an egg in their possession to distinguish them from ordinary rabbits. Play with these two general truths to produce the maximum humorous effect. The Easter Bunny with a basket pictured at right has gathered a few small eggs in his basket. The bunny in the picture at right didn't quite get the idea and thought he could still be an Easter Bunny if he made fried eggs. Also, if you look closely, all rules of symmetry are disobeyed, resulting in a rabbit that looks more deranged than cute.

1 To make a frying pan, start with a mushroomlike shape.

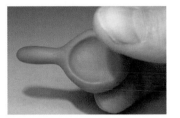

2 Press in the center of the thicker part with your thumb, while holding the other side with your index finger. Define the round inner edge of the frying pan with your fingernail. Rotate the pan, repeating the same action.

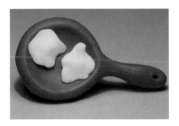

3 Add two white amoebas.

4 Add the yolk—two squished balls of yellow clay. Yummy! Note that the bunnies' legs are apart this time, so that they can serve as a support for the pan. The hands are, as usual, built around the item that the rabbit is holding.

The Three Easter Bunnies

A FIRE-BREATHING DRAGON

You are about to make a fire-breathing dragon. We won't go so far as to show you how to put the fire in it, but we'll use some wire to make it at least a little formidable. This is the first project where you will learn how to use armature to put polymer clay into whatever shape you want. Polymer clay, usually quite spineless, is pretty adamant on one point—it will not stand straight when you try to make a bow-legged elf with a beer belly. The mass of the torso would invariably crush the thin legs unless you use armature.

MATERIALS

2 blocks red clay

¼ block glow-in-the-dark clay

¼ block orange clay

⅛ block light brown clay

39" (1 m) 0.7 mm copper wire

Tin foil

TOOLS

Wire cutters

Flat-nosed pliers

Needle or safety pin

Small tapered-point clay shaper

Small cup-round clay shaper

Small tube

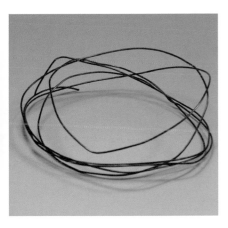 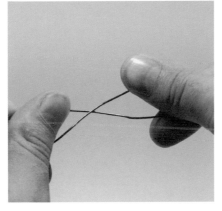 

▲ **1** To make the armature, or the skeleton, of the dragon, we will use any wire that is flexible enough to be manipulated with bare hands and strong enough to support some clay on it. The wire used here is ordinary copper wire. You will need about 39" (1 m) of wire and a pair of wire cutters.

Always try to use one piece of wire for the whole skeleton to avoid having to make complicated joints between several short pieces of wire. The small scale we are working on permits the use of a single piece of wire, because the wire does not have to be long. Using one piece of wire for the armature is a little like drawing without lifting the pen from the sheet, so you have to carefully plan the sequence of steps, making sure that the two ends of the wire remain loose until you reach the tail of the critter.

▲ **2** We are using relatively soft wire for two reasons. First, it's easy to manipulate, and second, because we can double it by twisting two halves together. Fold the long wire bit in half and, holding it as shown, start twisting it together.

▲ **3** Leave a loop at the end—because you have to (there is nowhere to hold the wire if you want to continue), and because this is where the head will be.

This simple technique of doubling the wire turns out to be priceless when it comes to armature. It allows you to regulate how long or short the double-wire bit will be, and you can also control its hardness and flexibility. The tighter you twist it together, the shorter and stronger the doubled wire will be. Last, but not least, the clay will cling better to an armature that is not as smooth as a single wire would have been had we left it that way.

TIP

About Armature

You don't need to spend too much time perfecting an armature. Armature is only an approximation of a critter's skeleton, not a clinical reconstruction of a skeleton. It is perfectly fine to make a rough and asymmetrical structure, as long as the deviations are small enough to be corrected by the clay coat afterwards.

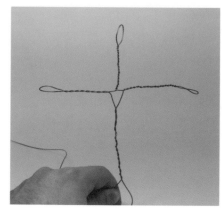

▲ **4** Referring to the photo, make two wings from the wire. Twist the two ends of the wire together below the wings.

▲ **5** Twist the wires of the two wings together to make a cross shape. Leave a little triangle in the middle, and twist the loose ends around each other for the last time.

▲ **6** Cut off the single loose ends of wire, and bend down the head loop and the wings, as shown. You will also need to get rid of the wing loops by squeezing them tightly together, perhaps with the help of a pair of flat-nosed pliers.

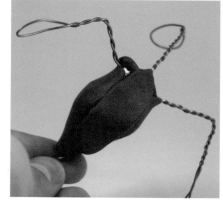

▲ **7** Wrap a piece of tin foil tightly around the central part of the cross to create more volume for the dragon's torso. Using tin foil for the core of the dragon allows us to create volume without creating a heavy mass; the finished critter will be lighter and you will save some clay. Of course, it is perfectly acceptable to use just clay to fill the empty stomach of the dragon if you wish. We are more concerned with appearance than essence—whatever you put inside a critter is acceptable, as long as the façade is pleasing to the eye. (You can leave a message to posterity on a small sheet of paper inside the dragon for when he finally breaks many years from now. It would be like putting a message in a flying opaque red bottle with scales and claws.)

▲ **8** Start covering the torso with clay of the color that you plan to use for the surface of the character.

▲ **9** Proceed in the same way for the limbs, until the whole thing starts looking like a bird of sorts. At this stage, the critter should have a round belly and a tapered tail.

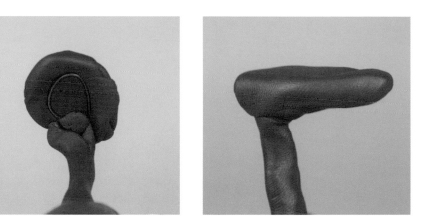

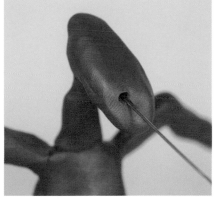

▲ **10** Cover the head loop until the neck and the head start looking like an upside-down boot. Make sure that the "heel" stands out. We will next work on the head—it is much more rewarding to put wings and scales on a critter that already has a face.

▲ **11** Using the needle, poke two nostrils in the upper-front part of the head. Rotate the needle a little to make the nostrils bigger.

▼ **12** Gently squeeze the dragon's muzzle, as shown, right under the nostrils to give them a droplike shape. You should only exert pressure on the upper half of the head, almost on the very surface, rather than squeeze on the sides.

▼ **13** Squeeze the dragon's snout between your index finger and thumb, as shown, to make it pointy. Then bend it down a little bit.

▼ **14** Gently pull while squeezing on the sides of the head to make it a little wider. The underside of the head should be more or less flat.

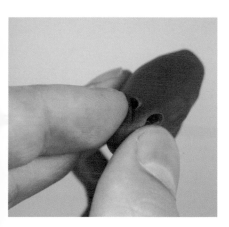

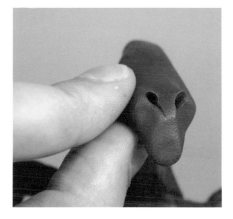

▶ **15** Carefully push down the head while holding the neck with your thumb. This manipulation has two goals: first, it flattens the top side of the head a little bit, and second, it makes it easier to look at the dragon. If the dragon's head were to remain strictly perpendicular to the body an observer would have to rotate the critter (or their own head) to get a full impression of it—they wouldn't be able to see all the important elements of the critter in one glance. When the head is bent down you can see both his head and his body at the same time.

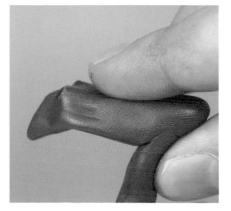

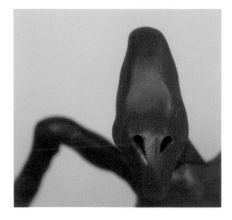

▲ **16** This is what the head looks like thus far.

▲ **17** Stick the tapered-point clay shaper in the nostrils to make them a little wider and to make the outside of the nostril stand out.

▲ **18** Put your finger, as shown, to flare the dragon's nostrils some more.

▼ **19** Use the clay shaper to put two holes in the upper part of the head. These holes will later serve as eye sockets.

We will now work on the wings. Working on different areas of a critter simultaneously can serve as a diversion and have a therapeutic effect—it is not unusual to get slightly bored when you concentrate on one area of a critter for a long time. As soon as you do not feel like dealing with a critter's nose anymore, feel free to turn to its feet, for instance. Remember that the purpose of all this is to have fun, and you should never let critter-making turn into another source of stress.

▲ **20** Attach a thick, flat piece of clay firmly to the wing's arm, as shown.

▼ **21** Start distributing the clay evenly until you fill up the whole space between the tip of the wing and the dragon's ribs. Be careful not to overthin the wing because there is no additional armature support that goes into it. An average thickness of about 1/10" (3 mm) is optimal.

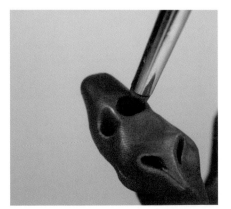

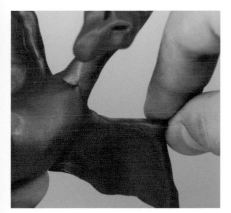

22 Pinch the wing elbow to make it pointier. This is the time to regulate the length of the lower and upper arms of the wing as well. Although there is armature on the inside, the clay that covers it does not need to follow the internal structure closely. Take advantage of this to make adjustments to the shape.

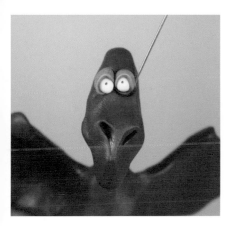

23 Wrap two pieces of glow-in-the-dark clay into orange clay, put them in the eye sockets, and poke two holes in them with the needle to create the dragon's eyes. Next, still using the needle, draw a curved line under each eye to accentuate it.

24 We will next make the lower jaw of the dragon. Start with a flat ellipse, then curve up the sides and form prongs, creating a shape like the one in the picture. Squeeze the two prongs so that they are flat in a direction perpendicular to the rest of the jaw. These prongs will help attach the jaw more firmly to the head.

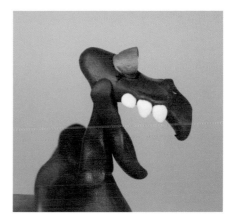

25 Attach the jaw to the dragon's head and to his neck. Now that the dragon's mouth is open, we should start putting teeth in it. Stick several irregularly shaped bits of glow-in-the-dark clay under the dragon's upper lip. The upper teeth should generally point downward, but to make them look jagged you can have them pointing in different directions.

26 Gently push the jaws further apart and insert teeth on the lower jaw. This set of teeth should point outward. We will soon give the dragon a tongue, and if the teeth point upward now, it will be more difficult to insert the tongue into the mouth later.

▲ 27 The tongue is made from a flat piece of light orange clay. Squeeze on the sides to curl it up a little bit. Then put the tongue inside the mouth, and raise the lower jaw teeth to surround it. (See the sidebar on "Adding Clay in Difficult Access Areas," page 225.)

▲ 28 Give the dragon cheeks just like the ones we gave every other critter so far. Remember that the kind of cheeks we use are often mouth corners, too, so make sure to place them at the appropriate spot where the upper and the lower jaws join. Here is what the dragon looks like at this stage.

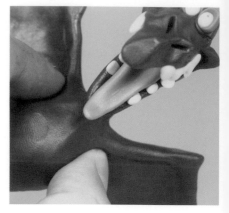

▲ 29 Squeeze the dragon's torso under the armpits so that the rounded belly protrudes even more.

▼ 30 With the tips of your fingers, pinch the lower part of the wings to create a few sharp points. A dragon's wing should look more like a bat's wing than a bird's wing. Two sharp points are enough to create that effect. The distances between these points should be slightly arched.

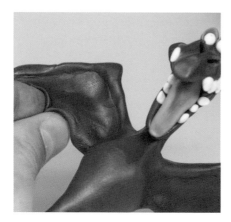 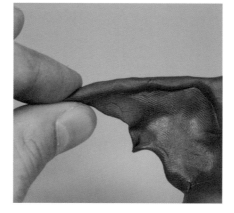

◄ 31 Sharpen the tip of the wings with your index finger and thumb, as shown.

◄ 32 This is what the tapered tail of the dragon looks like at this stage. If it has thinned a lot because you have been holding the dragon by the tail while working on the other parts of his body, you may have to make it a little thicker by wrapping an extra sheet of clay around it and smoothing out the seams with the clay shaper.

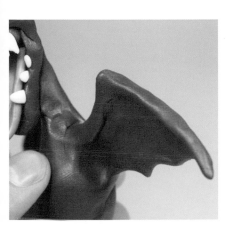

▲ 34 Push with your nail to define the part of the wing that has bones in it (what we have been referring to as the wing's arm). Slightly curve the skin surface of the wing.

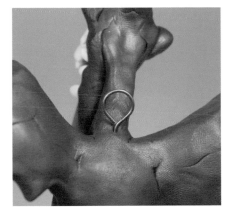

▲ 35 Turn the critter around. To create the suspension mechanism, put a loop of wire in his back. To make this mechanism stronger, you should take the wire bit out before baking the critter. After baking the critter, fill the hole with extra strength glue and stick the wire back in. Don't forget to add the glue because the critter's life will literally hang on a thread.

An alternative way of tackling the suspension mechanism is to make the hanging mechanism from part of the armature cross. It is up to you to determine which option suits you best.

▲ 33 By now you have probably realized that the dragon that we are making will indeed fly. In the next steps we will give him some mechanism by which he can be suspended in the air. There are many reasons for this choice. First of all, flying is an essential dragon characteristic. Second, a nonflying dragon would be more of a dinosaur, especially if you remove his wings (see the "Little Dinosaur" variation). And third, a winged dragon reduced to walking on the ground would look like a reptile and would have very little of the awe-inspiring quality that we are trying to achieve.

For all of these reasons, we will try to make the dragon look as if he is suspended in the air between two flaps of his powerful wings. Two concrete things you can do to achieve this—curve the tail slightly forward and to the side, and curve the lower arm of the wing.

▲ 36 The next series of steps is dedicated to giving our dragon a nice glow-in-the-dark (or white) façade, which will consist of several plates, gradually increasing in size as you go down the belly. Start with the smallest, elliptical plate, and place it on the neck, under the lower jaw.

▲ 37 Gradually increase the size of every following plate, sticking them to the body in such a way that they slightly overlap each other.

▲ 38 To make the legs, start with a chubby worm of clay. With your index finger and thumb, extract four toes, one at a time.

▲ 39 The leg should look like a tree with a thick trunk and four bare branches.

▲ 40 Group three of the little branches together and place the last one (the thumb) opposite them. Slightly bend the tips of the branches of the tree structure inward.

▼ 41 Bend the whole leg in the middle to make the joint, and do not forget to make the knee pointy. Following the same procedures, make one more leg.

▼ 42 Attach the legs to the body, toward the lower part. They shouldn't be hanging loosely in the air, but, rather, pointing up or forward because the dragon makes a physical effort to stay in the air—he is not relaxed.

▼ 43 Use the same technique to make the arms. The only differences are that the dragon's hand has only two fingers, and the arm is a lot smaller than the leg. We are exploiting the familiar theme of the disproportionately small arms of the Tyrannosaurus Rex to produce humorous effect.

▶ 44 Attach the arms to the body at shoulder height and, using a clay shaper, blend them into the body. The upper part of the arm and the elbow should be attached to the torso.

To make the critter more expressive and to create the impression of movement, try not to have both arms or both legs in the exact same position.

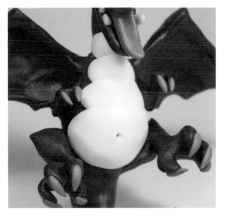

▲ **45** Let's give the dragon some claws. To make a claw from orange clay, roll a short clay worm, and mold one end to a point. Stick the claws firmly on the toes. They should point inward.

▲ **46** In the same manner, proceed with the claws for the hands, only make them a little smaller. Use the needle give the dragon a bellybutton in the center of the biggest and lowest breastplate

▲ **47** By this time, you have probably noticed that it has become increasingly difficult to hold the dragon while you work without affecting another part of it. The problem is that we are not working with a critter who is simply sitting on a large, flat bottom.

Try using the hold in the picture, where your thumb is on the dragon's tail and your index finger (and possibly middle finger) is on his back, between the wings.

▲ **48** Could this be Nessie, the Loch Ness monster?

Relax—this is just a series of triangles (the kind whose sides are not straight lines) that need to go on the dragon's head and back. Make them in different sizes, and make sure that they have one thicker side—the one that will be attached to the dragon's body.

▲ **49** Put two of the larger triangles on the sides of the dragon's head, as shown, until it starts looking like the tail of an airplane. Slightly tip up the very end of these new "wings."

◀ **50** Turn to the back of the critter. On his tail, apply a series of index-and-thumb squeezes along the center of the back of the tail. This zigzag shape that we are introducing will echo the triangles that we will place along the spine.

▲ **51** Place a small triangle on the tip of the tail, which by now should be pointing up. Make sure to strengthen the bond by using a clay shaper and smudge the tip of the tail into the triangle.

▲ **52** Place the little triangles along the dragon's back, down to where the zigzag pattern starts. Use smaller triangles toward the head and the tail, and use gradually larger triangles toward the center.

You have just completed the last stage of the sculpting process.

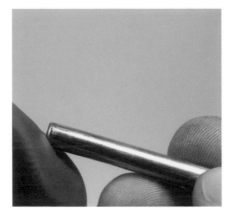

◄ **53** There still remain a few critical steps before we turn this creature into a real dragon. We need to give its skin some texture—a dragon without scales is no dragon.

To make the scales we will use any tool that would leave a circular imprint on the clay. We used a bit from a broken antenna but any other small tube shape, such as a straw, will do.

We will use only half of the tubular tool. Push half of the tube's cross section against the clay as shown to create a semicircle (experiment on a scrap piece of clay to practice). Repeat until you get a whole line of semicircles. Make another line of semicircles right above the first one with a lag of half a semicircle. Continue in this manner until you achieve a texture that looks like scales.

▲ **54** Apply the scale method to the dragon's body. Notice that you do not have to cover each square inch of the dragon with scales to make your point. Irregularly spaced patches of scales can be enough to create the desired effect.

▲ **55** Cover the wing's arm with scales, too, but leave the central part of the wing relatively smooth, so that you can draw in it with the needle to create the impression that the wing has some more sophisticated anatomy. Draw a few lines connecting the lower pointy tips with the wing's elbow.

▲ **56** When putting scales on the face, be particularly careful. If you put too much texture on the face the main facial features will not be as prominent as before. A few unfinished circles here and there will do.

▶ **57** Here is your finished charming monster. One last question remains—how can you bake it without flattening any part of it? You will need to make two cylinders of tin foil, so that the dragon can lie on his back with these cylinders going horizontally between his wings and the triangles in the middle of his back. These cylinders should be big enough to prevent the triangles or any other body part from touching the baking tray.

Bake the dragon following the clay manufacturer's instructions, and let it cool. For more tips on baking, see page 27.

TIP

Adding Clay in Difficult Access Areas

To put a piece of clay in an area where your fingers are too big to reach, use a clay shaper. Stick the bit of clay on the shaper's tip, insert it, push with the clay shaper to fasten it, and then withdraw the tool.

You can also use tools as a mediator when you are trying to get a piece of clay to stay on another piece of clay, but it stubbornly sticks to your finger instead. The fact that the bond between a tool and a bit of clay is much weaker than the one between two pieces of clay will work to your advantage.

The Order of Stickiness

Type of bond:	Strength of bond:
Clay to clay	Strong
Finger to clay	Medium
Tool to clay	Weak

Variation Idea
A Little Dinosaur

Dragons and dinosaurs are not all that different. By using the basic principles of this lesson and simplifying them, you are able to make this green little wingless character whose ancestors roamed the earth millions of years ago. It is nothing more than a small green wingless dragon baby.

One of the most popular fantasy characters is the wizard; usually an old bearded fellow with a pointy hat, a staff, and a magic crystal. Good or evil, wizards always have a lot of personality. This is the image we will try to capture in this lesson. The armature involved is quite simple, and we will practice embedding foreign objects in clay characters. This is the project in which we turn a marble into a magic crystal.

So put on your spell-proof helmet, and let's see what we can conjure up with some clay, a piece of wire, a bit from a chandelier, and an old marble.

MATERIALS

½ sheet flesh or beige clay
(we used Super Sculpey)

⅛ block glow-in-the-dark clay

⅛ block white clay

⅛ block black clay

1 block dark blue clay

1 block light blue clay

½ block red clay

¼ block yellow clay

⅛ block light brown clay

⅛ block dark brown clay

1 marble

1 hexagonal chandelier crystal/glass bead

15 ¾" (40 cm) 0.7 mm copper wire

TOOLS

Small tapered-point clay shaper
Small cup-round clay shaper
Needle or safety pin

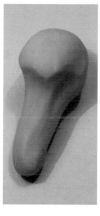

▶ **1** To make a shape like the one shown in the picture, roll a ball of clay and pull on one side of it. The oblong part will be the wizard's neck and the round one his head.

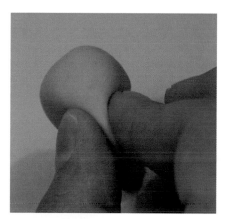

◀ **2** Perform the ingenious index-finger-and-thumb squeeze we have been using all along on the upper part of the head to generate the nose.

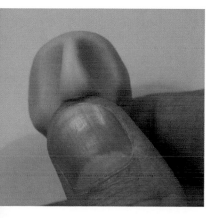

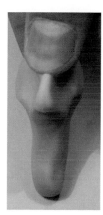

◀ **3** Push with your fingers, as shown, to define the length of the nose. A big nose has become an integral part of most wizard representations. Let's embrace this stereotype and bring it to a new dimension—forward, that is.

(Of course, you can go the nonconformist way and give this wizard a miniature, chipped nose. Then you can do away with the moth-eaten pointy hat and give him a baseball cap. And then you will have made a real wizard—one who has the ability to disappear! But what good is an invisible polymer-clay wizard? Doesn't everyone have tons of them in their closets? As you can see, this is getting slightly surreal, but such is our subject matter. Making a wizard is not for the weak at heart.)

▲ **4** Our goal is to give the wizard a characteristic profile, so from the very first steps, we should make sure that the nose does indeed stand out.

▲ **5** With the tip of the tapered-point clay shaper, make holes for the nostrils. These holes should yield bumps on the outside of the nose.

▼ **7** Behold the nose you have created!

▲ **6** Outline the outer nostrils with the other clay shaper, pushing up with your thumb as shown to give the wizard flared nostrils. Flared nostrils contribute to a more intense facial expression.

▲ **8** Put your fingers on the critter's neck, and push forward and up with your thumb, as shown, to separate the wizard's chin from his neck.

▼ **11** Repeat the above two actions several times to make the face look more wrinkled. Wizards have usually been around for a long time, so it is quite natural for them to carry the marks of their long, interesting lives.

▲ **9** Stick the cup-round clay shaper into the head, and drag some clay down, as shown. The purpose of this move (and the next few) is to make eye sockets and create bags under the wizard's eyes.

▲ **10** Stick the cup-round clay shaper above the newly created shape and repeat the action, only this time, try to capture a larger quantity of clay.

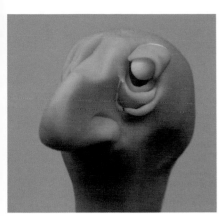

▲ **12** To make an eye, wrap a bead of glow-in-the-dark clay in flesh or beige clay, and place it on top of the uppermost eye bag, as shown. Leave a small hollow between the wrinkle and the eye to add to the magician's old age.

▲ **13** Cover one eye with an additional small piece of clay, on top of the inner part of the upper eyelid, to create the impression that the wizard is scowling.

▲ **14** Cover the other eye, too, only this time pinch the new piece of clay as shown. In doing this, we introduce an important asymmetry in the wizard's face—he looks as if he is raising an eyebrow. Raising an eyebrow is a widespread way of expressing powerful emotion among wizards.

▼ **15** Next, we will make the mouth. Insert the needle deep into the center of the face, right under and at a reasonable distance from the nose, leaving enough room for a big upper lip.

Using the tip of the needle as a lever, draw to one side and then the other to crack a smile on the wizard's face.

▶ **16** Here we used a random metal bit to open the mouth some more and then a clay shaper to widen it.

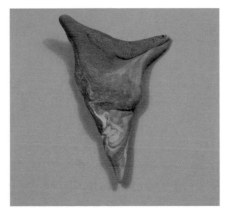

◀ **17** To create the beard, mix equal quantities of black and white clay, but do not knead until the color becomes uniform. We will use the half-mixed color to make a graying beard.

As for the shape of the beard, do not aim for perfection. The triangle you will make need not be perfect. This is only hair, after all, and as you know, hair is difficult to control and keep in order.

Note that the upper side of the beard triangle is a curve, which makes it easier to attach the beard to the face.

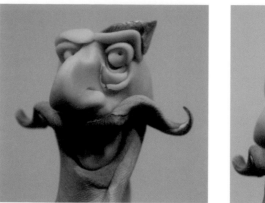

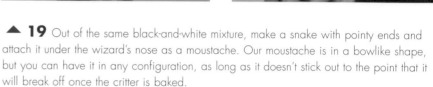

▲ 18 Attach the beard to the face, as shown. Now is also the time to insert a double or triple piece of wire through the neck, all the way into the head of the wizard. We are planning to make a tall critter, and he will need that rod of armature to keep him straight. We do not make any armature for the hands, because they will be close to the body.

▲ 19 Out of the same black-and-white mixture, make a snake with pointy ends and attach it under the wizard's nose as a moustache. Our moustache is in a bowlike shape, but you can have it in any configuration, as long as it doesn't stick out to the point that it will break off once the critter is baked.

Add thick eyebrows, as shown.

▼ 20 To make an ear, start with an irregular disk of clay. Then cut into it with your nail, as shown. Next, make a second cut vertical to the first one. Fold the clay along these cuts, and with your fingers sharpen the upper end of the ear, as shown.

Pointy elements are quite important when it comes to fantasy characters—pointy ears, pointy hats, pointy shoes, pointy fingers, and so on. Experiment with any creature you are making—add some pointy elements and see how it somehow acquires a fairy-tale-like quality.

 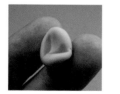

▲ 21 Before you finish the ear, make a small "joint," which will help us fasten it to the wizard's head. Extract this connecting bit out of the ear, as shown.

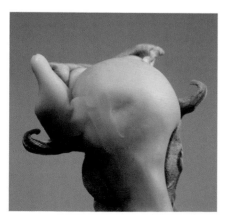

◀ 22 Stick the ear to the side of the head, and, using the tapered-point clay shaper, strengthen the bond.

▶ 23 This is what the ear looks like from the front. Note that it's quite large, relative to the nose.

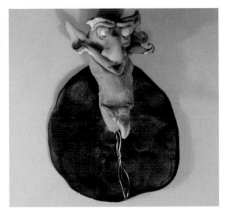

▲ 24 For the body of the wizard, make a thick, flat, elliptical shape of dark blue polymer clay, and place the head on top of it, as shown. To generate the volume of the body, wrap the wire bit and the neck in a dark blue burrito.

◀ 25 When you perform the wrapping procedure described in the previous step, use the top edge of the ellipse to give the wizard a collar. Have the back of the critter's neck stick to the blue "gown" (another word for burrito), but leave the whole collar slightly spread. Squeeze the blue clay tightly around the wire at the very end of the neck so that the flesh or beige clay and the blue clay can form a bond. Needless to say, the beard must be on top of the gown.

The base of the gown should be quite wide so that the wizard will be more stable.

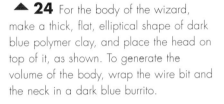

◀ 26 To make a pointy hat, make a cone of dark blue clay by rolling a piece of clay between your palms. Then place the pointy hat on the wizard's head. From the back, the hat should almost touch the collar. Try to cover as much head surface as you can without touching the face. Bend the hat forward a little, if necessary, to restore the critter's weight balance.

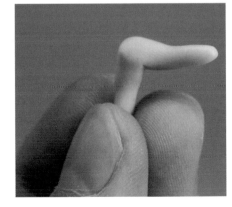

▲ 27 Use your thumb to put a dent on the wizard's torso. This is where you will soon insert the pointy end of a cone, similar to the one you made for the hat, which will be the wizard's sleeve. This time you'll make the cone of lighter blue.

▲ 28 Bend the sleeve into a 60-degree angle, and sharpen the elbow with your index finger and thumb.

▲ 29 Using flesh or beige polymer clay, make finger, like those shown in the picture; they are just rounded-end, right-angled clay worms.

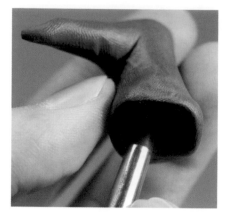

▲ **30** With the tip of a tapered-point clay shaper, dig into the base of the sleeve cone to make a "nest" for the fingers.

▲ **31** Insert the fingers into their nest by sticking two-thirds of the way into the inside of the sleeve, as shown. Notice how the thumb's upper part is slightly curved—this curve, in addition to its opposing position and its relative thickness, distinguishes the thumb from the other fingers. Make the tips of the other fingers a little pointier to increase the distinction between the fingers and the thumb.

▲ **32** Place a small marble in the wizard's hand. If you find a fancy marble, your wizard can only benefit, but even the most standard marbles—with the spirally thing inside—work great, because that spirally thing looks like a flame.

Group the three fingers so that their tips touch.

After baking the critter, apply a small drop of extra-strength glue between the marble—now promoted to a magic crystal—and the sleeve to keep the marble from rotating. The glue also makes the structure firmer.

▲ **33** Next we will make the wizard's staff. A staff is as essential to a wizard as a sword is to a knight.

We used a broken-off piece of a chandelier crystal, but if you don't have one handy, you can use a glass bead with a hole in it. Bend a piece of wire in two, and twist the ends around each other. Then run one of the ends through the hole in the crystal, as shown

▲ **34** Wrap a piece of light brown or gold-colored clay around the wire, and stick it firmly to the crystal. Try to cover the hole through which you ran the wire.

▲ **35** Roll a thin snake of dark brown clay, and squish it flat. Position it next to the double wire that forms the staff's backbone, and wrap the clay tightly around it.

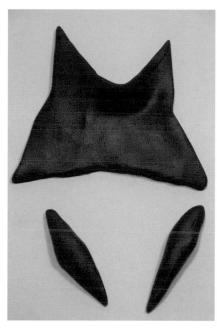

36 Following the instructions for the wizard's left hand, make a right one. Place the staff in it, and wrap the fingers around the staff. Attach the left sleeve firmly to the body. Stick the staff to the outer side of the collar. You can stick the lower end of the staff into the "fabric" of the wizard's gown. The more possible contact points you can create between the wizard and his magical instrument the better, because the figure is less likely to break if it has more support.

37 Using red clay, make a robe for the wizard with a shape roughly similar to that shown in the photograph. The two upper ends are supposed to go around the critter's neck.

Make two longish, pointy loaves of red clay for the critter's feet. Because the wizard is wearing a long robe, only his feet will be visible. Stick the wizard's body on top of the feet. The back of the feet may need to be squished flat by the bottom of the critter to maintain the wizard's balance.

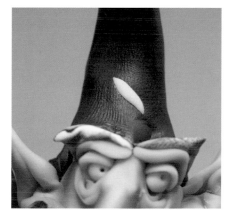

38 Roll out a short, thin yellow snake with sharp ends, and stick it on the wizard's hat, as shown. Flatten it a bit but be careful not to ruin the sharp ends. Then make another tiny yellow snake, and stick it perpendicular to the first one so that they can form a star. Add more evenly spaced stars all over the wizard's robe and hat.

Do not make the snakes too thin because they will look green on the blue surface. When you flatten an overly thin piece of yellow clay on a dark blue surface, the yellow clay becomes almost translucent and, as you may know from basic color theory, blue + yellow = green.

▶ **39** Wrap the two upper ends of the cloak around the wizard's neck, below his collar. The center of the cloak should cling to the back of the wizard. You can play with the ends of the cloak to create the impression that the wizard is standing in the wind.

▼ **40** Use the needle to draw some individual hairs on the wizard's beard, moustache, and eyebrows. Squish a small ball of flesh clay flat, and insert it into the wizard's mouth using a clay shaper. Then, using the needle, inscribe a line in the center of the tongue.

▼ **41** Pinch the wizard's nose one last time to make it pointier.

▼ **42** With the needle, add some finishing touches to the face—draw wrinkles around the eyes, put some marks on the nose.

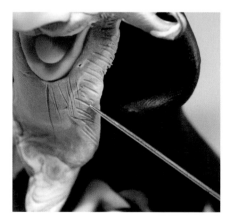

▶ **43** Roll out a small snake of flesh or beige clay, bend it into a moon shape, and attach it as a lower lip with the help of a tapered-point clay shaper. The lower lip makes the tongue appear more realistic.

◀ **44** Point the tips of the wizard's pointy shoes up to give the impression of better self-esteem. Adding a set of upper teeth is likely to produce a similar effect. Add a short snake of glow-in-the-dark clay right under the moustache, without covering the whole mouth, and use a needle to separate the individual teeth from each other, drawing toward the moustache.

◀ **45** Bake the wizard following the clay manufacturer's instructions, and let it cool. To be on the safe side, bake the critter lying on his back. Make cushions of tin foil to make it more comfortable and to prevent his posture from changing while in the oven. For more tips, on baking see page 27.

THE UNICORN'S LESS MAGICAL COUSIN

Or How to Make a Horse

This project provides another armature lesson, in which we will practice working with larger volumes of clay. The skills you will learn while making a horse are transferable to any four-legged character. Should you want to make a unicorn, for instance, all you have to do is make an emaciated white horse and put a horn in the middle of its forehead. If you want to make a tall two-legged critter with a tail, just think of it as a vertical horse.

2 blocks light brown clay
¼ block dark brown clay
⅛ block glow-in-the-dark clay
¼ block white clay
39½" (1m) 0.7 mm copper wire

Wire cutters
Needle or safety pin
Small tapered-point clay shaper
Small cup-round clay shaper

▲ **1** Start with a piece of wire approximately 39½" (1 m) long. As we did in when making the dragon, we will make the armature of the creature from a single piece of wire. Because a horse should ideally have four legs, making its wire skeleton will require a few more steps, but the basic armature principle of the twisted double wire remains the same.

▲ **2** Fold the piece of wire in the center, and twist both ends around each other until you have approximately 4" (10.2 cm) of double wire. This structure will be the neck of our horse. Make sure to leave the loop sufficiently large because it will serve as the armature for the horse's head.

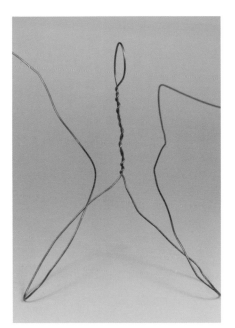

◀ **3** To make a leg, fold one of the two loose ends and twist it until the base of the neck. Once again, make sure to leave a loop at the end, around which we will build the hoof. You can make this loop small if you want your horse to be more graceful, although giving your horse big hooves will make it more solid, especially if it has one leg in the air. Excessively large hooves do not merely play a functional role; they are also essential in making the horse funnier. In this particular project we are going for an amusing horse that has one leg in the air.

Make another front leg.

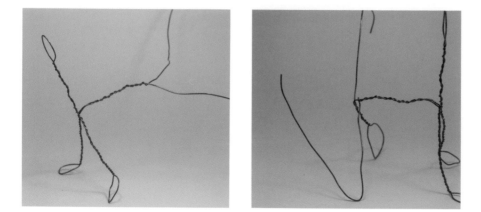

▲ **4** Twist the wires perpendicular to the neck and the front legs, working toward the rear legs. When you reach the desired length of this "spinal cord," bend the two loose ends down, fold them it half, and twist them back up to the horse's lower back.

▲ **5** We have left the loose ends sticking out to illustrate the fact that we do not use any additional wire for the armature. The main structure is finished now; the only remaining bit is the tail. To make the tail, twist the two ends around each other for the last time, and snip off the remaining single wire.

Raise one of the front legs, and bend it at the knee and at the ankle. This is a typical horse pose. (This could be a basic dog's pose, too. Consider making a dog based on the same armature as a possible extension of this project.)

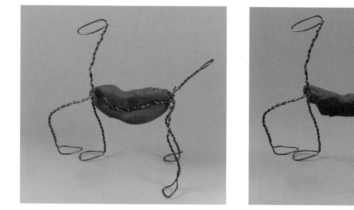

▲ **6** Once the armature is complete, we need to cover it. We will use just clay to create the volume of the horse. You can also use tin foil, especially if you are running short of clay or just want to make your horse lighter.

Using a piece of light brown clay, and proceed as shown.

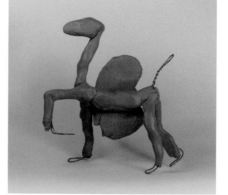

◀ **7** In the same way, proceed with the other body parts, covering them with a first layer of clay. Bear in mind that the horse's torso should be somewhat thicker than his limbs. Repeat with a second, thick layer. Cover the head, too, using an oblong piece of clay that is slightly thinner toward the front and thicker toward the back.

8 The aspiring horse will look like an ostrich unless you make his neck thicker, too.

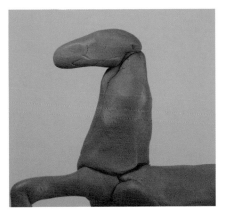

9 After all this covering with clay, the horse is a little flat and lacking in volume. To correct this and create the characteristic horse look, we will use the simplest geometrical shape—the circle. Out of several balls of clay, squish a few disks—four big ones for the horse's shoulders and hind legs, two medium ones for his cheeks, and two small ones for his nose. Stick these disks on both sides of the horse, as shown.

Ideally, these disks should be thicker in the center and thinner around the edges so that you can more easily blend them with their surroundings.

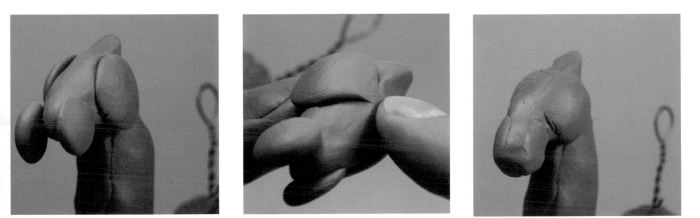

10 In this close-up of the head you can see why horses run so fast—clearly it is because their heads are apparently made of sports cars! Whether you find this logic compellingly persuasive or not, you will have to "hide" the car in the horse's head. To do this, gently smooth the periphery of the disk into the surrounding clay with your fingertip.

Pinch the back of the head with your index finger and thumb to create the impression of ears. We will add real ears later, but sometimes having a dummy body part on a critter helps you better see the direction in which things are going.

▲ ◀ 11 Apply the same smoothing technique to the other four disks. You will most probably end up with something that looks like the corner photo.

Notice that the hind legs bend backwards—it is as if this horse is actually a carnival costume with two men in it, men with huge knees. To avoid that illusion, just turn the horse's knee around. Now it looks as if it bends forward, which is somewhat closer to the true anatomy.

▲ 12 Here is what the horse looks like from the back. You can clearly see the shoulder volume and the volume of the buttocks, which was obtained by wrapping the disks around the previous thinned version of the horse.

◀ 13 At this stage, you need to make the horse's knees stand out. Tightly squeeze the clay above and below the wire inside the knees to make them more prominent.

▲ ▶ **14** To give the horse hooves, wrap a chunk of light brown clay around the wire feet to create a funnel. The hooves should have a rough, conical shape, the tip of which merges in the legs.

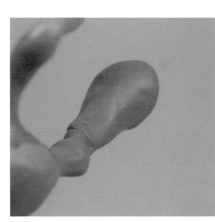

▲ **15** It's time for another round of smoothing and blending. The disks you used for the horse's buttocks need to make one whole with the thin leg that was there before. Use a clay shaper to remove seams and smooth the areas that are hard to reach.

▲ **16** To ensure the horse is stable, make sure that when you look straight from the back though the hind legs of the horse the front supporting leg is more or less in the middle.

A horse standing on three legs may seem a little less stable on a level surface, but, in fact, it is more stable because, according to basic geometry, any three points can lie in one plane, while any four points cannot. This is also why photographers use tripods instead of quadripods.

▲ **17** To correct problems, such as irregular distribution of clay and overthinned legs, use small, flat pieces of clay to create volume layer by layer. Ideally, you should use as few layers as you can, because you'll run a lower risk of ending up with a critter that looks like patchwork. The best way to merge additional layers with the whole is with your fingertips. The finger method also ensures that the shape that you are building on and the shape that you are adding will have the same texture.

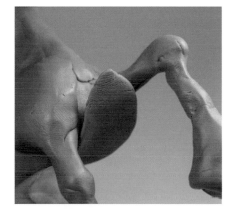

◀ **18** Add a new layer to the breast of the horse to make it look more powerful. That new layer should also be thicker in the middle with thinner edges.

▲ **19** A natural way of holding the horse while you work is by the torso (index finger on the back, thumb on the belly, or vice versa). Unfortunately, this grip is likely to have flattened it excessively. Add another thick layer to the horse's belly to make it a bit more swollen.

▶ **20** Wrap a piece of dark brown clay around the protruding wire tail. Fasten the clay part of this new tail firmly to the body, and arch it a bit. Hold the back of the horse's neck between your index finger and thumb, and with a series of short pinching moves, arch it a bit, too.

▲ **21** Use your fingernail to separate the hoof from the leg.

◀ **22** Now is the time to make sure that all of the hooves are the same size. Cut from the ones that are slightly bigger, and add to the ones that are smaller.

▶ **23** Back to the head. Fill the hollows between the horse's cheeks and under his nose with two small pieces of clay, using the tapered-point clay shaper to blend them with the rest of the head.

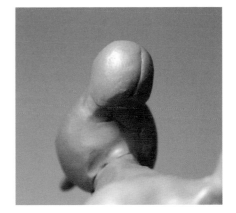

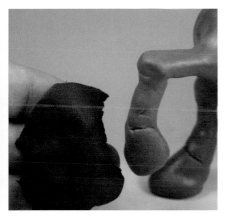

◀ **24** Make a thin, wide sheet of dark brown clay with which to cover the hoof. You may ask: "But why didn't we make the hooves out of dark brown clay in the first place?" Because we didn't think of it at the time. It is often impossible to plan everything in advance, so you have to make up things as you go. The most painless approach here is to cover the hoof with a thin layer of a different color, rather than take it out completely and replace it with a new one.

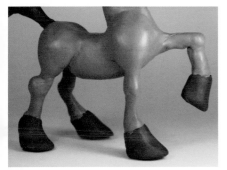

▲ **25** Our horse finally has shoes. Not horseshoes, though—only domesticated horses have horseshoes, and ours is a proud wild stallion. Besides, making horseshoes would be like nit-picking, so we'll leave that for the extra-zealous readers.

▲ **26** With the tip of your finger, smudge a little bit of the light-brown clay from the leg over the hoof. Make sure there are no air bubbles under the thin layer of dark brown clay. If there are any, poke a hole in them with the needle, and then gently press to flatten the bubble. Don't forget to cover the little hole.

▲ **27** Here is a general rear view of the horse. Note that his belly should be visible, as it is in the picture.

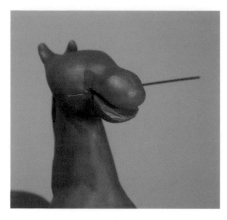

▲ **28** Add a band of dark brown clay along the back of the neck to give the horse a mane. Squeeze repeatedly with your index finger and thumb to attach it to the neck.

▲ **29** Open the mouth of the horse using a cutter blade or a needle.

▲ **30** Create holes to mark the prospective spots for the nostrils and the eyes. The eyes are usually wider apart than the nostrils.

◀ **32** Fill these holes with two beads of glow-in-the-dark clay. We didn't use eyelids this time, for a change, but you can always add them. The result is a horse with a less intense expression.

We also drew a few hairs on the forehead to experiment, but you won't see them in later steps.

▲ **31** Now, using the back of the clay shaper handle, make two holes into the head on top of the marks you created with the needle in the previous step.

◀ **33** Use the needle to underline the eye of the horse, as shown.

▶ **34** Remove the two dummy ears, and poke two holes in their place where you will next insert the real ears.

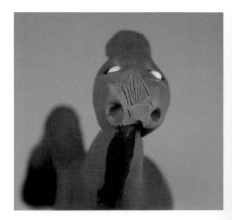

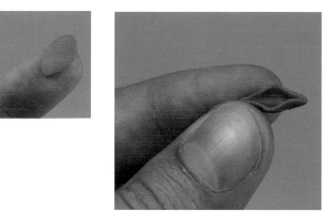

▲ **35** To make an ear, start with a small elliptical shape, and fold its ends until it starts looking like a boat.

▲ **36** Then insert the new ears in their respective holes, making sure they are well attached to the head. Continue the mane all the way to the forehead. Also widen the upper part of the nostrils, and make them slightly oblong.

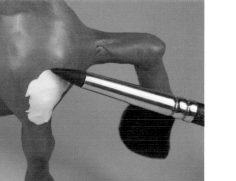

▲ **37** Fill the horse's mouth with tiny balls of clay, similar to the ones you used for the eyes. They will eventually become slightly rectangular as you push them. The lines you see going from the eyes down to the nose are another feature you can add.

▲ **38** Here is the head at this stage.

▲ **39** It's time to give this horse some pizzazz. Create some irregular, extra-thin patches of white clay (not glow-in-the-dark, but the opaque white), and distribute them here and there on the horse's body. Then, with a rolling motion of the tapered-point clay shaper, level the edges of the white patches. The white spots shouldn't stand out above the surface.

◀ **40** We thought it would be smart to put a white spot on the horse's forehead. Be careful not to overuse the small white patches, though—a horse is not the negative of a giraffe, nor does he have a skin condition.

◀ **41** Use the needle to draw some hairs on the horse's tail and on his hair. Notice the distribution of white patches we chose for the back of the horse.

42 Here is your finished beast of burden, er, I mean...noble animal!

Bake the horse a little longer than the clay manufacturer's instructions require at the appropriate temperature because a lot of clay went into this critter.

Variation Ideas
Mythical Unicorn
Making a unicorn is a direct and natural extension of the horse project, as we said earlier. Just remember to put a piece of wire in the horn.

Relaxing Giraffe
Four-legged animals need not always be standing up. Here is an example of how to make a giraffe sitting down in an almost human pose, using minimum armature. Notice how all his legs and tail are close to the body to minimize the potential risk of breaking.

THE MEDITATING SKELETON

What the skeleton we will learn how to make in this project does best is meditate—the process of going out into the woods, sitting under a tree for seven years, and doing nothing but thinking. Our skeleton's power of concentration is so amazing that he even glows at night! Of course, that might have more to do with the glow-in-the-dark clay we will exclusively use in this project rather than with the skeleton's brainpower.

We will learn first how to make a skull, and then we will explore the possible ways of combining bones into a body. Skeletons can be thought of as jigsaw puzzles, made up of hundreds of parts that need to be put together. Our concern, however, is with a more stylized skeleton, almost made of flesh and blood, so we will merge many of these puzzle bits together.

POLYMER CLAY ART

1 block glow-in-the-dark clay
3" (7.6 cm) 0.7 mm copper wire
1 miniature straw hat (optional)

Small tapered-point clay shaper
Needle or safety pin
Wire cutters

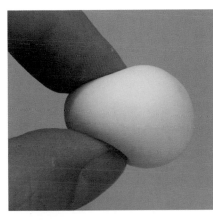

1 Make an egg shape or simply a ball by rolling a piece of clay between your palms. We used glow-in-the-dark clay because it has a nice bone color during the day. When you bake it really well (even if it turns slightly yellowish), it contributes to the true bone look of the skeleton.

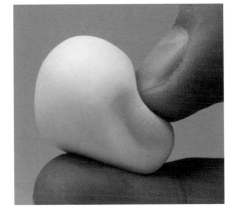

2 Squeeze half of the ball between your index finger and thumb, as shown. Refer to the picture to see the dents your fingers are supposed to leave on both sides of the skull. The idea is that a skull consists of an upper part—the cranium—which is round with a larger volume and a lower part—under the cheekbones and down to the lower jaw—which is more rectangular and generally narrower. We are now working on separating these two parts.

3 Push with your thumb on the back of the skull toward where the face will be. Exert counterpressure on the future face with your index or middle finger. You can use both hands if you find it easier. Just be sure to push with your thumb in a direction perpendicular to the face.

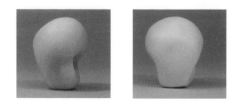

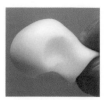

5 After the first couple of steps, the side and front views indicate that the lower, square part of the skull should lie not directly under the upper round one but aligned on one side.

4 This is a view of the back of the skull. Notice the marks that your thumbnail left during the previous step. You can also clearly see the two shapes starting to form—the wider upper part and the smaller, square lower part.

6 This series of steps is aimed at sharpening the distinction between the lower "box" and the upper "ball" that make up the skull. With the tips of your index finger and thumb, gently squeeze each edge of the lower jaw to make it sharper.

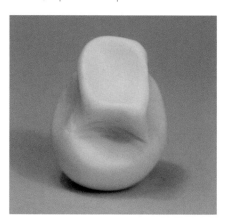

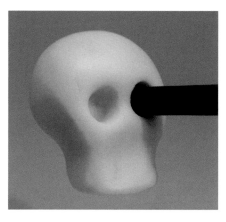

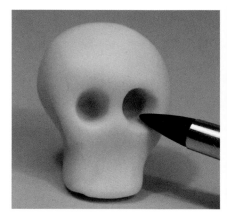

7 When you turn the skull upside down, the general box and ball distinction should be more or less visible. Right in front of you once again is the mark your thumbnail left on the back of the critter.

8 Using the clay shaper's handle, make two holes in the lower part of "the ball" for the eye sockets. These holes should be quite deep.

9 Use the tapered-point clay shaper, and, with a rotating motion, smooth the lower edges of the eyes sockets toward the cheekbones.

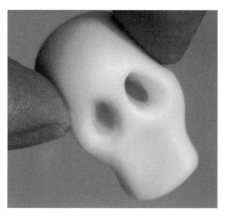

10 To make the temples, squeeze the forehead very gently between your index finger and thumb. Be careful to preserve the volume of the back of the head.

This move should have helped the cheekbones stand out.

11 Push down on the side of the eye sockets to make the cheekbones even more prominent.

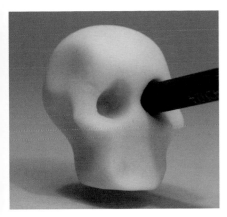

▲ **12** Stick the clay shaper handle into the eye sockets again to make them round—the previous procedures have probably distorted them somewhat. Notice this action's result on the cheekbones.

▲ **13** Drive the needle deep into the clay, and draw an inverted "V" to make the nose of the meditating skeleton. Think of it as writing—you need to go from left to right, without extracting the needle.

We are using only one color of clay for this project, so to shape the critter, we have to rely on the contrasts that occur when we create volume and draw in the clay. This is why we made the eye sockets, a few steps ago, and the nose so deep.

▲ **14** Make two balls of glow-in-the-dark clay small enough to sink to the bottom of the eye sockets.

A skull is by definition a scary dead head, but in this project the objective is to make a skull that defies that definition, a skull that looks alive and funny. Therefore, you have to give it real eyeballs to fill the hollows in his head. (Think of it as a biological paradox, just like the belly button of the bird.)

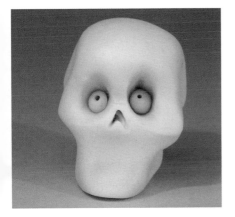

▲ **15** Insert the eyeballs into the sockets, and poke a hole in each one with the needle. You can also stick the ball on the tip of the needle first and then put it into the eye socket. Either way the result should be the same.

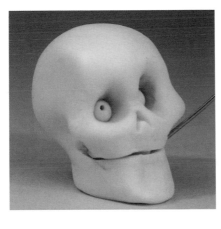

▲ **16** Skeletons have a reputation of always smiling. No doubt it must be easier for them. To allow our skull live up to the conventional standards, draw a huge smile on his face, starting from the side, as shown.

▲ **17** Make a mouth corner/cheek, just like the ones you made for the majority of the projects so far. This time, the mouth corner should be quite small to preserve the "ball and box" distinction. Add the corners to the skull.

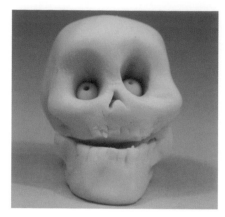

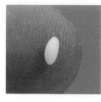

18 Use the pin to open the mouth a bit, and draw vertical lines on the upper and lower jaws to create the impression of teeth.

19 Make a couple of small grains of clay, as shown, and randomly add them to the lower and upper jaws. Our skull, perfect in every other respect, will have a couple of missing teeth.

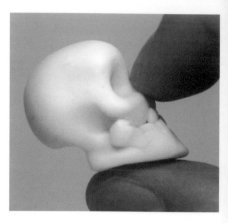

20 To give the skull a nicer profile, carefully push with your fingernail above the nose and between the eyes.

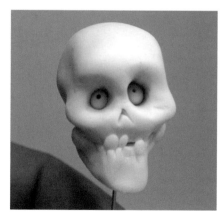

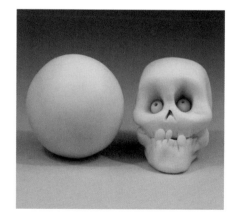

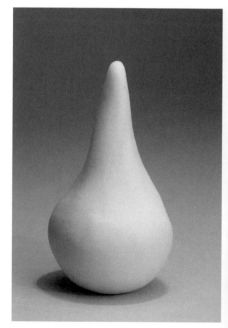

21 Here is the finished skull after the sculpting phase. Notice how the irregularly positioned teeth, the needle marks, and the actual clay bits complement each other to create the dental impression. Pinch the skull's chin to make it pointier.

22 Skeletons are often said to be quite skinny. This, however, need not always be the case, and for this project you will learn how to make a fellow with a belly. For a start, roll a ball slightly larger than the skull.

23 Rolling the ball between your fingers to elongate one end until the ball resembles a bulb. The tapered end will be the neck of the skeleton and the lower round end the torso.

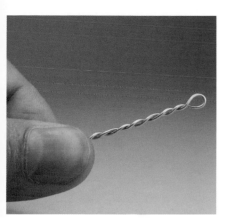

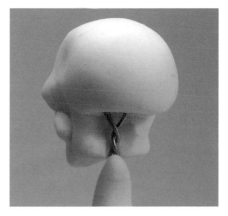

🔺 **24** To create the armature, bend 3" (7.6 cm) of wire in two, and twist both ends around each other.

🔺 **25** Stick the armature bit in the skeleton's body where the neck starts, and push it into the clay along the height of the neck. The loop of the armature bit should be on top; it will go into the skull.

🔺 **26** Cover the wire with the surrounding clay, leaving just the loop and the first twist naked. Carefully push the skull onto the wire neck until the wire disappears and the clay of the neck touches the lower jaw and the bottom of the cranium. Use the clay shaper to strengthen the clay joints between the skull and the neck.

🔻 **27** Here is the skeleton's profile so far.

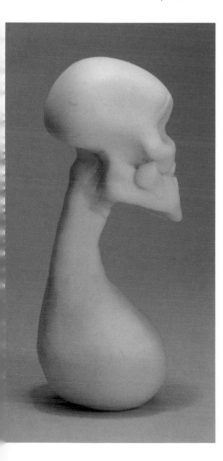

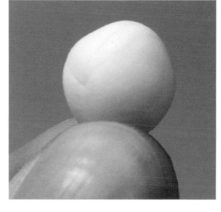

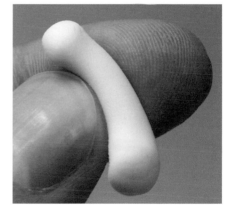

🔺 **28** Now that you have the torso and the head, you need some limbs. To have some limbs, you need some bones. To have some bones, you will need to make them, starting with a small ball of glow-in-the-dark clay.

🔺 **29** Roll the clay back and forth between your index finger and thumb until you have a shape with two "heads." To achieve such a shape, just hold the ball by the equator while rolling. You may find it easier to roll with the side of your fingertips rather than the center.

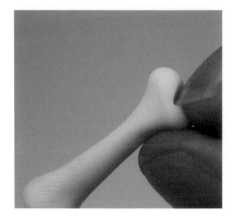

▲ **30** With the tip of your nail, cut into the oval end, as shown.

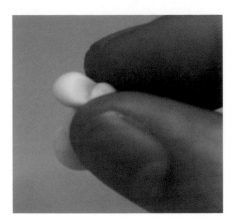

▲ **31** Holding the bone vertically, carefully squeeze the part that was just under your nail, not with the intention of flattening it but to restore the original width of the shape, which was slightly increased in the previous step.

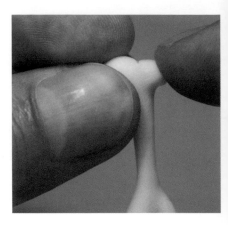

▲ **32** Holding the bone horizontally, push down a bit on one of the joints.

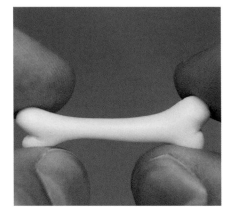

▲ **33** Here is the finished bone. You can gently pull on both ends to make it longer, but be careful because doing this will make the bone thinner as well. Proceed similarly with the rest of the bones.

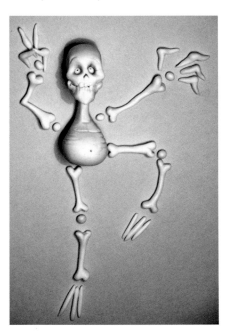

▲ **34** The first specimen of this type of skeleton was found after long and reluctant archaeological excavations somewhere very far away. The pose in which he was found suggests that he must have had interests other than meditation, for he was found in a ballet position, making a victory sign with his right hand. Nevertheless, scientists were able to decipher the map of his body and reconstruct him to the last detail.

We will use that same map to make our skeleton. Apparently, we need, all in all, six bones, six toes, eight fingers, two balls for the kneecaps, two for the shoulders, and two for the wrists.

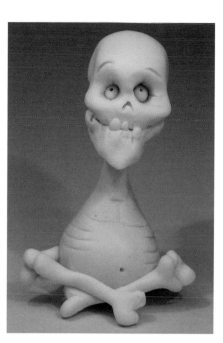

35 The skeleton will be sitting cross-legged in a typical meditative position. Firmly attach two of the bones to the body, as shown. The back end of the rear leg bone should be sticking to his bottom. The middle of that bone should be attached to the side of his body, and the other end should be attached to the front leg bone. The front leg bone's middle is attached to the critter's belly. Try to have as much contact surface between the bones and the body as possible, so that the skeleton will be less likely to break.

36 Repeat the same steps for the other leg. This time, the front leg bone is attached to the belly and to the front leg bone of the other leg.

At this point we were tempted to give the skeleton ribs, a belly button, and a chest, as well as eyebrows, using the needle. This drawing stage can take place at any moment of the critter-building process, although it usually comes last.

37 To add feet to the skeleton, first connect the three toes of each foot together, and then stick them to the lower ends of the front leg bones and under the knees, as shown. Once again, try to maximize the contact surface.

38 This is the index finger and thumb of the skeleton's hand. Stick their tips and bases firmly together. You will next attach them to the arms of the skeleton, for which we have already made the bones.

39 The arm of the skeleton is a bone that is simply bent in the middle and attached at shoulder height. It should follow the torso, with the forearm resting on the skeleton's thigh. The wrist should almost rest on the knee.

Attach the combination of index finger and thumb that you just made to the back of the skeleton's hand, as shown.

40 Turn the critter around, and add the other fingers, paying meticulous attention to how well they are attached to the bones of the hand and the knees. Because we do not use any armature for the arms and legs, it is to be expected that the fragile skeleton would not survive a nosedive from your work surface to the floor. However, we still have to ensure that the skeleton's parts do not come off in the morning breeze.

Add the small balls of clay for the kneecaps, the foot joints, and one of the shoulders. Leaving the other shoulder without a small ball makes the skeleton appear as if not all of his parts were found, which makes a more credible critter.

41 Trace the backbone using the clay shaper.

44 The last thing to do when making a skeleton is to turn off the lights to see if he has reached the desired level of enlightenment from his meditation practices.

Bake the character following the clay manufacturer's instructions, and let it cool. For more tips on baking, see page 27.

42 Use the needle to add a cosine graph on the skeleton's skull. Also, outline his eyebrows again, and draw two fine lines under his eyes.

43 In this optional step, weave a miniature straw hat, and place it on the skeleton's head after you have baked him.

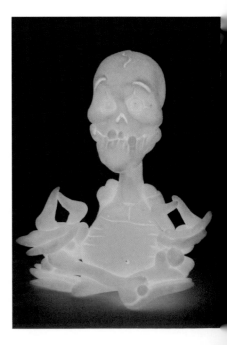

TIP

Regular White Eyeballs
To achieve a different glow-in-the-dark effect, you can make regular white clay eyeballs. Then two dark holes for the skull's eyes will appear when you turn off the lights.

Variation Ideas
Bird Skeleton
This chubby bird skeleton is largely made following the bird lesson. The only alterations are the use of glow-in-the-dark clay, the creation of deep eye sockets, and the use of a structure similar to that of the skeleton's feet for the wings.

Quadruped Animal Skull
Animal skulls are generally more elongated and have other bony bits protruding from their surface, such as horns. Prominent cheekbones and excessively large teeth are a must. You can also put two holes in the upper part of the forehead to make ear sockets.

Skeleton with a Ball and Chain
Making a skeleton with a ball and chain is a natural extension of the skeleton project. Creating the ball and chain is essentially the same process as the one we used to make the knight's mace. Be sure that the leg bone to which the chain is attached is a little thicker, because it will have to host the wire attachment.

Ghoulish Gang

Whether Santa is an imaginary character or a real one has long been a subject of debate. In my opinion, he is the only *real* creature I could not resist including in this book.

The Santa character is made exclusively of clay—no armature and no embedded objects go into him. You will learn how to make a generic Santa, complete with a red coat, a Christmas tree, and a present, but if you are creating him in the middle of July, feel free to give him a pair of shorts and flip-flops.

MATERIALS

1 block red clay
½ block flesh or beige clay
⅛ block glow-in-the-dark clay
1 block white clay
¼ block dark green clay
⅛ block brown clay
¼ block yellow clay
⅛ block pink clay

TOOLS

Small tapered-point clay shaper
Small cup-round clay shaper
Needle or safety pin

▲ **1** Red polymer clay is the messiest color of them all. The pigment in the red clay tends to color your fingers when knead it, and unless you are working next to the sink and washing your hands every two seconds, you are likely to leave red fingerprints all over the other light-colored polymer clays you use. It is strongly recommended that you first complete the red bits of the character and then move on to all the rest.

Start with a ball of red clay that will form the body of Santa.

▲ **2** With your thumb, press on the upper end of the ball to create a shape like the one in the photograph. The head will soon lie here; the thin, elongated upper end will be the collar of Santa's coat. The round part will be his belly.

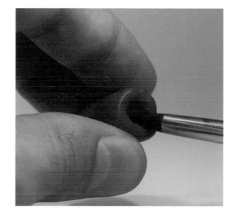

3 Make three conical shapes of red clay. Two of them, the arms, should have a smaller base, be slightly higher, and be bent in the middle. The third one, for the hat, should be straight and somewhat shorter, with a larger base.

◄ **4** With a rotating movement, use the tapered-point clay shaper to make holes in the bases of the arms. We will insert the fingers in these holes later.

You can wash your hands now; we are done with the red clay for the moment.

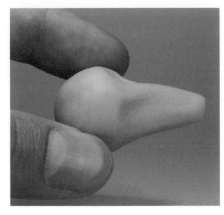

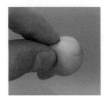

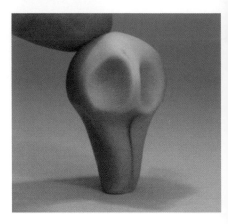

▲ **5** Roll a ball of flesh or beige clay a little bit smaller than the one you made for the body. Then, holding it with the fingers of your left hand, as shown, pull on one of the ends to elongate it.

▲ **6** This is roughly the shape you should have obtained after the last step. The round part will be the head, and the long, narrow part will be the neck, which will serve two functions—first, it will provide a holding place while you are working on the face, and second it will connect the critter's body to the head.

▲ **7** Perform an index-finger-and-thumb squeeze on the head to start extracting the nose. Make sure there is a fair amount of clay between your fingers, because Santa should ideally have a big nose. The line going from the end of the nose that you see in the picture is unintended, but we will not bother to remove it.

▼ **8** After the vertical squeeze, make a horizontal one. Then, using the nose as an axis, rotate the head, making a series of short squeezes, until you get a shape like this one.

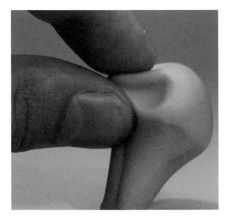

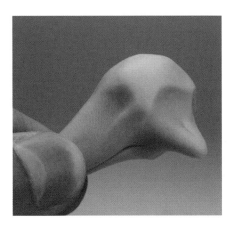

▼ **10** Push horizontally until your thumbnail defines the lower end of the nose

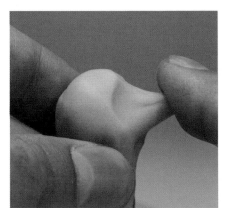

◀ ▲ **9** Clearly, if the nose keeps up its expansion, our critter will look more like Pinocchio than Santa. Push the nose back to make it rounder and bulkier.

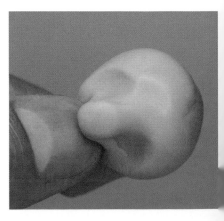

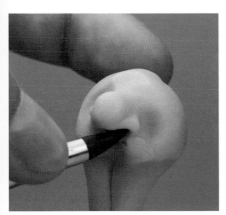

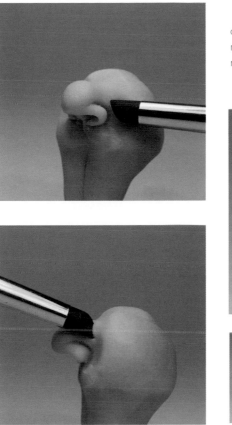

▲ **11** A nose, as we have seen before, traditionally consists of a protruding bit, the holes of the nostrils, and the outer nostrils. Here, as usual, we take care of the nostrils in one step. Stab the protruding bit with the tip of the tapered-point clay shaper, as shown, to generate the inner and outer nostrils.

◀ **12** Add a finishing touch on the outside of the nose with the tip of the cup-round clay shaper, making the nostrils more prominent. Consider the nose done.

▲ **13** Using the round-cup clay shaper, prepare the ground for the eyes, as shown. Repeat this action to make the ripples of clay for the bags under the eyes.

▼ **14** Using the clay shaper's handle, open wide the critter's mouth. Don't worry, he won't be screaming the whole time—just until we give him a beard and moustache. Make two eyes of glow-in-the-dark polymer clay wrapped in flesh or beige clay, and insert them in their appropriate places.

▼ **15** A beard is actually made of a white croissant. To make the croissant, use off-white clay rather than sparkling white to minimize the risk of red fingerprints showing (see tip on page 266 for directions on making off-white clay). The croissant should have some volume.

▲ **16** To make the moustache, roll a snake of clay, making the middle thinner than the rest. This part will go under the nose, and we want Santa to be able to breathe.

▲ **17** Attach the beard to the head, with the ends of the croissant pointing up.

▲ **18** Then add the moustache, curving the ends around the cheeks. You may have to adjust the thinness of it.

▼ **19** With the tips of your index finger and thumb, gently squeeze, as shown, to create the pointy ends of the moustache. Then push with your thumb on the sides of the face to make the cheeks stand out. The moustache and beard are just hair that covers the face and should, therefore, follow some general facial features, which is why we still need to create a volume that can be interpreted as cheeks. Finally, push the croissant toward the nose to close the mouth.

▼ **20** To make the ears, take a small bit of clay, as shown, and fold it in half.

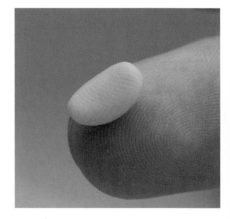

▶ **21** Attach the ear to the head, and using the tapered-point clay shaper, blend the upper part of the ear into the side of the head. The head is mostly done now, and we will return to the costume.

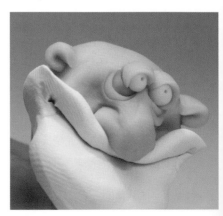

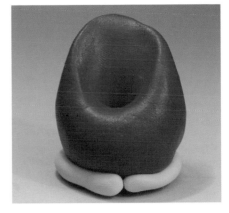

▲ **22** Using the clay shaper's handle, make a hole in the body where you will put the head. Hold the body with your left hand while making the hole with your right one.

▲ **23** Using your right hand, roll a snake of white clay with round ends to decorate the lower part of the coat. All these right hand/left hand instructions can help you avoid leaving red fingerprints and making fewer trips to the sink. If you are left-handed, just do the reverse, making sure to use different hands for the red and white clays.

▲ **24** Wrap the white snake around the lower edge of the coat, as shown, until the two ends meet at the front. If the white touches the working surface, Santa will appear to be wearing a long coat. If the white snake is at the "equator" of the belly, it will seem as if he is wearing some sort of pants.

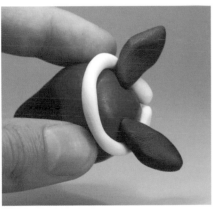

▲ **27** Now for the Christmas tree. Using dark green polymer clay, make a big disk, a medium disk, and a small base cone. The two little green balls will be the "stairs" between the different "floors" of the Christmas tree.

▲ **26** Attach the head to the body, putting the neck into the hole you made. If the neck is too long to fit, you may have to shorten it. So far, we have a Santa with a body and a head. We just need to give him arms. He needs arms to hold stuff, but we need to put that stuff on first and then put the hands around it.

▲ **25** Make two loaves of brown clay for the feet, and attach them to the body, as shown. The feet should be apart, because they will serve as props for the objects Santa will be holding.

▲ **28** Squeeze the two disks repeatedly while rotating them, as shown, to give them an irregular shape. Your squeezes should not overlap each other. Do the same to the base of the cone.

▲ **30** To complete the tree, make a hole on the bottom of the big disk, and insert a small brown polymer clay peg in it. The trunk of the tree has a purely functional role to play—it will not be too visible on the outside, but it will help fasten the tree to the body.

▲ **29** The idea, as you have probably already guessed, is to build the Christmas tree layer by layer: layer one, the big disk; layer two, the medium disk; layer three, the small base cone. To connect the layers, add one of the small green balls between each layer.

▲ **31** Stick the lowest layer of the tree above the white snake on Santa's coat, making sure to achieve maximum contact surface. The trunk should end up at the corner where the foot joins Santa's bottom.

▲ **32** Use the clay shaper's handle to make a hole at shoulder height where you will soon put the arm holding the tree.

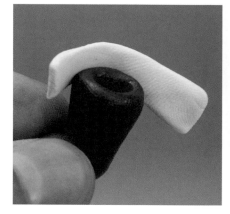

▲ **33** Wrap a flat, rectangular white sheet of clay around one of the prefabricated arms to make a cuff. Make sure that the two ends of the white cuff are close to each other.

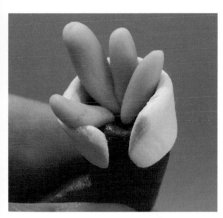

▲ **34** Roll three short, chubby clay worms for the fingers and one for the thumb, and insert them in the sleeve, as shown, fastening them to the white and the red clay simultaneously.

▲ **35** Attach the arm to the body, as shown. Each finger should rest on the tree, and the upper part of the arm should stick to the torso.

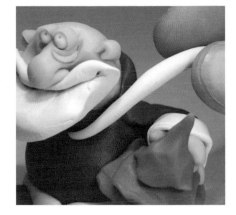

▲ **36** Let's give Santa a white collar. Roll a white snake with two pointy ends long enough to wrap around the critter's neck. Add it to the neck, starting from the front, as shown.

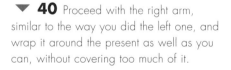

◄ **38** Roll a very thin snake of pink polymer clay, and wrap it around the box, as shown. Press on it lightly until it flattens. Do the same in the perpendicular direction, so that the pink ribbon forms a cross on the top of the present.

▲ **37** Santa usually carries a big bag full of presents for everyone, but our Santa will have a more personal approach—he'll be carrying just one present, for you. Make a cube of yellow polymer clay. If your cube does not have straight lines, don't bother to straighten them; you can always blame it on the wrapping paper.

▼ **39** Attach the packed present to the body and the foot.

▼ **40** Proceed with the right arm, similar to the way you did the left one, and wrap it around the present as well as you can, without covering too much of it.

41 The making of the hat is very much like the making of the arms. Wrap a piece of white clay around the wide end and set it on the head. In the picture you can see we played with the position of the tip of the hat. Give Santa a nice big white pom-pom on the end.

This is also the step in which you add the buttons to Santa's coat. Draw a line with the needle to indicate where the coat is buttoned. Then put several white disks of clay along that line. Push lightly with the clay shaper's handle in the center of each disk to form a small circular dent, and poke four buttonholes in a square formation in the center of each button.

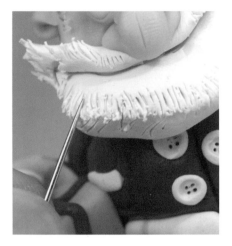

42 Use the tip of the needle to draw hairs on the beard and the moustache. You can draw the hairs on the edges of the beard to create a fuzzy impression.

This is also the time to draw wrinkles near the bottom-outer corners of the eyes. Add corners to the mouth and eyebrows on the white band of the hat. Draw a pocket on the coat, next to the present, and put a white bit on top of it to create the impression of an elaborate costume. Make some vertical marks on the Christmas tree, and draw a patch in the very center of the hat.

You are almost finished. The last thing to do is to decorate the Christmas tree—just put small, multicolored clay balls all over it. Bake Santa following the clay manufacturer's instructions, and let him cool. For more tips on baking, see page 27.

TIP

Off-White and Sparkling White

To make an off-white color for the beard, you can mix some flesh or beige clay with some sparkling white clay. The flesh or beige clays do not have enough pigment to drastically change the white color, but they can mute it a little bit.

The Universal Hat of Santa

This is probably obvious, but you can put small red-and-white Santa hats on all the ordinary critters you didn't give away before the start of the Christmas season to turn them into very appropriate Christmas gifts.

Variation Ideas
The Christmas Tree Has Had Enough

Now that you know how to make a Christmas tree, you just need to give it a face, some arms, and an ax to make it come to life. When making the trunk, use a cone with a wider base rather than a cylindrical shape so that your tree can stand firmly on its feet. We use short pin as armature for the ax's handle.

A More Earthly Santa

To make a Santa with some real purchasing power, place a coin in one of his hands and a bag with a patch in the other. The pom-pom is bigger this time, and we used a short piece of wire to connect it to the hat. You can also put a dollar sign on the sack instead of a patch to emphasize the point you are making.

Santa Imposter?

AFTERWORD FOR FIGURE CREATION

How Far Can and Should Critter-Making Go?
Working on Details and Making Stories with Your Characters

Critter-making can go very far; one is either tempted to go into the most minute details of a critter or get caught up in making an intricate set to provide a context for the character they have created. Putting your italicized initials on every gray hair on your goblin's head would be an example of the former, and making a highway that leads to the castle where your knight dwells in the middle of a forest, on an island, in a sea, on a planet, in a universe in a parallel polymer-clay dimension would be an example of the latter. As you can see, even the very sentence that describes the process of going to these two extremes is long and confusing.

Of course, going to extremes can be a lot of fun and is definitely worth trying at some point, but do not forget that there is a middle road you should explore:

When the random passerby looks at your creation, the character's highlights should be more or less apparent, and only then should there be enough detail to keep the viewer's interest for a while. It is better, for example, to spend more time giving a creature a big crooked nose and a huge unibrow than to meticulously put all the 365 stitches that it usually takes to fasten a patch on a sleeve.

By analogy, a finished character should be expressive enough on its own to stimulate the onlooker's imagination. Making an auxiliary setting may provide the context, but that context should be first and foremost suggested in the character itself.

If you followed all the lessons in this book you may have built a whole cast of characters with which to stage your own fairy tale. Take advantage of the fact that many of the characters are compatible—you can make a knight on a horse fighting a dragon, a wizard with a raven (the generic bird, in black) perched on his shoulder, a Santa with a helper elf and a reindeer (using the horse lesson and the armature technique for the antlers), a clumsy troll with a bird on his head…you get the idea. Here is an example:

Sir George Tickles the Dragon

To build this scene we used the horse and dragon lessons as they appear in this book. The only new character is the knight. To make a rider out of the knight, we used simple armature—an inverted "Y" of wire—to provide support for the legs. For the spear, we attached a feather to one end of a wooden stick with the help of some very thin red wire.

Gallery

Ice cream served with this beautifully decorated scoop can only taste sweeter. You can make a scoop like it by following the project directions.

Artist: Mona Kissel

These elegant bracelets illustrate how effectively Mona Kissel uses the
acrylic floor wax technique.

Gallery

Tearing effects give an aged look the lozenge beads in this necklace.

Artist : Ellen Marshall

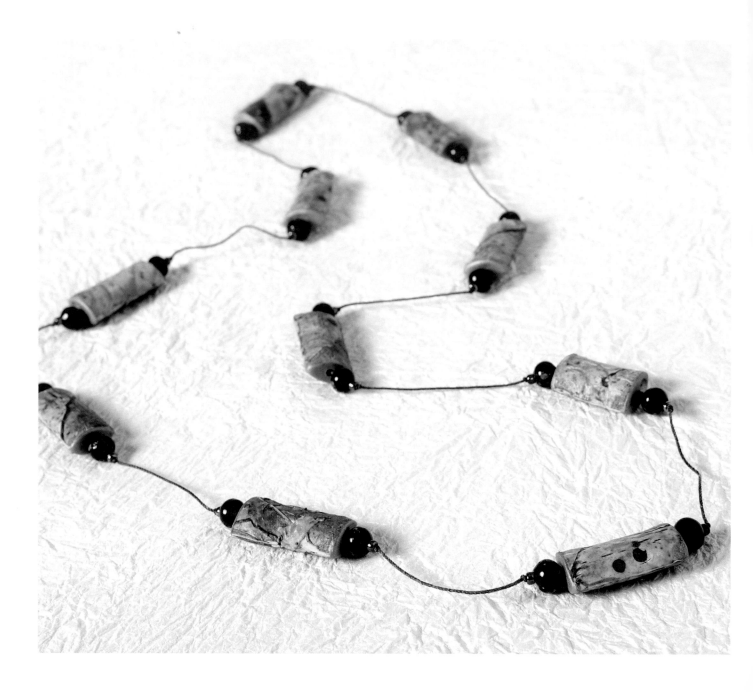

These necklaces feature paint and pastel applications.

Artist : Ellen Marshall

Gallery

This necklace is a marriage of metal-wire wrapping and textured clay highlighted with mica powder. The clay was textured with stamps from Era Graphics.

Artist: Ellen Marshall

Subtle applications of ink and pastel color soften the hard contour of this necklace.

Artist: Ellen Marshall

Gallery

Vibrant colored clay-on-clay is featured in this pin.

Artist: Ellen Marshall

Acrylic media and metallic paint combine to create the quilted effect on this pin.

Artist: Ellen Marshall

Gallery

These pins are miniature collages of decorated sheets of clay.

Artist: Ellen Marshall

Exquisite seed-bead fringe and polymer clay ornaments (by the author) combine beautifully in this necklace.

Artist: Leslie Pope

Gallery

This artist pioneered the application of silk-screening on polymer clay and introduced methods for building Japanese-style inro.

Artist: Gwen Gibson

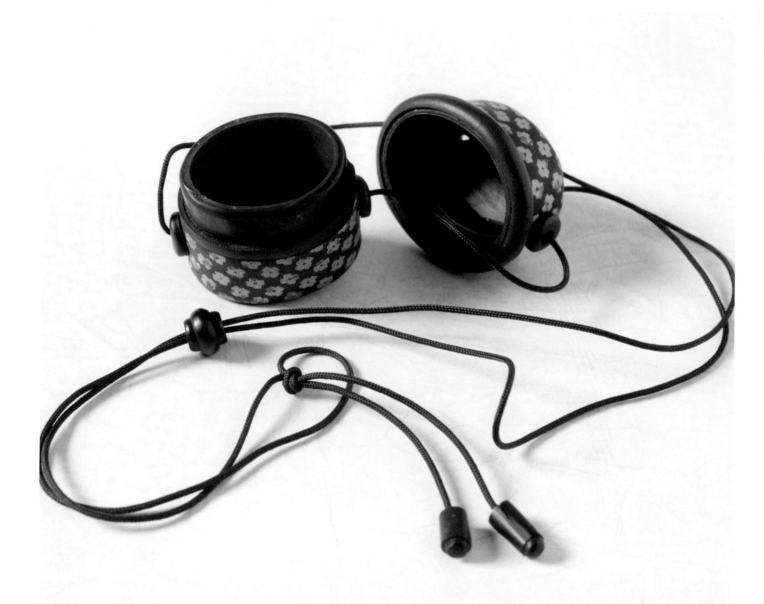

Gallery

This artist works with both polymer clay and fiber. She uses surface design in her mixed-media artwork.

Artist: Andi McDowell

Gallery

Stamping and caning applications are featured in this necklace.

Artist: Ellen Marshall

This artist applied her considerable talent as a fiber artist toward designing and making this roll bag. The bag is ornamented with hand-dyed fabric triangles and the author's heart-shaped polymer ornaments.

Artist: Judith Rose Lapato

Gallery

The light weight of this bracelet belies its marble-like finish.

Artist: Sue Springer

This artist has created ancient-looking, Asian-style boxes with fitted lids.
The surface treatment is translucent clay combined with embossing
powder and acrylic paint heated with an embossing gun.

Artist: Martha Aleo

Gallery

Celie Fago

Exploring a new material, in this case Precious Metal Clay, can produce strikingly original work. The malleability of the clay contrasts with crisp carved textures and complex forms in these distinctive bracelets and pendants. The polymer clay elements were produced with related and visually harmonious techniques, including photo transfers and carving.
Photos: Robert Diamante

Jacqueline Lee

Love for ancient and exotic art pervades these pins and pendants. Using acrylic paint, metallic powders, and handmade molds, Lee has developed meticulous techniques to produce work that evokes the ancient Far East lacquer and wood pieces in modern clay. Elements are molded in clay, assembled and adhered with glue or TLS. *Photos: Jacqueline Lee*

Nan Roche

Mokumé gané is a versatile technique. The effects vary depending on the color, transparency, and pearlescence of the clays used. For the pieces below, a sheet made of contrasting layers of opaque clay was pressed into shallow molds and later carved or sanded away, revealing dramatic graphic patterns. A weathered look was achieved by applying a metal patina as the last step of construction. *Photos: Chris Roche*

Dayle Doroshow

When is a book not a book? When it's a dream. Doroshow's evocative figurines, boxes, and plaques hold secret messages, treasures, and wishes in hidden compartments. Techniques combine sculpture, caning, doll making, and book arts. *Photos: Don Felton*

Elise Winters

This master of form and color explores new ways to combine polymer clay with other materials. The screen holds a thin sheet of tinted translucent clay embellished with gold leaf. In the cinched pin, a ring of vermeil encircles a core of subtly color-blended polymer clay and a skin crazed iridescent acrylic paint.

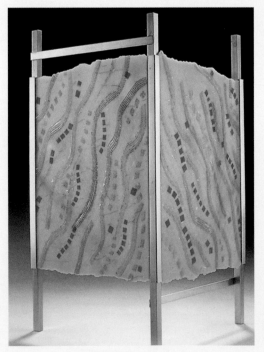

Barbara Morrison

Energy and sprit are embodied here. Wirework and beading embellish these colorful figures. *Photos: Patrick Clark*

Liz Mitchell

Polymer clay, transfer images, and paint were used to produce these distinctive books and frames. *Photos: Ralph Gabriner*

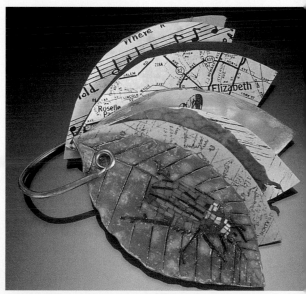

Dorothy Greynolds

These streamlined pieces make the most of the luster of pearl clays. In the pendants and earrings, paper-thin cut-out shapes in contrasting colors are applied to pearl or black bases and rolled in. *Photos: Dorothy Greynolds*

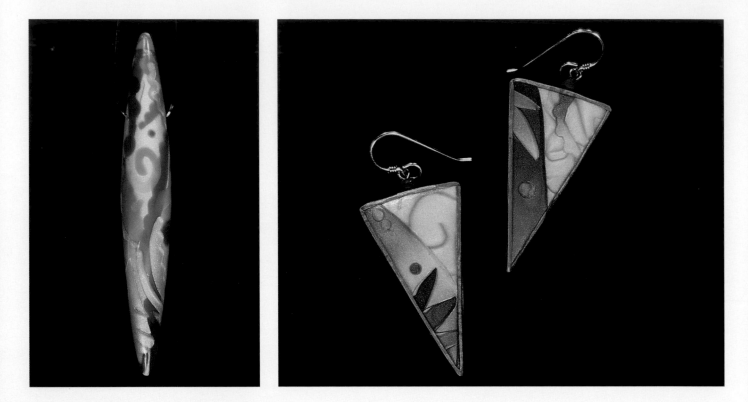

Dotty McMillan

How many decorative techniques can you spot in these Oriental looking pieces? Just for starters, the kaleidoscope employs image transfers, molded pieces, and antiquing, while the lively figures (concealing recycled prescription vials) are clothed in mokumé gané and chrysanthemum cane slices.

Patricia Klamser

Large, beautifully crafted evening purses bring the small traditional Japanese inro boxes into the world of modern fashion. They are formed over wooden shapes and ornamented with hand-painted and silk-screened imagery, as well as veneers featuring metallic clay effects, carving, and texturing. *Photos: Rob Vinnedge*

Judy Kuskin

In these unusual mixed-media necklaces and wall pieces, found objects like driftwood, shells, and feathers contrast with polymer clay design elements. These diverse pieces employ many techniques, including carving, backfilling with contrasting-colored clay, molding, texturing, mokumé gané, canework, crackling, patinas, and antiquing. *Photos: Roger Schrieber*

Liz Tamayo

Voyages of imagination, discovery, and delight are memorialized in these complex hinged albums. The "postcards" are polymer clay, too, and made with transfers as well as paint and patinas. *Photos: Don Felder*

Gwen Gibson

Innovation is Gibson's hallmark, from the Tear-Away technique "cave art" brooch to the silk-screened lentil beads, bracelet, and pendant. The transfer image on the pendant (lower left) was made on the back of a paper-thin sheet of translucent clay, tinted, laid over crackled metal leaf on clay, baked, and highly polished. *Photos: Robert Diamonte*

Maj-Britt Cawthon

Polymer clay adapts just as easily to bold, geometric modern designs as it does to traditional imagery and imitating ancient artifacts. Mokumé gané and simple canes are used to decorate the big, bold, elegant beads in these necklaces. *Photos: John Bonath*

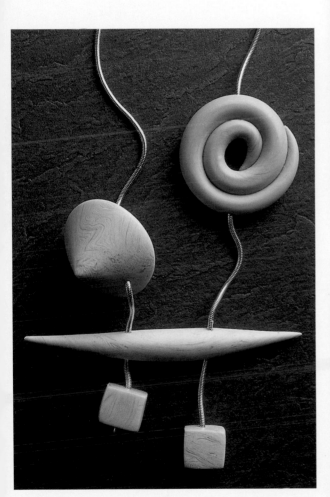

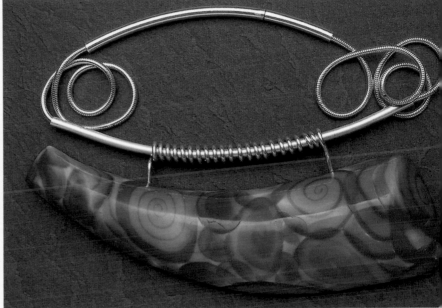

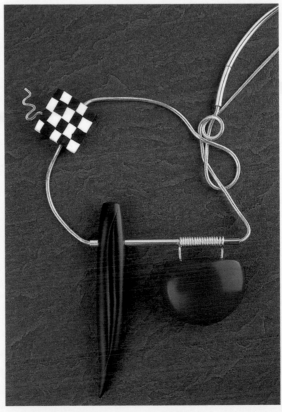

Standard PMC Frame Project Templates

Textured Silver Frame with Inset
(see page 188)

These templates show the before and after firing sizes of five sample rectangles. The larger size in each set (left) represents the "before firing" size. The smaller size in each set (right) shows the 28% shrinkage of standard PMC. If you roll standard PMC out to a height of 3 cards, you'll use approximately the portion of an ounce listed under each "before firing" size.

¾ of an oz.

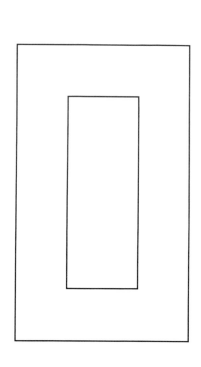

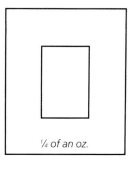

¼ of an oz.

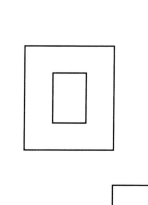

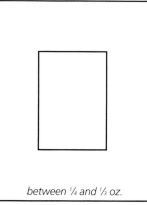

between ¼ and ⅓ oz.

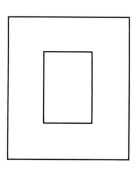

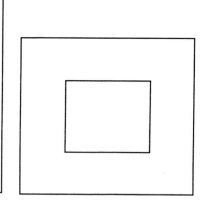

½ of an oz.

⅛ of an oz.

Diagram for Cutting Accurate Frame Windows

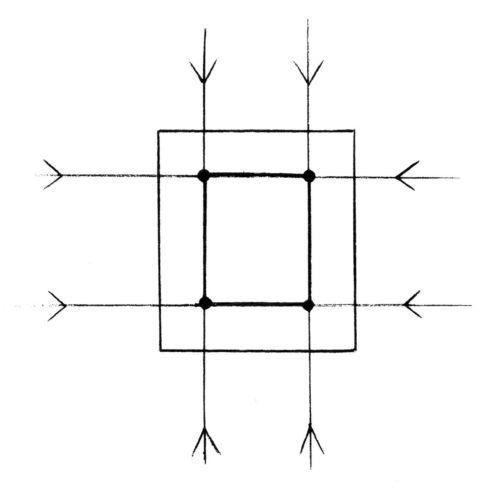

Bird Box Pendant (see page 192)

Use a diagram like the one shown here to help cut the window accurately. Cut the rectangle for the front of the box and place it on a scrap of plastic. Position it precisely on the diagram and follow the arrow lines in at each corner to find the spot to poke the four holes. Then, using a craft knife, cut the window out using the four holes as guides.

Template

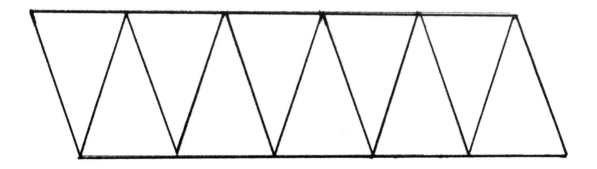

Triangle Bracelet (page 98)

Contributing Artists/Resources

Martha Aleo
817 South 10th St.
Philadelphia, PA 19147
marthaaleo@yahoo.com

Meredith Arnold
Moonenstars Unlimited
110 N. 201 St.
Shoreline, WA 98133-3012
206.542.3405
marnold@nwlink.com

Jody Bishel
548 Wakelee Ave.
Ansonia, CT 06401-1226
203.735.5879
jbishel@aol.com

Maj-Britt Cawthon
11715 West 18th Ave.
Lakewood, CO 80215
303.274.7565
mbcawthon@att.net

Dan Cormier
RR1, Site 24, C67
Gabriola Island, BC V0R1X0
CANADA
hoco@island.net

Dayle Doroshow
Zingaro
P.O. Box 354
Fort Bragg, CA 95437
707.962.9419
dayledoroshow@hotmail.com

Celie Fago
RR 1 Box 376
Bethel, VT 05032
806.234.5428
celie@adelphia.net

Gwen Gibson
216 Bayview St.
San Rafael, CA 94901
gwen@gwengibson.com

Linda Goff
1204 S. Fir
Olympia, WA 98501
Wire4Clay2@aol.com

Dorothy Greynolds
5678 Eldridge Dr.
Waterford, MI 48327
248.683.1107
claywear@yahoo.com

Susan Hyde
Susan Hyde Designs
3920 Sunnyside Ave. N.
Seattle,WA 98103
206.281.1559
shd2clay@aol.com

Mona Kissel
749 Nadenbousch Lane
Martinsburg, WV 25401
monak@airphotographics.com

Patricia Klamser
308 20th Ave. S.
Seattle, WA 98144
206.322.8819
pklamser@hotmail.com

Judy Kuskin
2527 32nd Ave. S.
Seattle, WA 9814
206.725.2725
jkuskin@hotmail.com

Judith Rose Lapato
3104 Addison Court
Bensalem, PA 19020
jslapato@aol.com

Jaqueline Lee
1645 S. 350 E.
Springville, UT 84663
801.489.6226
jaquelinelee@mail.com

Ellen Marshall
2420 Montrose St.
Philadelphia, PA 19146
215.752.0360
larrine@msn.com

Andi McDowell
5664 Vantage Point Rd.
Columbia, MD 21044
andi_mcdowell@yahoo.com

Dotty McMillan
7060 Fireside Dr.
Riverside, CA 92506
909.780.4056
dcmcmillan01@earthlink.net

Livia McRee
livia@liviamcree.com

Liz Mitchell
101 Upper Kingtown Rd.
Pittstown, NJ 08867
908.735.5710
lizzez@ptd.net

Barbara Morrison
717 Hiberta St.
Missoula, MT 59804
406.721.6159
tmw717@hotmail.com

Leslie Pope
LesliePope@yahoo.com

Elissa Powell
Elissahearts
1731 Santa Cruz Ave.
Santa Clara, CA 95051
elissahearts@yahoo.com

Margaret F.H. Reid
2 Stone House
Howey
Llandrindod Wells
Powys LD1 5PL
UNITED KINGDOM
(44) 1597 825517
mfhreid@polyopol.kc3ltd.co.uk

Nan Roche
4511 Amherst Rd.
College Park, MD 20740
301.864.1805
nan@nanroche.com

Leigh S. Ross
Polymer Clay Central
610 5th Ave.
Bradley Beach, NJ 07720
732.776.6576
sincereleigh@polymerclaycentral.com

Georgia Sargeant
2400 Virginia Ave. NW, #C-1017
Washington, DC 20037
202.223.0777
georgiapeach@erols.com

Sue Springer
69 Hamilton St.
Chalfont, PA 18914
suespringer@comcast.net

Liz Tamayo
2926 Holyrood Dr.
Oakland, CA 94611
510.530.7249
LizzeeT@aol.com

Elise Winters
56 Adams Ave.
Haworth, NJ 07641
201.501.0520
winterse@aol.com
Valerie Wright
4370 Hickory Wood Dr.
Columbus, OH 43228
valkatdesigns@hotmail.com

Valerie Wright
4370 Hickory Wood Dr.
Columbus, OH 43228
valkatdesigns@hotmail.com

AATRICECO
12244 N. 84th Place
Scottsdale, AZ 85260
phone: 888.484.1999
www.atriceco.com
Airbrush supplies and accessories

Accent Import Export, Inc.
1501 Loveridge Rd.
Box 16
Pittsburg, CA 94565
phone: 800.989.2889
sean@fimozone.com
www.fimozone.com
general supplies, "Magic Leaf" patterned leaf,
molds, stamps, books, crackle finishes, and
adhesives

Airbrush City, Inc
24 S. Jarom Lane
Nampa, ID 83687
phone: 208.461.9191
www.airbrushcity.com
Airbrush equipment, accessories, technical
assistance

American Art Clay Co. Inc.
4717 West 16th St.
Indianapolis, IN 46222
phone: 800.374.1600
fax: 317.248.9300
catalog@amaco.com
www.amaco.com
general supplies, push molds, and tools

Angelwings Enterprises
3065 N. Sunnyside Ave
Fresno, CA 93727
phone: 800.400.3717
www.radiantpearls.com
Primary Elements Coloring System- Polished
Pigments and other products

Clay Factory, Inc.
P.O. Box 460598
Escondido, CA 92046-0598
phone: 877.728.5739
clayfactoryinc@clayfactoryinc.com
www.clayfactoryinc.com
general supplies, Cernit, and ripple blades

Clearsnap Inc
P.O. Box 98
Anacortes, WA 98221
phone: 800.448.4862
www.clearsnap.com
Fluid chalk pigment inks and other products

Create An Impression
56 E. Lancaster Ave.
Ardmore, PA 19003
phone: 215.645.6500
www.createanimpression.net
Earthtone rubberstamps, other
rubberstamping and paper arts materials

Diane Maurer
P.O. Box 78
Spring Mills, PA 16875
phone: 814.422.8651
www.dianemaurer.com
Wood graining combs, paste paper and
marbling supplies

Dick Blick
P.O. Box 1267
Galesburg, IL 61402
phone: 800.828.4548
www.dickblick.com
Lascaux acrylic paints (see www.lascaux.com
for international sources) and other artist
supplies

Golden Artist Colors, Inc
188 Bell Road
New Berlin, NY 13411
phone: 607.847.6154
www.goldenpaints.com
Acrylic paints and media

Gwen Gibson Designs
216 Bayview Street
San Rafael, CA 94901
phone: 415.454.3246
www.gwengibson.com
Photo-EZ stencils- ready-made and stencil-
making kits. Online tutorials

Heart in Hand Studio
9825 Tarzana Lane
Las Vegas, NV 89129
www.heartinhandstudio.com
Poly Bonder and other tools for polymer clay

Homecrafts Direct
P.O. Box 247
Leicester, LE1 9QS UK
phone: 44.0116 251.0405
post@speccrafts.co.uk
www.speccrafts.co.uk
general supplies, Formello, tools, and cold
enamels

Letraset Limited
Kingsnorth Industrial Estate
Wotton Road
Ashford Kent, TN23 UK
44-(0) 1233 624421
www.letraset.com
Promarkers, Tria markers, other products

Metalliferous Inc.
34 West 46th St.
New York, NY 10036
phone: 888-944-0909
Precious metal clay

Mindstorm Productions, Inc.
2625 Alcatraz Ave., Suite 241
Berkeley, CA 94705
phone: 510.644.1952
fax: 510.644.3910
burt@mindstorm-inc.com
www.mindstorm-inc.com
Instructional videos

Over the Rainbow
ABN: 37 212 817 463
PO Box 495
Ascot Vale, Victoria
Australia 3032
phone: 03.9376.0545
fax: 03.9376.4489
Heather.Richmond@overtherainbow.com.au
www.overtherainbow.com.au
A full range of polymer clay products, tools,
Lumiere paints, and Pinata inks

PMC Tool and Supply
1 Feeder St.
Lambertville, NJ 08530
phone: 609.397.9550
Precious metal clay

Polymer Clay Central
website: www.polymerclaycentral.com
The biggest Internet portal dedicated to
polymer clay art: A great online resource for
beginners and advanced clayers alike—a
treasury of all kinds of polymer clay-related
information. PCC's forum is a meeting place
for many artists of the international polymer
clay community.

Polymer Clay Express
13017 Wisteria Drive
Box 275
Germantown, MD 20874
phone: 800.844.0138
fax: 301.482.0610
www.polymerclayexpress.com
general supplies, all brands of clay, and hard-
to-find items

The Polymer Clay Pit
British Polymer Clay Guild
Meadow Rise, Low Road
Wortham, Diss
Norfolk, IP22 1SQ UK
phone: 44.01379.646019
fax: 44.0139.646016
claypit@heaser.demon.co.uk
www.heaser.demon.co.uk/claypit.htm
general supplies and Creall-therm

Prairie Craft Company
P.O. Box 209
Florissant, CO 80816-0209
phone: 800.779.0615
fax: 719.748.5112
vernon@pcisys.net
www.prairiecraft.com
general supplies, Kato clay, NuBlade Kato
and Marxit Kato tools

Raydec Creations
Warkworth, Ontario, Canada
phone: 705.924.3903
fax: 705.924.3872
Arts, Crafts and Hobby Services
Craft Supplies and Equipment Hobby
Products and Supplies

Red Castle Inc.
Phill Schloss
P.O. Box 39-8001
Edina, MN 55439-8001
phone: 877.733.2278
www.red-castle.com

Rio Grande
7500 Bluewater Rd. N.W.
Albuquerque, NM87121
phone: 800.545.6566
Precious metal clay

Rossdale Pty Ltd.
137 Noone Street, Clifton Hills
VIC 3068, Australia
Premo, Sculpey

Staedtler (Pacific) Pty Ltd.
P.O. Box 576, 1 Inman Road
Dee Why, NSW 2099, Australia
phone: 2-9982-4555
Fimo

Stewart Gill, LTD
Unit 13, Elgin Industrial Estate
40 Dickson St.
Fife, KY12 7SN Scotland, UK
www.stewartgill.com
Byantia Cloisonne and other paints and
materials. USA sources:
www.meinketoy.com, www.puffinalia.com

Royal Sovereign Ltd
7 St.Georges Industrial Estate
White Hart Lane
London, N22 5QL
info@royal-sovereign.com
Magic color inks USA source:
www.jerrysartarama.com

About the Authors

Ellen Marshall has worked with polymer clay for more than a decade. She is a past cochair of the Philadelphia Area Polymer Clay Guild, which she cofounded, and a past president of the National Polymer Clay Guild. Ellen has been teaching polymer-clay craft for several years and has been published in the magazines *Polymer Café* and *Step-by-Step Beads.*

Georgia Sargeant started drawing, sewing, and building things as a child and never stopped. After studying studio arts in college, she became a graphic artist, reporter, and editor. From 1997 to 2001 she was the editor of the quarterly newsletter of the National Polymer Clay Guild, where she featured and wrote about leading polymer clay artists from around the world. She has been working with polymer clay for more than a decade and loves to learn and teach new techniques.

Celie Fago began working in polymer clay in 1991 after years of working as a painter and sculptor. Her jewelry combines polymer clay with precious metal clay. She's a highly regarded, generous, and innovative teacher who has done groundbreaking work combining these materials. She's one of six senor instructors of precious metal clay worldwide and was invited by master metalsmith Tim McCreight to be Mitsubishi's PMC liasion to the polymer clay community in 1999. Celie and Tim's intermediate video, *Push Play for PMC,* is available from the author or whereever craft videos are sold.

Livia McRee is a craft designer and writer, and a former editor at Handcraft Illustrated magazine. She's author of *Easy Transfers for Any Surface, Quick Crafts, and Instant Fabric,* among others. Her work has been published online, and she has contributed to several how-to craft books.

Dinko Tilov has been creating amazing 3 to 5 inch (8 to 13 cm) creatures using polymer clay and mixed media ever since he was a child. His unique characters have been featured on polymer clay websites, in newsletters, galleries, and in a calendar. He has lived and studied in Bulgaria (where he is from), France, and the United States. Much of his prolific work can be viewed at his website: www.dinkos.com.